CREATIVITY

CREATIVITY

Editor
David E. Carter

COLLINS|DESIGN

An Imprint of HarperCollins*Publishers*

HarperCollins books may be purchased for educational, business, or sales promotional use.
For information, please write: Special Markets Department, HarperCollins Publishers Inc.,
10 East 53rd Street, New York, NY 10022.

First Edition

First published in 2006 by:
Collins Design
An Imprint of HarperCollins*Publishers*
10 East 53rd Street
New York, NY 10022
Tel: (212) 207-7000
Fax: (212) 207-7654
collinsdesign@harpercollins.com
www.harpercollins.com

Distributed throughout the world by:
HarperCollins*Publishers*
10 East 53rd Street
New York, NY 10022
Fax: (212) 207-7654

Jacket & book design by Designs on You!
Suzanna and Anthony Stephens

Library of Congress Control Number: 2006921702

ISBN-10: 0-06-113743-X
ISBN-13: 978-0-06-113743-3

Printed in China by Everbest Printing Company through Four Colour Imports, Louisville, Kentucky.

First Printing, 2006

$\mathscr{P}$RINT

$\mathcal{T}$Vc/FILM/VIDEO

$\mathcal{N}$EW MEDIA

Creativity 35.

It seems like years with numbers divisible by 5 are a good excuse to look back, to reflect on "how things were."

The first Creativity Annual was published in 1972. Things were very different then—in so many ways. Graphic design was mostly a black-and-white world. (Full color printing was very expensive, as well as very time consuming.)

In 1972, the term "great creative work" was usually attached to a big city address such as New York, Chicago, or San Francisco. (It's hard to imagine that LA wasn't considered to be much of an "ad center" 35 years ago.) London had outstanding work then, but globalization hadn't come along so the rest of Europe basically had "local" ads. And Asia was still considered to be "third world," especially for creative work.

In 1972, nobody would have imagined that Portland, Minneapolis, Boston, and Atlanta would someday be highly regarded ad centers. Not to mention Rome, Hong Kong, Seoul, and a lot of other places.

Back then, typography was either: a) bad, or b) very expensive, and time consuming, taking as much as two weeks to get type set at a big-city "type house." THEN have it mailed back to you. (FedEx? It wouldn't appear for a long time.)

Somewhere along the way, the Mac arrived and changed the creative world. Doing great creative work was no longer connected to a postal code.

For 35 years, the Creativity Annual has been at the forefront of these changes.

We were among the first to produce a 400-page annual, with every page in process color.

We were among the first to recognize the work of creative people from all over the world, not just a few select cities.

What will the future hold for the creative world? Who knows? But one thing is certain: the Creativity Annual will continue to be at the forefront of recognizing change, and we will continue to focus on the new tools, and the people who produce great creative work with those new tools.

The Creativity Awards

Register online.

www.creativityawards.com

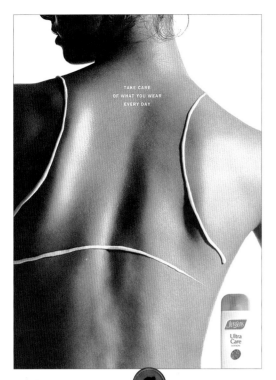

creative firm
Taxi Canada Inc.
Montréal, (Québec) Canada
creatives
Stephane Charier, Patrick Chaubet,
Maxime Patenaude
client
KAO Brands Canada (Jergens)

creative firm
D'Adda Lorenzini Vigorelli, BBDO
Rome, Italy
creatives
Giampietro Vigorelli
client
Universal Studios Networks Italy

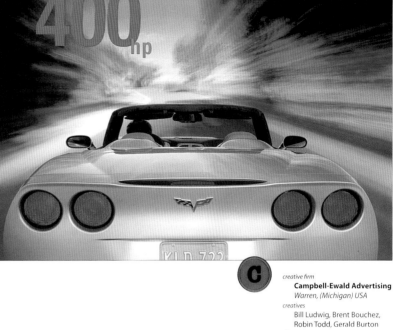

creative firm
Campbell-Ewald Advertising
Warren, (Michigan) USA
creatives
Bill Ludwig, Brent Bouchez,
Robin Todd, Gerald Burton
client
Chevrolet

creative firm
Bohan Advertising/Marketing
Nashville, (Tennessee) USA
creatives
Kerry Oliver, Kevin Hinson,
David Bailey
client
Grande Ole Opry

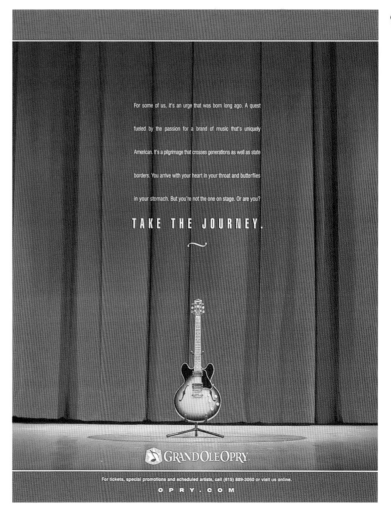

creative firm
Campbell-Ewald Advertising
Warren, (Michigan) USA
creatives
Bill Ludwig, Mark Simon, Debbie Kamowsky,
Marni Burns, Mike Conboy, Neville Anderson,
John Dolab
client
Kaiser Permenante

10

creative firm
Portfolio Center
Atlanta, (Georgia) USA
creatives
Josh Dimarcantonto, Shannon Kaiser
client
Healthy Choice

creative firm
Rodgers Townsend
St. Louis, (Missouri) USA
creatives
Tom Hudder, Mike McCormick,
Evan Willnow
client
Joe Rocket

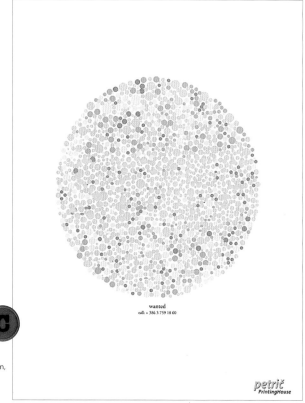

creative firm
Futura DDB
Ljubljana, Slovenia
creatives
Žare Derin, Zoran Gabrijan,
Miha Grobler
client
Printing House Petrič

creative firm
Dieste Harmel & Partners
Dallas, (Texas) USA
creatives
Dieste Harmel & Partners
Creative Team
client
Tropicana Dole

creative firm
Campbell-Ewald Advertising
Warren, (Michigan) USA
creatives
Bill Ludwig, Brent Bouchez,
Tom Cerroni, Joe Godard
client
Chevrolet

creative firm
MARC USA
Pittsburgh, (Pennsylvania) USA
creatives
Ron Sullivan, Laurie Habeeb,
Danielle Caruso
client
Mohawk Flooring

11

creative firm
Grey Worldwide
New York, (New York) USA
creatives
Tim Mellors, Mike Ryniec,
Mark Catalina, Jonathan Klein
client
New York Jets

creative firm
Bald & Beautiful
Venice, (California) USA
creatives
Luis Camano,
Cameron Young
client
Aspen Dental

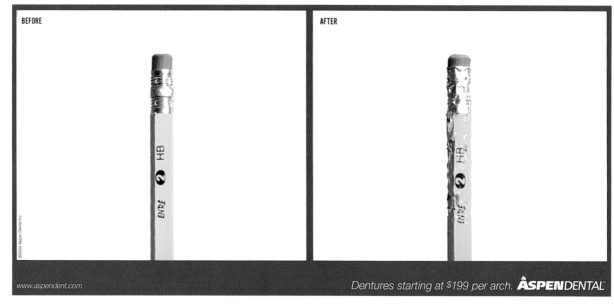

BEFORE

AFTER

©2004 Aspen Dental Inc.

www.aspendent.com

Dentures starting at $199 per arch. **ÂSPEN**DENTAL™

12

GEORGES DUBŒUF

CHARDONNAY

Réserve

creative firm
Hampel Stefanides
New York, (New York) USA
creatives
Tom Kane, Chris Collins,
Daniel Smith
client
Georges Duboeuf Climbing

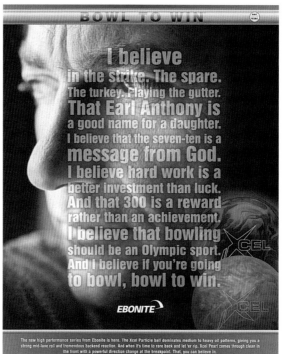

BOWL TO WIN

I believe
in the strike. The spare.
The turkey. Playing the gutter.
That Earl Anthony is
a good name for a daughter.
I believe that the seven-ten is a
message from God.
I believe hard work is a
better investment than luck.
And that 300 is a reward
rather than an achievement.
I believe that bowling
should be an Olympic sport.
And I believe if you're going
to bowl, bowl to win.

EBONITE

XCEL

The new high performance series from Ebonite is here. The Xcel Particle ball dominates medium to heavy oil patterns, giving you a strong mid-lane roll and tremendous backend reaction. And when it's time to rare back and let 'er rip, Xcel Pearl comes through clean in the front with a powerful direction change at the breakpoint. That, you can believe in.

BALLS / BAGS / GLOVES / ACCESSORIES / COACHING PRODUCTS / EBONITE.COM

creative firm
Bohan Advertising/Marketing
Nashville, (Tennessee) USA
creatives
Kerry Oliver, Kevin Hinson,
Ray Otterson, David Bailey
client
Ebonite Bowling

186mph

creative firm
Campbell-Ewald Advertising
Warren, (Michigan) USA
creatives
Bill Ludwig, Brent Bouchez,
Robin Todd, Gerald Burton
client
Chevrolet

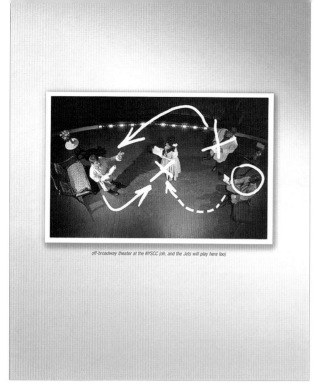

off-broadway theater at the NYSCC (oh, and the Jets will play here too)

creative firm
Grey Worldwide NY
New York, (New York) USA
creatives
Tim Mellors, Mike Ryniec,
Mark Catalina, Jonathan Klein
client
New York Jets

creative firm
Nickelodeon Creative Resources
New York, (New York) USA
creatives
Jon Lease, David Hamed,
Russell Hicks

creative firm
Revolución
New York, (New York) USA
creatives
Alberto Rodriguez, Roberto Pedroso,
Abby Lee
client
Palm Bay Imports

creative firm
021 Comunicaciones
Mexico City, Mexico
creatives
Gabriel Flores, Dahian Rau, Paco Gutierrez,
Mariana Ortiz, Vladimir Nabor, Gabriel Flores,
Veronica Trujillo, Angel Martinez
client
Hyatt

13

SHIPPING WITHOUT THE SCHLEPPING.

When you can't come to the Post Office,™ let the Post Office come to you. Just go to usps.com, where you can print labels, pay for postage, and your carrier will pick up your packages for you. To learn more, visit usps.com/clickship. It's just one more way the U.S. Postal Service™ is working for you.

UNITED STATES POSTAL SERVICE.

©2004 United States Postal Service. Eagle symbol is a registered trademark of the United States Postal Service.   usps.com

creative firm
Campbell-Ewald Advertising
Warren, (Michigan) USA
creatives
Mark Simon, Marcia Levenson, Dan Ames
client
The United States Postal Service

14

UN MESE DEDICATO ALLE DONNE. PREPARATEVI.

A MARZO, OGNI SERA ALLE 21, DARIO VERGASSOLA E DAVID RIONDINO PRESENTANO LA PIÙ ECCITANTE RASSEGNA DI FILM DEDICATI ALLE DONNE. DA THELMA & LOUISE AD ELIZABETH, DA LA RAGAZZA DI NASHVILLE A FUNNY GIRL, DA LEZIONI DI PIANO A LA MIA AFRICA. BASTA DIGITARE 320 SUL TELECOMANDO.

| IN ONDA SU SKY | CANALE 320 | studiouniversal.it | La Tv del cinema da chi fa cinema |

Studio UNIVERSAL

creative firm
D'Adda Lorenzini Vigorelli, BBDO
Rome, Italy
creatives
Giampietro Vigorelli
client
Universal Studios Networks Italy

creative firm
Dieste Harmel & Partners
Dallas, (Texas) USA
creatives
Dieste Harmel & Partners
Creative Team
client
Tropicana Dole

Location is everything.

MOHAWK
Mohawk makes the room

HARDWOOD • CERAMIC • LAMINATE • RUGS • 1-800-2-MOHAWK • MOHAWKFLOORING.COM

creative firm
MARC USA
Pittsburgh, (Pennsylvania) USA
creatives
Ron Sullivan, Laurie Habeeb,
Danielle Caruso
client
Mohawk Flooring

creative firm
Hampel Stefanides
New York, (New York) USA
creatives
Tom Kane, Chris Collins,
Daniel Smith
client
Yellow Tail Wine

creative firm
Nickelodeon Creative Resources
New York, (New York) USA
creatives
David Hamed,
Russell Hicks

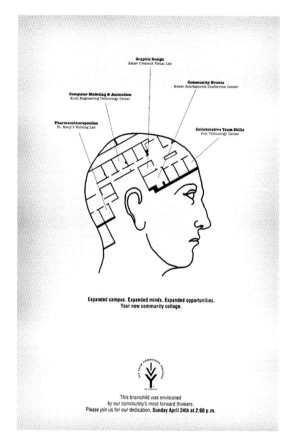

creative firm
Keller Crescent Advertising
Evansville, (Indiana) USA
creatives
Randall L. Rohn, Keith Rios,
Nancy Kirkpatrick
client
Ivy Tech

15

creative firm
Grey Worldwide NY
New York, (New York) USA
creatives
Tim Mellors, Mike Ryniec,
Mark Catalina, Jonathan Klein,
Jonathan Kantor
client
New York Jets

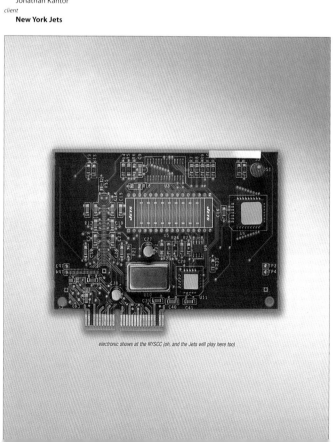

Naughty and Nice.

The legendary Tequila Rose, the passionate combination of strawberry cream liqueur with a splash of the finest tequila. The same great original naughtiness you have always loved is now available in a stunning new bottle.

More Naughtiness.

You'll be tempted by two new Tequila Rose family members, Cocoa Cream and Java Cream. These naughty siblings combine the succulent tastes of chocolate or coffee with the same strawberry cream you love from the original Tequila Rose. Get ready for more naughtiness in Fall 2005.

Visit us at TequilaRose.com

creative firm
Sagon-Phior
Los Angeles, (California) USA
creatives
Sagon-Phior
client
McCormick Distilling Co.

You really need a vacation.

HYATT
HOTELS & RESORTS
M E X I C O

For reservations, call 9138 1234

creative firm
021 Comunicaciones
Mexico City, Mexico
creatives
Gabriel Flores, Dahian Rau, Paco Gutierrez,
Mariana Ortiz, Vladimir Nabor, Gabriel Flores,
Veronica Trujillo, Angel Martinez
client
Hyatt

creative firm
Keller Crescent Advertising
Evansville, (Indiana) USA
creatives
Randall L. Rohn,
Keith Rios
client
Evan Williams

16

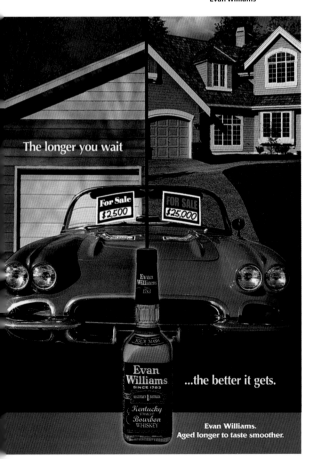

The longer you wait

For Sale $2,500   FOR SALE $25,000

Evan
Williams
1783

Evan
Williams
SINCE 1783

...the better it gets.

Kentucky
STRAIGHT
Bourbon
WHISKEY

Evan Williams.
Aged longer to taste smoother.

creative firm
MARC USA
Pittsburgh, (Pennsylvania) USA
creatives
Ron Sullivan, Laurie Habeeb,
Danielle Caruso
client
Mohawk Flooring

Fantastic voyage.

CARPET • HARDWOOD • CERAMIC • LAMINATE • RUGS • 1-800-2-MOHAWK • MOHAWKFLOORING

MOHAWK
Mohawk makes the room

BEFORE

AFTER

www.aspendent.com

Dentures starting at $199 per arch. **ÂSPEN**DENTAL™

creative firm
Bald & Beautiful
Venice, (California) USA
creatives
Luis Camano,
Cameron Young
client
Aspen Dental

17

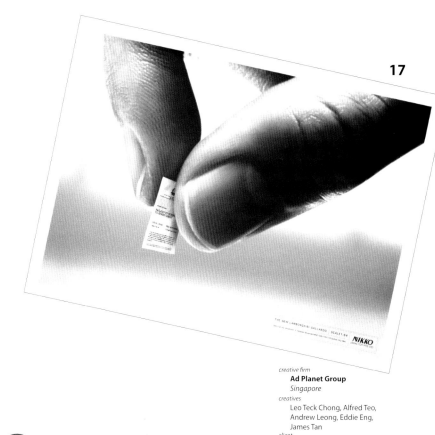

creative firm
Ad Planet Group
Singapore
creatives
Leo Teck Chong, Alfred Teo,
Andrew Leong, Eddie Eng,
James Tan
client
Nikko Asia Toys Pte Ltd

creative firm
Dieste Harmel & Partners
Dallas, (Texas) USA
creatives
Dieste Harmel & Partners Creative
Team
client
Frito Lay

creative firm
Campbell-Ewald Advertising
Warren, (Michigan) USA
creatives
Bill Ludwig, Brent Bouchez,
Robin Todd, Gerald Burton
client
Chevrolet

creative firm
021 Comunicaciones
Mexico City, Mexico
creatives
Gabriel Flores, Dahian Rau, Paco Gutierrez,
Mariana Ortiz, Vladimir Nabor, Gabriel Flores,
Veronica Trujillo, Angel Martinez
client
Hyatt

creative firm
D'Adda Lorenzini Vigorelli, BBDO
Rome, Italy
creatives
Giampietro Vigorelli,
Luca Scotto Di Carlo
client
**Universal Studios
Networks Italy**

creative firm
Portfolio Center
Atlanta, (Georgia) USA
creatives
Josh Dimarcantonto, Shannon Kaiser
client
Healthy Choice

You really need a vacation.

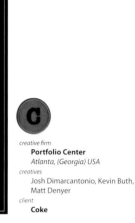

creative firm
Portfolio Center
Atlanta, (Georgia) USA
creatives
Josh Dimarcantonio, Kevin Buth,
Matt Denyer
client
Coke

19

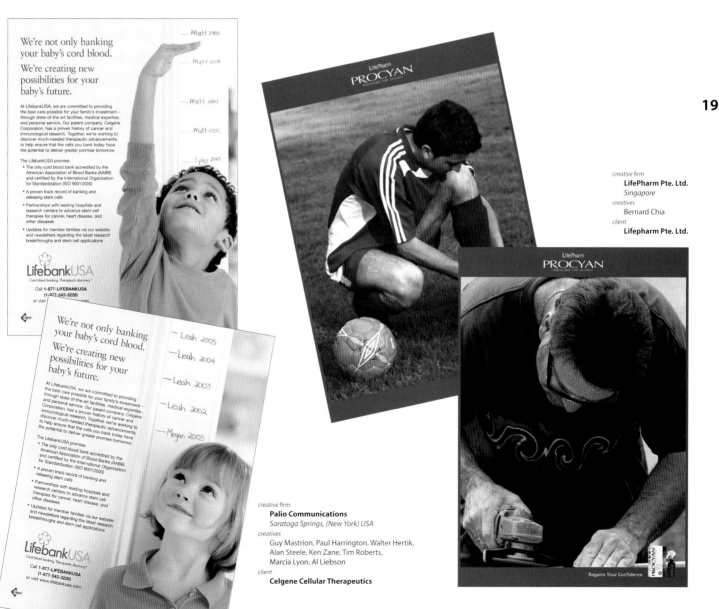

creative firm
LifePharm Pte. Ltd.
Singapore
creatives
Bernard Chia
client
Lifepharm Pte. Ltd.

creative firm
Palio Communications
Saratoga Springs, (New York) USA
creatives
Guy Mastrion, Paul Harrington, Walter Hertik,
Alan Steele, Ken Zane, Tim Roberts,
Marcia Lyon, Al Liebson
client
Celgene Cellular Therapeutics

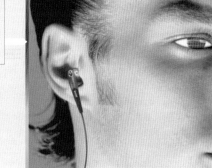

creative firm
Campbell-Ewald Advertising
Warren, (Michigan) USA
creatives
Bill Ludwig, Jim Gorman, Joe Puhy,
Craig Marrero, Robin Todd, Joe Godard,
Chris Grenier, Buddy Higgs
client
Chevrolet

creative firm
Portfolio Center
Atlanta, (Georgia) USA
creatives
Ashley Powell, Mark Sikes
client
Shure Electronics

20

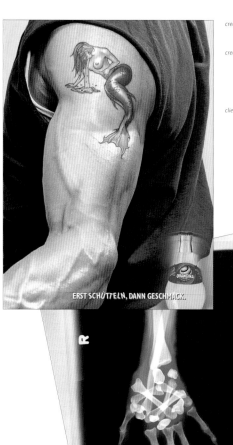

creative firm
Y&R Germany
Frankfurt, Germany
creatives
Christian Daul,
Horst Becker,
Norbert Huebner,
Lothar Mueller,
Stefanos Notopoulos
client
**Apollinaris &
Schweppes GmbH**

creative firm
AdVantage Ltd
Hamilton, Bermuda
creatives
Sami Lill, Faye Farley
client
Cuarenta Bucaneros

Look more successful than you really are.

If smoking cigars is an art form,
then we are an art gallery.

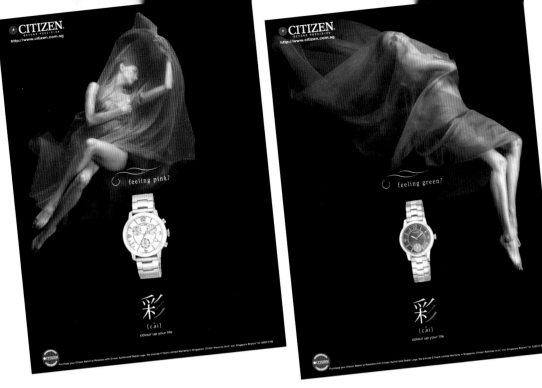

feeling pink?

彩
[căi]
colour up your life

feeling green?

彩
[căi]
colour up your life

creative firm
Planet Ads and Design Pte. Ltd.
Singapore
creatives
Hal Suzuki, Michelle Lauridsen
client
Citizen Watches (H.K.) Ltd.

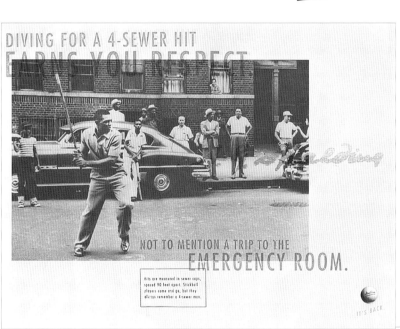

DIVING FOR A 4-SEWER HIT
EARNS YOU RESPECT

NOT TO MENTION A TRIP TO THE
EMERGENCY ROOM.

IT'S BACK

creative firm
Portfolio Center
Atlanta, (Georgia) USA
creatives
Matt Sharpe,
Coleen Wilson
client
Spalding

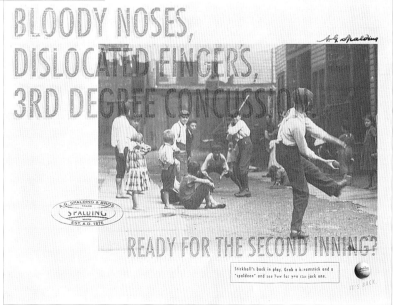

BLOODY NOSES,
DISLOCATED FINGERS,
3RD DEGREE CONCUSSIONS.

READY FOR THE SECOND INNING?

Stickball's back in play. Grab a broomstick and a
"spaldeen" and see how far you can jack one.

IT'S BACK

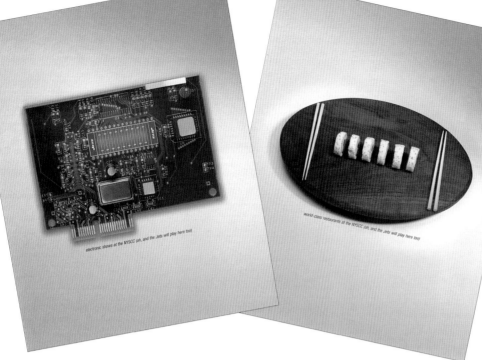

creative firm
Grey Worldwide
New York, (New York) USA
creatives
Tim Mellors, Mike Ryniec,
Mark Catalina, Jonathan Klein
client
New York Jets

creative firm
Portfolio Center
Atlanta, (Georgia) USA
creatives
Howard Hill,
Matt Denyer
client
Kirin Khiban

22

creative firm
Glitschka Studios/Prejean Lobue
Salem, (Oregon) USA
creatives
Von R. Glitschka, Brent Pelloquin,
Glen Gauthier
EasyClosets.com

You really need a vacation.

You really need a vacation.

creative firm
021 Comunicaciones
Mexico City, Mexico
creatives
Gabriel Flores, Dahian Rau, Paco Gutierrez,
Mariana Ortiz, Vladimir Nabor, Gabriel Flores,
Veronica Trujillo, Angel Martinez
client
Hyatt

23

SAVE FOR A RAINY DAY. INVEST FOR A RAINY DECADE.
H&R BLOCK
financial advisors
Don't predict, prepare

RIGHT WHEN YOU THINK YOU HAVE EVERYTHING WORKED OUT,
YOUR KIDS WILL GO AND DO SOMETHING STUPID.
LIKE GET INTO GRAD SCHOOL.

H&R BLOCK
financial advisors
Don't predict, prepare

creative firm
Portfolio Center
Atlanta, (Georgia) USA
creatives
Brent Deschene, Jason Arentsen
client
H&R Block

creative firm
RT&E Integrated Communications
Wilmington, (Delaware) USA
creatives
Rick Clemons,
Matt Caspari
client
Riverfront Development Corporation

Bag the brown bag.

JOE'S CRAB SHACK   IRON HILL   HARRY'S

HEAD FOR THE RIVER.

RIVERFRONT
WILMINGTON

SOUTH MADISON STREET, WILMINGTON, DELAWARE
302.425.5000 RIVERFRONTWILMINGTON.COM
GREAT SHOPPING • GOOD EATS • BLUE ROCKS BASEBALL • THE ARTS

Take an unannounced vacation.

HEAD FOR THE RIVER.

RIVERFRONT
WILMINGTON

SOUTH MADISON STREET, WILMINGTON, DELAWARE
302.425.5000 RIVERFRONTWILMINGTON.COM
GREAT SHOPPING • GOOD EATS • BLUE ROCKS BASEBALL • THE ARTS

IN 1920, HE FINISHED SECOND IN HOMERS.
THE PHILADELPHIA PHILLIES FINISHED FIRST.

11 seasons with over 40 homeruns and a total of 714 has forever placed Babe into baseball's record books. Learn more about the man who transformed a struggling sport into America's pastime.

The Babe Ruth Museum at Camden Station
216 Emory Street Baltimore, MD 21230
410-727-1539 or visit www.baberuthmuseum.com

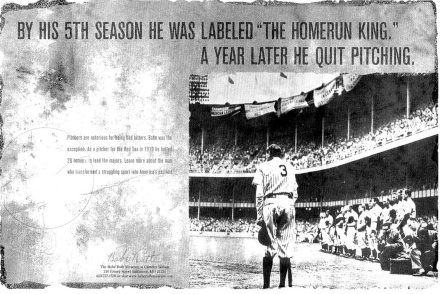

BY HIS 5TH SEASON HE WAS LABELED "THE HOMERUN KING."
A YEAR LATER HE QUIT PITCHING.

Pitchers are notorious for being bad hitters. Babe was the exception. As a pitcher for the Red Sox in 1919 he belted 29 homers to lead the majors. Learn more about the man who transformed a struggling sport into America's pastime.

The Babe Ruth Museum at Camden Station
216 Emory Street Baltimore, MD 21230
410-727-1539 or visit www.baberuthmuseum.com

24

creative firm
Portfolio Center
Atlanta, (Georgia) USA
creatives
Josh Dimarcantonio, Pat Horn
client
Babe Ruth Museum

Conquer the corporate jungle.
Gear up. The UD MBA.

Information sessions: Wednesday, April 7 & Thursday, May 13, 2004 5:30 – 7pm
Goodstay Center, University of Delaware, Wilmington Campus
2600 Pennsylvania Avenue. 302.831.2221

www.emba.udel.edu   302.831.2221

It's where you're going that counts.

Fast track.
Equipped for peak performance. The UD Executive MBA.

It's where you're going that counts. And you'll get there faster with an EMBA from the University of Delaware.
Our five nine-week semesters give you the skills to take advantage of professional opportunities — without missing a beat in your current position. Accelerate your career. With a fast track UD EMBA. Celebrating 50 years of developing some of the finest MBA talent in the country.

UD EMBA Information Sessions:
Wednesday, April 28 5:30 – 7pm
University of Delaware
Goodstay Center in Wilmington, 2600 Pennsylvania Avenue

www.emba.udel.edu   302.831.2221

It's where you're going that counts.

creative firm
RT&E Integrated Communications
Wilmington, (Delaware) USA
creatives
Rick Clemons,
Michael Bense
client
University of Delaware

IMAGINE.
HEART CARE THAT STARTS BEFORE YOU EVER GET TO THE HOSPITAL.

THE RIGHT CARE. RIGHT HERE. At El Camino Hospital's Heart and Vascular Program, we believe the best cardiac care starts with a commitment to complete cardiac care. That's why we offer a range of preventive, healthy heart seminars and screenings. They work hand in hand with our range of innovative surgical and non-invasive cardiac procedures. As well as with our unique cardiac/pulmonary rehab programs. How, you're probably asking, can a local community hospital be dedicated to such a complete continuum of cardiac care? Because we answer to the community, not corporate interests. So our physicians and staff are empowered to build the best cardiac programs and services right here, where you need them. El Camino Hospital's Heart and Vascular Program. Here for your heart.

EL CAMINO HOSPITAL
MOUNTAIN VIEW, CA

FREE HEALTHY HEART PACK.* CALL 800-216-5556 OR VISIT
ELCAMINOHOSPITAL.ORG/HEART TODAY TO GET YOURS.

*While supplies last

WHAT'S POWERFUL?
PHYSICIANS EMPOWERED.

THE RIGHT CARE. RIGHT HERE. When illness is the enemy, you need to put your most powerful resources on the job. That means physicians and staff who can make decisions. Authorize treatment. And get you back to feeling better. Because we answer to the community, not corporate interests. So our physicians and staff are free to deliver the care they know is right. Right for you. That's why they choose to work here. That's why you should choose to come here.

EL CAMINO HOSPITAL
MOUNTAIN VIEW, CA

TO FIND AN EL CAMINO HOSPITAL PHYSICIAN,
CALL 800-216-5556 OR VISIT WWW.ELCAMINOHOSPITAL.ORG.

creative firm
Publicis Dialog
San Francisco, (California) USA
creatives
Alex Grossman,
David Popino,
Jonathan Butts
client
El Camino Hospital

400 hp

4.2 0-60

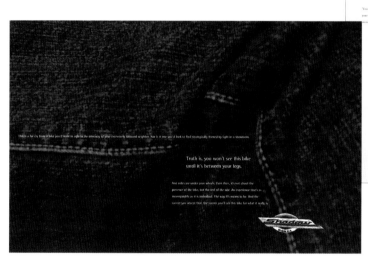

Truth is, you won't see this bike
until it's between your legs.

25

TAKE CARE
OF WHAT YOU WEAR
EVERY DAY

creative firm
Pure Design Co. LLC
Leverett, (Massachusetts) USA
creatives
Dan Mishkind, Graeme Ritchie,
Josef Kottler, Peter Einstein
client
Boiron USA

26

creative firm
Portfolio Center
Atlanta, (Georgia) USA
creatives
Josh Dimarcantonio,
Matt Denyer
client
Napster

creative firm
Portfolio Center
Atlanta, (Georgia) USA
creatives
Josh Dimarcantonio, Ashlea Powell,
Matt Denyer, Steve Nichols

My son flunked
out of school and his
girlfriend is pregnant.
Yesterday he totalled my
car and he doesn't even
have a license.

Otherwise he's a great boy!

I was in a traffic
jam for two hours
this morning,
my boss gave
me a hard time,
and I just found out
I've forgotten my
wife's birthday.

Otherwise it's been a great day!

creative firm
Futura DDB
Ljubljana, Slovenia
creatives
Žare Kerin, Zoran Gabrijan,
Miha Grobler, Janez Pukšič
client
Kratochwill

creative firm
Portfolio Center
Atlanta, (Georgia) USA
creatives
Pat Horn,
Matt Denyer
client
Aetna

creative firm
Portfolio Center
Atlanta, (Georgia) USA
creatives
Brent Deschene
client
Old Town Canoes

27

creative firm
D'Adda Lorenzini Vigorelli, BBDO
Rome, Italy
creatives
Sara Portello, Alessandro Fruscella,
Glon Pietro Vigorelli
client
Universal Studio Networks Italy

creative firm
VH1
New York, (New York) USA
creatives
Nigel Cox-Hagen, Phil Delbourgo,
Nancy Mazzei, Adam Vohlidka,
Jimmy Fingers, Traci Terrill,
Beth Wawerna, Hugh Kretschmer,
O'Neil Edwards, George Philhower
client
VH1

Apricot Baby Oil

Banana Hand Creme

28

Today Quinn...

voted for his favorite new ba
remixed the *Drake & Josh* th
shopped for vintage comic b
and then "tooned" his guitar

all between chord progressio

welcome to the futu

For the past 26 years, Nickelodeon has been finding innovative ways to connect ki
to what's new, what's now and what's next. Keeping up with kids keeps Nickelodeon

Today Julian...

mixed his own cd
battled for the inner sphere
watched some *SpongeBob*
and then checked last night's scores

all on his way to school.

welcome to the future

For the past 26 years, Nickelodeon has been finding innovative ways to connect kids
to what's new, what's now and what's next. Keeping up with kids keeps Nickelodeon #1.

NICKELODEON

It's time to discover true nature.

It's time to discover true nature.

It's time to discover true nature.

My personality isn't compartmentalized—why should my life be? I live in a big open loft space. It's great for parties because there aren't many corners for herding people into a single conversation for half the night. All boundaries are blurred, and every part of the space—every person there—is connected, open to a diversity of thought and action. It's not just about me and my little corner of the world. That's the way I want to live and work because that's how I think the world works.

Love how you see the world.

izzy

We only speak to the 2.31% of the population.

AboveMedia. A media company exclusively for an AB+ target.

C

creative firm
BBK Studio
Grand Rapids, (Michigan) USA
creatives
Yang Kim, Michele Chartier,
Kristin Tenant
client
izzydesign

creative firm
Parsons Brinckerhoff
New York, (New York) USA
creatives
Ana Tiburcio-Rivera,
Tom Malcolm
client
Parsons Brinckerhoff

creative firm
021 Comunicaciones
Mexico City, Mexico
creatives
Gabriel Flores, Dahian Rau
client
AboveMedia

29

full speed ahead!

PB Ports & Marine
draws on the experience
and multidisciplinary skills
of 9,000 professionals in
150 offices worldwide
to provide
comprehensive
services for ports and
marine facilities.
For more information,
call 212-465-5000 or visit
www.pbworld.com/ports.

PB PARSONS BRINCKERHOFF

For career opportunities in ports & marine planning,
design and construction-phase services, please visit
w w w . p b w o r l d . c o m

CONSIDER YOUR NATIONAL RETAIL NETWORK. **Consider the dots connected.**

GOING BEYOND THE CALL. SBC

creative firm
Rodgers Townsend
St. Louis, (Missouri) USA
creatives
Tom Hudder, Tom Townsend,
Evan Willnow
client
SBC Communications, Inc.

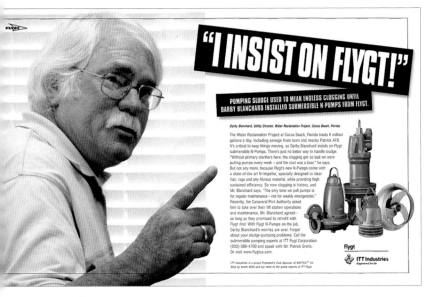

we invite you to see the "worst reel" in the business.

www.worstagencyreel.com

For beauty that lasts...

We bring you the best in organic fruit. Ma[...]link, call Organics Unlimited at (619) 710-0658 or visit www.organicsunlimited.com

creative firm
Oster and Associates
San Diego, (California) USA
creatives
Ben Duarte, Barbara Squires,
Terri Henry, Karin Oster
client
Organics Unlimited

creative firm
Rodgers Townsend
St. Louis, (Missouri) USA
creatives
Tom Hudder, Scott Lawson,
Mike Dillon, Evan Willnow
client
SBC Communications, Inc.

31

LONDON PACKAGING DINNER
FOR PACKAGING, DESIGN AND PRINT

BLACK TIE   THURSDAY 19TH MAY, 2005 7.30PM FOR 8.00PM
THE SAVOY, THE STRAND, LONDON, WC2R 0EU

INVITE

creative firm
**Turner Duckworth London
& San Francisco**
London, England
creatives
David Turner, Bruce Duckworth,
Christian Eager, Andy Grimshaw,
Reuben James
client
London Packaging

creative firm
Y&R SF
Sausalito, (California) USA
creatives
Al Mumtaz,
Walt Denson
client
Hitachi

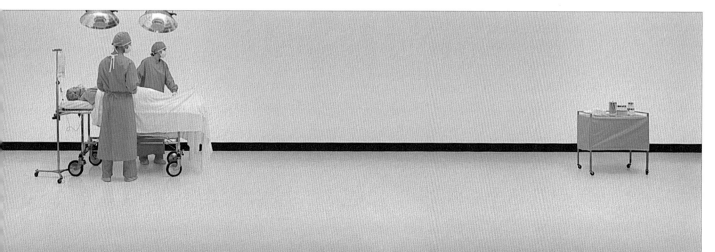

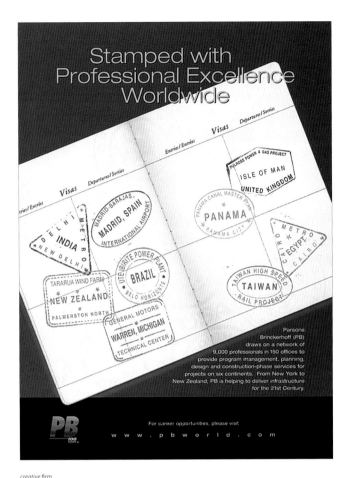

32

**Size D cups,
neurotic peeing dogs
and a funeral,**

now there's ideas for life.

Panasonic ideas for life

SLUDGE PROBLEMS? WHO YOU GONNA CALL?

SLUDGE BUSTERS

33

TELLER
LINE
FORMS
HERE

Consider the dots connected.

Because life doesn't stop at the bathroom door.

**Give your customers a reason to trade up
with new STAINMASTER® bath rugs.**

With over 90% brand recognition, the STAINMASTER® brand is one
of the most well-known consumer brands. Now it's available in the bath!
And research confirms that consumers are willing to pay more
for a bath rug when it carries the STAINMASTER® brand.

STAINMASTER® bath rugs. A beauty of an offering.

Step Forward™

INVISTA™

STAINMASTER® LYCRA® TEFLON® CORDURA® COMFOREL® COOLMAX® TACTEL® SUPRIVA™

WE CONTRIBUTED TO THIS MEMORIAL. BUT OTHERS PAID FOR IT.

SBC

creative firm
Rodgers Townsend
St. Louis, (Missouri) USA
creatives
Tom Hudder,
Scott Lawson,
Tom Townsend,
Evan Willnow
client
SBC Communications, Inc.

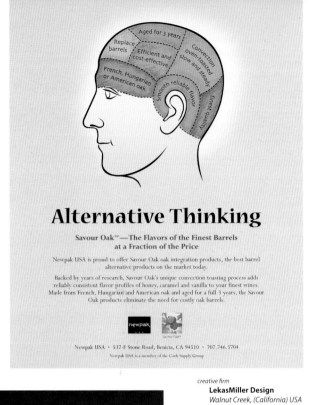

Alternative Thinking

Savour Oak™ — The Flavors of the Finest Barrels
at a Fraction of the Price

Newpak USA is proud to offer Savour Oak oak integration products, the best barrel
alternative products on the market today.

Backed by years of research, Savour Oak's unique convection toasting process adds
reliably consistent flavor profiles of honey, caramel and vanilla to your finest wines.
Made from French, Hungarian and American oak and aged for a full 3 years, the Savour
Oak products eliminate the need for costly oak barrels.

Newpak USA • 537-F Stone Road, Benicia, CA 94510 • 707.746.5704
Newpak USA is a member of the Cork Supply Group

creative firm
LekasMiller Design
Walnut Creek, (California) USA
creatives
Lana Ip, Tina Lekas Miller
client
Newpak USA, Inc.

34

creative firm
Brohard Design Inc.
Purcellville, (Virginia) USA
creatives
William Brohard
client
CompTel/ASCENT

The **NEW POWER** in Telecommunications

Register at: www.comptelascent.org

February 8-11, 2004
Anaheim Convention Center
Anaheim, California

CompTel ASCENT
ALLIANCE
Convention + Expo | Spring 2004

creative firm
Y&R SF
Sausalito, (California) USA
creatives
Al Mumtaz, Walt Denson
client
Hitachi

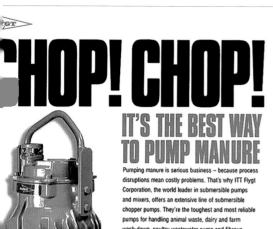

CHOP! CHOP!

IT'S THE BEST WAY TO PUMP MANURE

Pumping manure is serious business – because process disruptions mean costly problems. That's why ITT Flygt Corporation, the world leader in submersible pumps and mixers, offers an extensive line of submersible chopper pumps. They're the toughest and most reliable pumps for handling animal waste, dairy and farm wash-down, poultry wastewater sump and fibrous waste applications. Eliminate waste and inefficiency in your manure pumping applications. Choose Flygt's submersible chopper pumps. Learn more about Flygt submersible chopper pumps, mixers and other innovative hydraulics – and why they're best for your application. Call Mr. Bob Domkowski at 203-380-4700 for details. Or visit our website at www.flygtus.com

A unique swept-back impeller chops solids 175 times per second – turning them into small easy-to-pump pieces.

Flygt

ITT Industries
Engineered for life

creative firm
St. Vincent, Milone & O'Sullivan, Inc.
New York, (New York) USA
creatives
Rick St. Vincent, Edward Leighton,
Michael Podwill
client
ITT Flygt Corporation

Consider the dots connected. The end-to-end voice over IP solution we designed for Crate and Barrel features a unified IP messaging platform and the most advanced hardware available. The new system will save them a bundle on maintenance, management and wiring, while easing the cost and complexity of adding features or employees. And it's already improving productivity, helping over 400 associates make millions of customers feel right at home. To find out more, go to sbc.com/dots. **GOING BEYOND THE CALL.**

SBC

creative firm
Rodgers Townsend
St. Louis, (Missouri) USA
creatives
Tom Hudder, Scott Lawson
Mike Dillon, Evan Willnow
client
SBC Communications, Inc.

creative firm
Fixation Marketing
Washington, (D.C.) USA
creatives
Bruce E. Morgan, Randy Guseman,
Joe Younger
client
National Association of Broadcasters

35

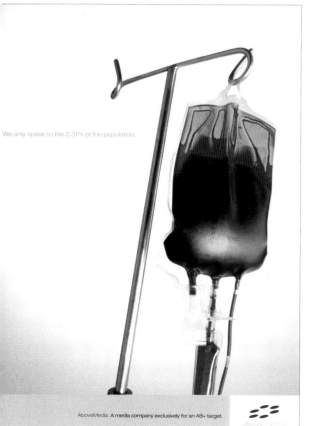

We only speak to the 2.31% of the population.

AboveMedia. A media company exclusively for an AB+ target.

above media

creative firm
021 Comunicaciones
Mexico City, Mexico
creatives
Gabriel Flores, Dahian Rau
client
AboveMedia

POSITIVELY DIFFERENT

COMING THIS NOVEMBER
NAB POST+ NEW YORK

Advanced training in the latest production and post-production techniques combined with a showcase of the latest content creation technologies from the biggest names in the industry — right in the heart of the Big Apple. Prepare yourself for a positively different event experience. If you are a professional video or film editor, Web developer, producer, director, graphic designer, animator, visual effects artist, sound designer or DVD producer... this is the East Coast show you've been waiting for.

www.nab.org/conventions

NAB POST+
NEW YORK
The NAB Post+Production Show

Future Media Concepts

Experience Comes With Age

Since 1995, we've had a simple vision —deliver exceptional engineering services. Now, we are the fastest-growing engineering firm in the mid-Atlantic region. We owe our success to our clients and dedicated employees. Give us a call. We're ready to put our expertise to work for you.

Bowman
CONSULTING

ENGINEERING | PLANNING | SURVEYING | ENVIRONMENTAL CONSULTING
T 703.464.1000 www.bowmanconsulting.com

Emphasize Embellishment

Embellish it as you like. Embossing, stamping, precision perfect printing. Elegant intricate detail or sophisticated simplicity, almost anything you can imagine Rivercap can realize for you. Not only is our product beautiful, our service is impeccable. Rivercap. Our premium tin capsule is the ultimate finishing touch to your premium bottle of wine. Period.

newpak USA   RIVERCAP USA
A DIVISION OF NEWPAK USA

537-F Stone Road, Benicia, CA 94510 • Phone 707.747.3630 • Fax 707.746.7471

creative firm
LekasMiller Design
Walnut Creek, (California) USA
creatives
Lana Ip, Tina Lekas Miller
client
Newpak USA, Inc.

creative firm
021 Comunicaciones
Mexico City, Mexico
creatives
Gabriel Flores, Dahian Rau
client
AboveMedia

creative firm
Hinge Inc.
Reston, (Virginia) USA
creatives
Juan Plaza, Steve Uzzell
client
Bowman Consulting

creative firm
Rodgers Townsend
St. Louis, (Missouri) USA
creatives
Tom Hudder, Scott Lawson
Mike Dillon, Evan Willnow
client
SBC Communications, Inc.

36

We only speak to the 2.31% of the population.

AboveMedia. A media company exclusively for an AB+ target.   abovemedia

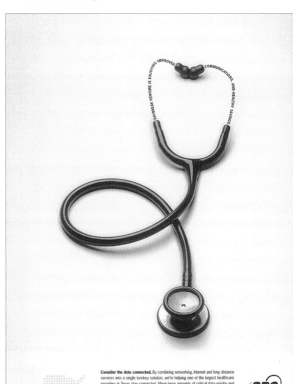

Consider the dots connected. By combining networking, Internet and long distance services into a single turnkey solution, we're helping one of the largest healthcare providers in Texas stay connected. Move large amounts of critical data quickly and reliably. Adapt to long-term growth efficiently. And save money along the way – more than $1 million over the next three years. Find out more about how we're helping Daybreak Venture connect the dots at sbc.com/dots. **GOING BEYOND THE CALL.**

SBC

creative firm
Hoffman/Lewis
San Francisco, (California) USA
creatives
Sharon Krinsky, Ronda Dunn,
Anne Lewis
client
Bank of the West

37

creative firm
HBO Creative Services
New York, (New York) USA
creatives
Gary Dueno, Tony Viola,
Venus Dennison
client
HBO

Fantastic voyage.

greener   greener

"I love what you've done with yourself."

MOHAWK
Mohawk makes the room

1 gig RAM   1 gig RAM

RAZOR WIRE WILL
NOT DETER THE NEW
GENERATION OF INVADER.

Consider the dots connected.
Intelligent networks interwoven and
working together. Not only can we
design, deliver and manage an integrated data network,
we'll help you keep it safer and more secure. Access
granted for the good guys. Access denied for everyone
else. Across firewalls. Across checkpoints. Across America.
To learn more, talk to your SBC account representative
at 1-866-SBC-FEDS or go to sbcfeds.com.

GOING BEYOND THE CALL. SBC

INFINITE REINFORCEMENTS,
AT YOUR SERVICE.

Consider the dots connected.
It's time to reap the benefits of
IP convergence. Data and voice
solutions, customized and secure. We can design,
deliver and manage your network while helping you
improve day-to-day operations while protecting what
must be protected. Across barracks. Across branches.
Across America. To learn more, talk to your SBC account
representative at 1-866-SBC-FEDS or go to sbcfeds.com.

GOING BEYOND THE CALL. SBC

creative firm
Greenfield/Belser Ltd.
Washington, (D.C.) USA
creatives
    Burkey Belser, Jonathan Bruns,
    Joe Walsh, Alan Sciulli
client
    DecisionQuest

OUT OF ORDER →

When
did
you
realize
the
jury
missed
all
your
signs?

While you work the facts and the law, we help you
understand themes and strategies, community attitudes,
alternative courtroom graphics, witness effectiveness
and likely jury reactions. At all six steps of litigation,
we can help you make your message clear. Study
every step at *decisionquest.com,* or call Judy Leon or
Steve Teller at *202-408-3000.*

THE BEST CASE SCENARIO™   DECISIONQUEST
A BOWNE COMPANY

creative firm
Rodgers Townsend
St. Louis, (Missouri) USA
creatives
    Tom Hudder,
    Luke Partridge,
    Mike McCormick,
    Evan Willnow,
    Susan Howells
client
    SBC Communications, Inc.

40

How
could
we
know
public
opinion
would
crush us?

While you work the facts and the law, we help you understand themes and strategies, community attitudes, presenta-
tion options, witness effectiveness and likely jury reactions.
At all six steps of litigation, we can help you minimize
downside risks. Study every step at *decisionquest.com,*
or call us at *1-877-8-Decision.*

THE BEST CASE SCENARIO™   DECISIONQUEST
A BOWNE COMPANY

baustahlgewebe gmbh
DIE SEELE DES BETONS

STAUDAMM

creative firm
RTS Rieger Team GmbH
Leinfelden-Echterdingen, Germany
creatives
    Boris Pollig, Shadi Satrapi,
    Martin Uhl
client
    Baustahlgewebe GmbH

baustahlgewebe gmbh
DIE SEELE DES BETONS

TUNNEL

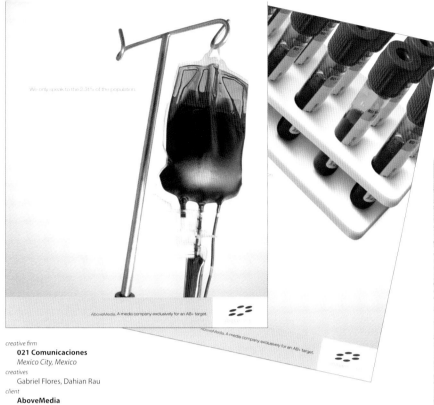

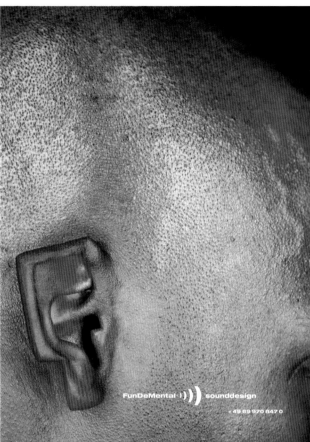

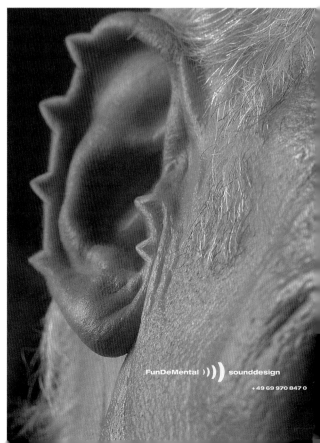

IT ALL STARTS WITH STEER MANURE.
WE TURN IT INTO HORTICULTURAL ART.

MIRAMAR
Wholesale Nurseries, Inc.

DEPENDABLE. ACCESSIBLE. CAPABLE. RESPONSIBLE.
WE'RE AN ABLE BUNCH. AND OUR PLANTS ARE GREAT TOO.

MIRAMAR
Wholesale Nurseries, Inc.

CITY COUNCILS.
COUNTY SEATS.
CAPITOL FLOORS.

Consider the dots connected.
Everybody will soon be working better together. We can design and deliver managed, intelligent networks. Reliable and secure solutions, customized for government applications and reducing capital expenditures. Across jurisdictions. Across county lines. Across America. To learn more, send us an email at gov@sbc.com.

GOING BEYOND THE CALL.

SBC

LOCAL HOSPITALITY.
CIVIC RESPONSIBILITY.
PUBLIC SECURITY.

Consider the dots connected.
More than ever, local governments have complicated network security needs. We can design, deliver and manage a data integration system that brings it all together. Redundancy for greater security, assistance with quick response and disaster recovery to help government prepare for almost any scenario and maintain the public safety. Across neighborhoods. Across communities. Across America. To learn more, send us an email at gov@sbc.com.

GOING BEYOND THE CALL.

SBC

creative firm
Rodgers Townsend
St. Louis, (Missouri) USA
creatives
Tom Hudder, Luke Partridge
Mike McCormick, Evan Willnow
client
SBC Communications, Inc.

43

Today Julian...

mixed his own cd
battled for the inner sphere
watched some *SpongeBob*
and then checked last night's scores

all on his way to school.

welcome to the future

NICKELODEON

Today Quinn...

voted for his favorite new band
remixed the *Drake & Josh* theme
shopped for vintage comic books
and then "tooned" his guitar

all between chord progressions.

welcome to the future

NICKELODEON

For the past 26 years, Nickelodeon has been finding innovative ways to connect kids to what's new, what's now and what's next. Keeping up with kids keeps Nickelodeon #1.

Everything under the sun.

The Logomark brand has long been established as the one source for the most extensive selection of quality promotional

Logomark
www.logomark.com

BASICS Bettoni Bettoni Crystal

creative firm
IE Design + Communications
Hermosa Beach, (California) USA
creatives
Cya Nelson, Marcie Carson,
Kenny Goldstein
client
Logomark, Inc.

Every color in the rainbow.

At Logomark, the sky is the limit.
From bright red travel mugs to cool blue key chains, we have a variety of items to choose from in all of your favorite colors. Logomark is the source for the most extensive selection of quality promotional items. But look to our value for the real pot of gold at the end of rainbow.

Logomark
www.logomark.com

BASICS Bettoni Bettoni Crystal E OPTCOM

creative firm
**Nickelodeon Creative
Resources**
New York, (New York) USA
creatives
David Hamed,
Russell Hicks

CONSIDER YOUR NATIONAL RESERVATIONS NETWORK. Consider the dots connected.

GOING BEYOND THE CALL? **SBC**

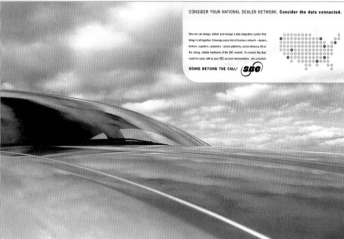

CONSIDER YOUR NATIONAL DEALER NETWORK. Consider the dots connected.

GOING BEYOND THE CALL? **SBC**

44

creative firm
Rodgers Townsend
St. Louis, (Missouri) USA
creatives
Tom Hudder, Tom Townsend,
Evan Willnow
client
SBC Communications, Inc.

Work like this never goes out of style.

Into the latest gadget? Chances are, Marger Johnson was part of it. We patent ideas across a wide variety of industries. We defend intellectual property cases for startups and market leaders alike. And inventors consider us colleagues. That is no fad.

01 Full-Color Display
Indigm Display Corporation
San Francisco, CA

Work like this never goes out of style.

Into the latest gadget? Chances are, Marger Johnson was part of it. We patent ideas across a wide variety of industries. We defend intellectual property cases for startups and market leaders alike. And inventors consider us colleagues. That is no fad.

Magnification 550x

PermaFiche™

07 PermaFiche™
Serenity Technologies, Inc.
Aloha, Oregon

12 BiGHA
BiGHA
Corvallis, Oregon

Turning invention into advantage.
1030 SW Morrison Street, Portland, Oregon USA · 97205-2626 · 503.222.3613
www.techlaw.com

Marger Johnson & McCollom

creative firm
Greenfield/Belser Ltd.
Washington, (D.C.) USA
creatives
Burkey Belser, Charlyne Fabi,
Jennifer Myers, Alan Sciulli
client
Marger Johnson & McCollom, P.C.

creative firm
RTS Rieger Team GmbH
Leintelden-Echterdingen, Germany
creatives
Ute Witzmann, Siegfried Schaal
client
Voith Paper

VOITH
Engineered reliability.

think in paper

VOITH
Engineered reliability.

think in paper

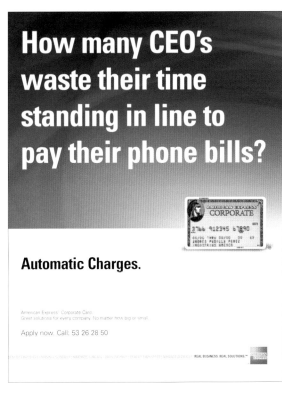

How many CEO's waste their time standing in line to pay their phone bills?

Automatic Charges.

American Express® Corporate Card.
Great solutions for every company. No matter how big or small.

Apply now. Call: 53 26 28 50

REAL BUSINESS. REAL SOLUTIONS.™

creative firm
021 Comunicaciones
Mexico City, Mexico
creatives
Gabriel Flores, Ivan Pedraza
client
American Express Corporate Card

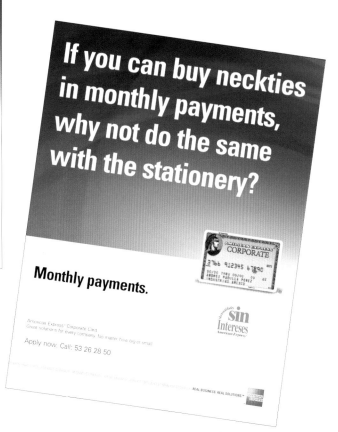

If you can buy neckties in monthly payments, why not do the same with the stationery?

Monthly payments.

American Express® Corporate Card.
Great solutions for every company. No matter how big or small.

Apply now. Call: 53 26 28 50

sin Intereses
American Express

REAL BUSINESS. REAL SOLUTIONS.™

45

creative firm
Qualcomm
San Diego, (California)
USA
creatives
Christopher Lee,
Frank Bernas,
Dean Sipe,
Eric Myer,
Anthony Eng
client
Qualcomm, Brazil

>>> El carisma de 3G

Carisma; simplemente se tiene o no. La red 3G inalámbrica lo tiene. Tan sólo observe a su alrededor y verá que en todas partes la gente se asombra por la atractiva variedad de aplicaciones de datos inalámbricas que son posibles gracias a las normas 3G CDMA2000 y WCDMA (UMTS). Mediante las redes 3G, no sólo puede conversar con otras personas, también tiene acceso a Internet, correo electrónico y servicios GPS, además de poder descargar música, juegos, timbres personalizados y protectores de pantalla.

Para conocer más sobre el carisma de 3G,
visite www.3GVidaEN.com hoy mismo.

QUALCOMM

>>> La seguridad de 3G

Seguridad—no es algo que deba analizar a posteriori. Basada en complejas técnicas de codificación digital, las redes 3G inalámbricas proporcionan un entorno de comunicaciones móviles seguro que Wi-Fi no puede igualar. Mediante las redes 3G, como CDMA2000 o WCDMA (UMTS), puede trabajar en línea o enviar y recibir correo electrónico desde ubicaciones remotas, sin poner en riesgo su seguridad o privacidad. Además, las redes 3G inalámbricas proporcionan una conectividad de alta velocidad que permite tener acceso a una red privada virtual (VPN) en forma rápida y conveniente.

Para conocer más sobre la velocidad de
3G, visite www.3GVidaIT.com hoy mismo.

QUALCOMM

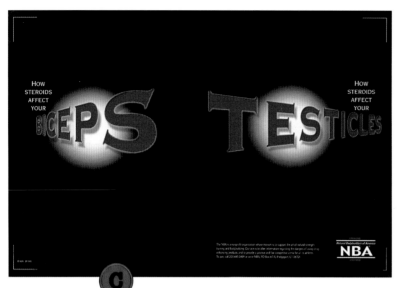

creative firm
Schneider Art & Design
Fairfield, (Connecticut) USA

creative firm
The Humane Society of the United States
Washington, (D.C.) USA
creatives
Paula Jaworski, Susan Washington
client
The Humane Society of the United States

creative firm
Publicis Dialog
San Francisco, (California) USA
creatives
Alex Grossman, Lotus Child,
Tom Kavanaugh
client
Shanti

creative firm
021 Comunicaciones
Mexico City, Mexico
creatives
Gabriel Flores, Dahian Rau
client
Aeromexico

46

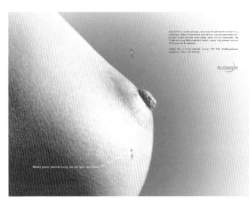

Translation of the headline:
Not every hardening is so easy

Mamazone e.V. - women and genomics against breast cancer, "Hardening"

The Brief
Fundraising and influencing the public opinion for Mamazone e.V. an organisation which fights against breast cancer and for mammography screening programs.

The Solution
A doublepage press ad with an oversized breast, where the staple at the magazine centerfold becomes part of the creative execution. It stands for an obvious, easy-to-spot "hardening". The illness can be discovered by early detection mammography in the millimeter range, long before it can be felt by touch.

The Results
20% more incoming donations versus pre-campaign period. Significant increase in awareness for Mamazone e.V. in

EVEN GOD WAS A **SILENT** SPECTATOR THIS TIME.
SUNAMI
BREAK THE **SILENCE,** DON'T BE A MERE SPECTATOR.

It may take several days, weeks or years for the victims to come back to normalcy.
Help them by contributing to UNICEF TSUNAMI RELIEF FUND.
www.unicef.org

creative firm
Deepak Advertising Agency
Indore, (Madhya Pradesh) India
creatives
Sachin Upadhyay, Mohd Vahid Khan,
Ashwath Ramchandran
client
UNICEF

creative firm
Y&R Germany
Frankfurt, Germany
creatives
Christian Daul, Monika Spirkl,
Micael Hess
client
Mamazone

47

creative firm
McCann Erickson Korea
Seoul, Korea
creatives
YC Kim, RH Lee
client
UNICEF Korea

creative firm
Oster and Associates
San Diego, (California) USA
creatives
Ben Duarte, Barbara Squires,
Terri Henry, Karin Oster
client
San Diego Foundation

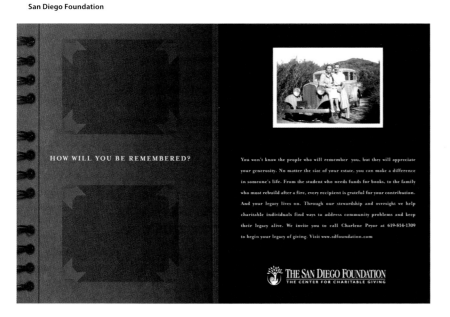

HOW WILL YOU BE REMEMBERED?

You won't know the people who will remember you, but they will appreciate your generosity. No matter the size of your estate, you can make a difference in someone's life. From the student who needs funds for books, to the family who must rebuild after a fire, every recipient is grateful for your contribution. And your legacy lives on. Through our stewardship and oversight we help charitable individuals find ways to address community problems and keep their legacy alive. We invite you to call Charlene Pryor at 619-814-1309 to begin your legacy of giving. Visit www.sdfoundation.com

✦ THE SAN DIEGO FOUNDATION
THE CENTER FOR CHARITABLE GIVING

엄마, 어딨어요?

아빠는? 형, 누나는요..?

친구들은 다 어디로 갔죠?

우리 집과 내가 다니던 학교는요?

도대체 내가 살던 세상이 어떻게 된 거죠...?

이번 쓰나미로 혼자가 된 "끄리아니"로부터...

그는 혼자가 아니었습니다
당신의 손길만 함께 한다면,
지금도 혼자가 아닙니다

unicef ✿
유니세프한국위원회
KOREAN COMMITTEE FOR UNICEF

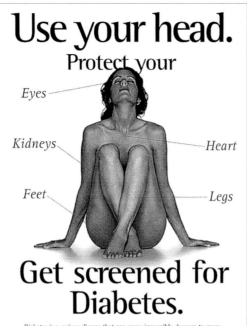

creative firm
Janet Hughes and Associates
Wilmington, (Delaware) USA
creatives
Felice Croul,
Joyce Williams
client
Delaware Pharmacist Society

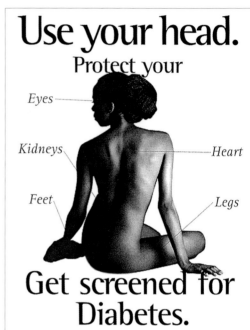

48

creative firm
Y&R Germany
Frankfurt, Germany
creatives
Christian Daul, Horst Becker,
Norbert Huebner, Lothar Mueller,
Stefanos Notopoulos
client
Sharkproject E.V.

"If I were a giant panda would you help protect my environment?"

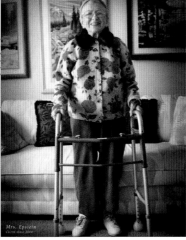

"If I were a bald eagle would you help me be free?"

At ElderHelp our purpose is to provide the elderly with the assistance they need to remain in their own home. Their home is more than where they live, it is their life. It is where they store memories of family and friends, youth and infancy. Take away their home and you take away their individuality, their independence and eventually their will to live. Help us support the elderly in their work to keep their home. To remain where they belong, for more information call (619) 284-9281 or visit www.elderhelpofsandiego.org

ElderHelp

creative firm
Oster and Associates
San Diego, (California) USA
creatives
Ben Duarte, Barbara Squires,
Terri Henry, Karin Oster
client
Elderhelp

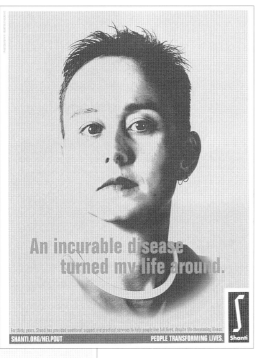

An incurable disease turned my life around.

SHANTI.ORG/HELPOUT   PEOPLE TRANSFORMING LIVES.   Shanti

creative firm
Publicis Dialog
San Francisco, (California) USA
creatives
Alex Grossman, Lotus Child,
Tom Kavanaugh
client
Shanti

49

- SMALL BUSINESS OWNER
- PTA MEMBER
- FATHER OF TWINS

INVEST IN FUTURES

How can we support the power and possibility of a new generation? By creating a world in which he can be an architect and an active dad. A world in which he can be involved and successful in his work, home and community life.

Help create tomorrow's world by re-imagining today's — through the eyes of a child — in the Ms. Foundation for Women's annual Take Our Daughters And Sons To Work® Day. It's more than a day. It's the power and possibility of a new generation.

Please visit our Web site at www.DaughtersandSonstoWork.org or call 1.800.676.7780 to learn how to participate in **Take Our Daughters And Sons To Work®** Day on April 28, 2005.

Take Our daughters and sons TO WORK
MS. FOUNDATION FOR WOMEN

Breast cancer showed me how strong I am.

- ARCHITECT
- VOLUNTEER FIREFIGHTER
- CARES FOR ELDER PARENT

creative firm
Suka Design
New York, (New York) USA
creatives
Brian Wong, Chris Vanauken,
Deborah Schupack
client
MS. Foundation for Women

INVEST IN FUTURES

How can we support the power and possibility of a new generation? By creating a world in which she can be an architect and a volunteer firefighter. A world in which she can be involved and successful in her work, home and community life.

Help create tomorrow's world by re-imagining today's — through the eyes of a child — in the Ms. Foundation for Women's annual Take Our Daughters And Sons To Work® Day. It's more than a day. It's the power and possibility of a new generation.

Please visit our Web site at www.DaughtersandSonstoWork.org or call 1.800.676.7780 to learn how to participate in **Take Our Daughters And Sons To Work®** Day on April 28, 2005.

For thirty years, Shanti has provided emotional support and practical services to help people live full lives, despite life-threatening illness.

Consumer Newspaper Ads, single

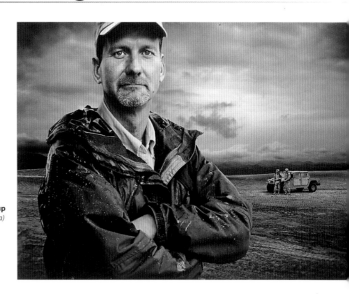

creative firm
The Richards Group
Sausalito, (California)
USA
creatives
Jeff Hopfer,
Walt Denson
client
Haliburton

From one power company to another, thank you for a truly amazing season.

Ameren

50

creative firm
Rodgers Townsend
St. Louis, (Missouri) USA
creatives
Tom Hudder, Scott Lawson,
Mike McCormick
client
Ameren UE

creative firm
Griffo
Belém, (Pará) Brazil
creatives
Antônio Natsuo, Renato Brito, Sergio Bastos
client
ORM

creative firm
Y&R Germany
Frankfurt, Germany
creatives
Christian Daul, Uwe Marquardt, Monika Sprkl
client
Praxis Fuer Paartherapie Dr. Grosrurth

96

www.couple-therapy.org

THE ORM AWARD FOR NEW ADVERTISING TALENT.

FOR THOSE WHOSE TALENT COMES DIRECT FROM THE CRADLE.

www.orm.com.br

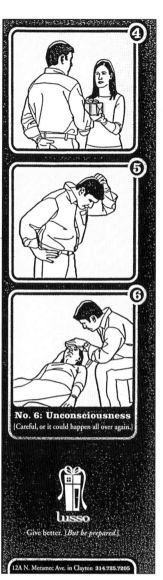

creative firm
Rodgers Townsend
St. Louis, (Missouri) USA
creatives
Tom Hudder,
Luke Partridge,
Kris Wright,
Mike McCormick
client
Lusso

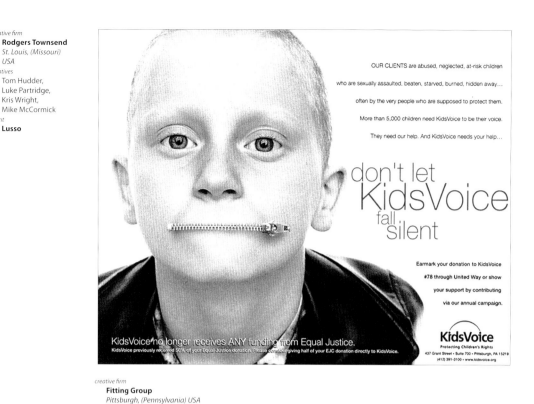

OUR CLIENTS are abused, neglected, at-risk children

who are sexually assaulted, beaten, starved, burned, hidden away...

often by the very people who are supposed to protect them.

More than 5,000 children need KidsVoice to be their voice.

They need our help. And KidsVoice needs your help...

don't let
KidsVoice
fall
silent

Earmark your donation to KidsVoice

#78 through United Way or show

your support by contributing

via our annual campaign.

KidsVoice
Protecting Children's Rights
437 Grant Street • Suite 700 • Pittsburgh, PA 15219
(412) 391-3100 • www.kidsvoice.org

KidsVoice no longer receives ANY funding from Equal Justice.
KidsVoice previously received 50% of your Equal Justice donation. Please consider giving half of your EJC donation directly to KidsVoice.

creative firm
Fitting Group
Pittsburgh, (Pennsylvania) USA
creatives
Michael Henry
client
KidsVoice

creative firm
Hoffman/Lewis
San Francisco, (California) USA
creatives
Sharon Krinsky, Chris Toffoli,
David Swope, Jeff Billig, Scott Leeper
client
Wild Oats Natural Marketplace

51

creative firm
Mendes Publicidade
Belém, (Pará) Brazil
creatives
Oswaldo Mendes,
Maria Alice Penna
client
Banco da Amazônia

PALMAS PRA PALMAS !

Palmas, a última capital planejada do Século XX no
País, está entre as primeiras que mais crescem.
Parabéns, Palmas, pelo desempenho e pelo aniversário.

O MELHOR DO BRASIL
É O BRASILEIRO

BANCO DA AMAZÔNIA
Excelência por natureza

BR**SL**
UM PAÍS DE TODOS
GOVERNO FEDERAL

20 DE MAIO.
ANIVERSÁRIO
DE PALMAS.

"O melhor do Brasil é o brasileiro" provém de obra de Câmara Cascudo.

Like a regular grocery store.
Only with real food.

JUST BECAUSE PEOPLE WILL EAT SOMETHING DOESN'T MAKE IT FOOD.
Today, most supermarkets are so focused on profitable "products" they've forgotten what real
food is. Case in point — the processed stuff in a squirt can they call cheese. And the multi-
hued sugar stuff they call cereal. Today, in place of cheeses,
chocolates, beef and fruit, you find shelves of artificial "cheesy,"
"chocolaty," "beefy," and "fruity." We don't know about you, but
we find that fishy.

IF YOU ARE WHAT YOU EAT, WE ARE
WHAT WE SELL.
Wild Oats has strict standards for what we'll allow
in our stores. We only feature natural products
that contribute to the health and well-being of
our customers. That eliminates everything with artificial colors, flavors, and
preservatives. That also means no meat from animals raised on antibiotics,
artificial growth hormones or animal byproducts. We don't buy from socially
and environmentally unhealthy factory farms. And you won't find hydrogenated
oils or genetically modified ingredients in our food, anywhere in the store.

GET A HEALTHY TASTE OF REALITY.
So what's left? Just the finest, freshest, natural and organic products from
around the world. From local produce to rare and exotic fruits and herbs.
From the highest-quality all-natural meats to
the freshest seafood (though if a species is being
overfished, we won't buy it). As well as
a mind-expanding collection of cheeses
and olives, freshly baked breads, and aisles of packaged foods and
health products. Just like a regular grocery store — but it's all real.
Nothing artificial.

Come and see for yourself. The more you know about Wild Oats,
the less you're going to want to shop anywhere else.

Brad Dillman, Cheese Supervisor

DID YOU KNOW?

Baked Goat Cheese Salad

WILD OATS
NATURAL MARKETPLACE

To find the Wild Oats nearest you, call 800-494-WILD or go to www.wildoats.com

Become a better cook.
Buy better food.

YOU CAN ONLY BE SO GOOD WITH SO-SO INGREDIENTS

TO FIND BETTER FOOD, LOOK FOR A BETTER FOOD STORE.

ANY QUESTIONS?

DID YOU KNOW?

Linguine with Capers, Olives, Tomatoes, Basil & Feta

INGREDIENTS

PREPARATION

WILD OATS
NATURAL MARKETPLACE

To find the Wild Oats nearest you, call 800-494-WILD or go to www.wildoats.com

52

The best thing to happen to prostate care since

Introducing Daily Prostate Positioning. This is state-of-the art technology for those who have been diagnosed with prostate cancer. The Cancer Treatment Group can pinpoint radiation treatment with astonishing accuracy, unheard of until today, so only the tumor is zapped, and healthy tissue is left untouched. It is the only place in Northwest Indiana to have this technology. It is the only place to go for the best treatment with the best results.

Cancer Treatment Group
in association with Methodist Hospital
For more information call 219-945-1050 or visit www.CancerTreatmentGroup.com

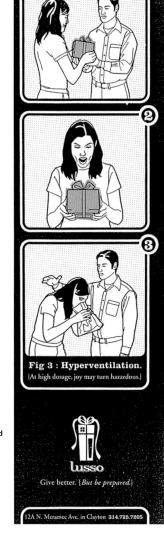

Fig 3 : Hyperventilation.
{At high dosage, joy may turn hazardous.}

lusso

Give better. {But be prepared.}

12A N. Meramec Ave. in Clayton 314.725.7205

WHOSE BRIGHT IDEA WAS IT TO PUT THE MAN IN BLACK?

MANUEL AT THE FRIST

FRIST CENTER FOR THE VISUAL ARTS®

Manuel: Star-Spangled Couture December 17 - May 22
Image is everything for America's icons and our newest exhibition offers an intimate look at clothing that helped create the stage presences for Johnny Cash, Marty Stuart, Dolly Parton and others. Also on display is a personal "thank you" to America from Manuel — a collection of 50 jackets representing each state.

919 Broadway, Downtown Nashville · 615-244-3340 · www.fristcenter.org

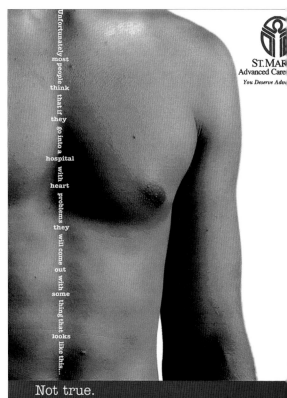

Unfortunately most people think that if they go into a hospital with heart problems they will come out with something that looks like this...

ST. MARY
Advanced Care
You Deserve Adva

Not true.
The advances in heart care are phenomenal. And St. Mary's is leading the way. With advanced imaging, drug-e
stents. Endoscopic vein-harvesting. Same day procedures. So major heart problems don't always means major sur

22c: Fractured Humerus
(Hysteria and hugging do not mix.)

lusso

Give better. (But be prepared.)

124 N. Meramec Ave. in Clayton 314.725.7205

Summer is how you make it!
at Délifrance, we're making it...

Longer...

Brighter!

Cooler...

Délifrance.

53

Guess who just flew in
from the coast.

OUR ENTIRE SEAFOOD SECTION IS FIRST CLASS.

FISH FOR COMPLIMENTS.

NOTHING WATERED DOWN ABOUT OUR COMMITMENT.

Garlic Peppered Shrimp

DID YOU KNOW?

WILD OATS
NATURAL MARKETPLACE
Better Food. Pure & Simple.™

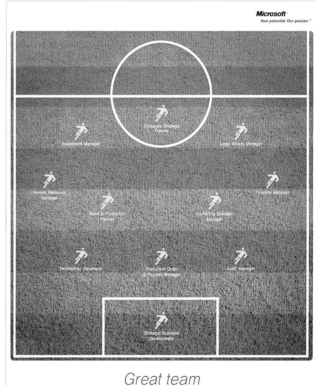

Microsoft
Your potential. Our passion.™

Great team
Great solution

Microsoft Enterprise Project Management Solution   Microsoft Office

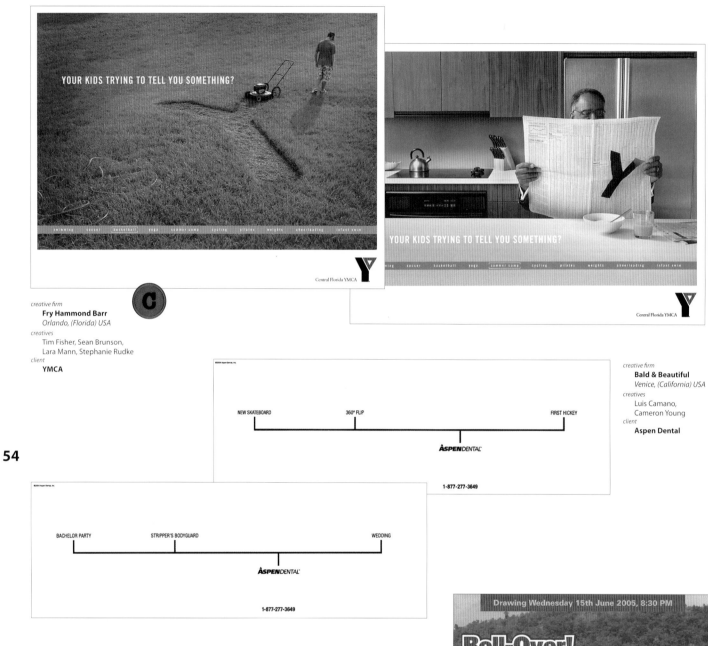

YOUR KIDS TRYING TO TELL YOU SOMETHING?

swimming   soccer   basketball   yoga   summer camp   cycling   pilates   weights   cheerleading   infant swim

Central Florida YMCA

NEW SKATEBOARD   360° FLIP   FIRST HICKEY

ÂSPENDENTAL

1-877-277-3649

BACHELOR PARTY   STRIPPER'S BODYGUARD   WEDDING

ÂSPENDENTAL

1-877-277-3649

54

Drawing Saturday 11th June 2005, 8:30 PM

**Even I could
get lucky...**

YOU CAN WIN
$3,800,000
This Week's Estimated Jackpot

National

Drawing Wednesday 15th June 2005, 8:30 PM

**Roll-Over!
Roll-Over!**

YOU CAN WIN
$4,200,000
This Week's Estimated Jackpot

National Lottery On-Line

Play LOTTO plus today!

Diamonds are
produced from years
of heavy pressure.

Funny, so are
marriage proposals.

SWISS TIMING
Watchmakers & Jewellers

Because
her eyes
already do
sparkle.

SWISS TIMING
Watchmakers & Jewellers

creative firm
Advantage Ltd
Hamilton, Bermuda
creatives
Sami Lill, Karen Martin,
Susan Tang Petersen
client
Swiss Timing

55

*Are you better at measuring powdered sugar
than blood sugar?*

You've just learned you have diabetes....now what?

Joslin Diab
affiliate at St. Mar

creative firm
Keller Crescent Advertising
Evansville, (Indiana) USA
creatives
Randall L. Rohn,
Lee Bryant
client
Joslin Diabetes Center

*Do you spend more time with paint chips,
than test strips?*

There are an alarming number of people with diabetes
who struggle to keep health as their top priority.

Joslin Diabetes Center
affiliate at St. Mary's

You can't ignore it away. If you have diabetes, you must take control of
it, before you lose control of your life. We know it's hard to do on your
own. Let us help. We're Joslin Diabetes Center at St. Mary's.

Joslin is a complete center for treatment and research of diabetes.
• A full-time Board Certified Endocrinologist on staff. Dr. Zouhair Bibi.
• Diabetes education and self-management program.
• A foot clinic, specializing in diabetes-related problems.
• Exercise and weight loss programs.
• Dietitians and nutritionists to help in meal planning.

The Joslin Diabetes Center in Boston is the world-renowned leader in
the treatment of diabetes and is affiliated with Harvard Medical School.

Call us at 485-1814.

ST.MARY'S
Advanced Care Hospital
You deserve advanced care.

LAUNCHES A SUMMER OF HEROES!

SUPER EDITION

**Don't Miss The
Premiere of
SPIDER-MAN®* 2
Tomorrow,
June 4, 8PM ET/PT**

SPIDER-MAN 2
on Cinemax

cinemax

**THIS SUMMER, CINEMAX BRINGS YOU OVER
A BILLION DOLLARS IN BOX OFFICE HITS!**

creative firm
HBO Creative Services
New York, (New York) USA
creatives
Ana Racelis,
Venus Dennison
client
HBO

A GOURMET DINNER SO EXCLUSIVE EVEN THE LOBSTERS NEED INVITES.

the Reefs
SOUTHAMPTON BERMUDA

AFTER TRYING THE TAPAS YOU COULD TRY THE FREE SALSA LESSONS. (SHOULD YOU BE ABLE TO MOVE)

the Reefs
SOUTHAMPTON BERMUDA

creative firm
Advantage Ltd
Hamilton, Bermuda
creatives
Sami Lill, Sheila Semos,
Faye Farley
client
The Reefs

(Week One Of Rehab)

(Week Two Of Rehab)

(Week One Of Rehab)

(Week Three Of Rehab)

(Week Five Of Rehab)

(Week Four Of Rehab)

The most crucial step in recovery...

Our Cutting-Edge Approach To Injury Recovery...

ST.MARY'S
Advanced Care Hospital
& Rehabilitation Institute
You deserve advanced care.

creative firm
Keller Crescent Advertising
Evansville, (Indiana) USA
creatives
Randall L. Rohn, Keith Rios,
Nancy Kirkpatrick
client
St. Mary's

56

creative firm
**Planet Ads and
Design Pte. Ltd.**
Singapore
creatives
Eunice Ng,
Michelle Lauridsen
client
TTS Eurocars Pte. Ltd.

www.fiat.com.sg

Stilo

FIAT STILO **FIAT**

You'll see it and

FIATCROMA **FIAT**

THE LIBERAL IS THE NEWSPAPER WITH THE HIGHEST NEWSPAPER SALES RATE IN THE NORTH/NORTHEAST.
IT'S ON OF THE 35 LARGEST NEWSPAPER PUBLISHERS IN LATIN AMERICA. IF YOU ADVERTISE ANYWHERE ELSE, MAN, YOU'RE CRAZY

THE LIBERAL IS ONE OF THE 8 LARGEST NEWSPAPER PRINTERS IN BRAZIL. IT IS ALSO RANKS 18TH AMONGST THE MOST READ PAPERS IN THE COUNTRY. WHOEVER JUMPS INTO THE FRAY WITHOUT IT IS SURE TO BE THE UNDERDOG."

O LIBERAL

creative firm
Griffo
Belém, (Pará) Brazil
creatives
António Natsuo, Edgar Cardoso,
Sergio Bastos
client
O Liberal

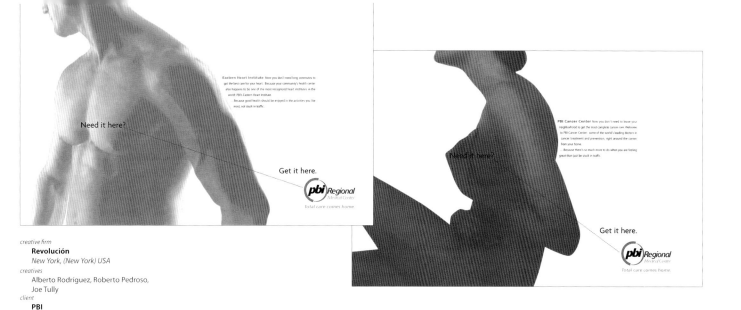

Eastern Heart Institute Now you don't need long commutes to get the best care for your heart. Because your community's health center also happens to be one of the most recognized heart institutes in the world: PBI's Eastern Heart Institute.

Because good health should be enjoyed in the activities you like most, not stuck in traffic.

Need it here?

Get it here.

pbi Regional
Medical Center
total care comes home.

PBI Cancer Center Now you don't need to leave your neighborhood to get the most complete cancer care. Welcome to PBI Cancer Center: some of the world's leading doctors in cancer treatment and prevention, right around the corner from your home.

...Because there's so much more to do when you are feeling great than just be stuck in traffic.

Need it here?

Get it here.

pbi Regional
Medical Center
Total care comes home.

creative firm
Revolución
New York, (New York) USA
creatives
Alberto Rodriguez, Roberto Pedroso,
Joe Tully
client
PBI

creative firm
Griffo
Belém, (Pará) Brazil
creatives
Antônio Natsuo, Beth Mendes,
Vera Souza
client
TV Liberal

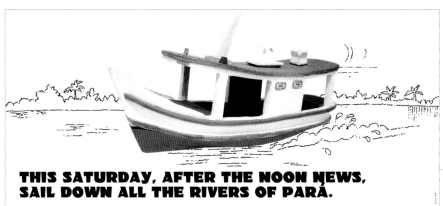

THIS SATURDAY, AFTER THE NOON NEWS, SAIL DOWN ALL THE RIVERS OF PARÁ.

THIS SATURDAY, AFTER THE NOON NEWS, TAME THE TRAILS OF PARÁ.

creative firm
Griffo
Belém, (Pará) Brazil
creatives
Antônio Natsuo, Edgar Cardosa,
Sergio Bastos
client
ORM

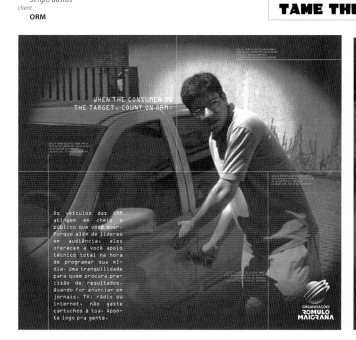

WHEN THE CONSUMER IS
THE TARGET, COUNT ON ORM.

Os veículos das ORM atingem em cheio o público que você quer. Porque além de líderes em audiência, eles oferecem a você apoio técnico total na hora de programar sua mídia. Uma tranqüilidade para quem procura precisão de resultados. Quando for anunciar em jornais, TV, rádio ou internet, não gaste cartuchos à toa. Aponte logo pra gente.

ORGANIZAÇÕES
ROMULO MAIORANA

WHEN THE CONSUMER IS
THE TARGET, COUNT ON ORM.

Os veículos das ORM atingem em cheio o público que você quer. Porque além de líderes em audiência, eles oferecem a você apoio técnico total na hora de programar sua mídia. Uma tranqüilidade para quem procura precisão de resultados. Quando for anunciar em jornais, TV, rádio ou internet, não gaste cartuchos à toa. Aponte logo pra gente.

ORGANIZAÇÕES
ROMULO MAIORANA

PUBLICIDADE RIMA COM LIBERDADE.

Antes de 1920, foram lançados, nos Estados Unidos, o
aspirador de pó, o fogão elétrico e a geladeira também
elétrica, que levaram 34 anos para chegar a todos os
lares americanos.

Décadas depois, o televisor levou menos
de 8 anos*.

Hoje, os produtos só precisam que suas
campanhas cheguem à mídia para o mercado
absorver a novidade, que logo torna-se lugar-
comum.

Foi o que aconteceu recentemente com
o celular.

A diferença chama-se publicidade
comercial.

Para confirmar a tese, o "Pravda", de
Moscou, vem em nossa ajuda informando,
no fim da década de 80, ainda em pleno
regime comunista, que era estimado em
37 bilhões de horas/ano o tempo gasto
nas filas pelos soviéticos.

Quase 200 horas/ano por adulto!
Esperando para fazer compras!
As lojas eram todas do Estado.
Não havia concorrência. Por isso, não
anunciavam, não informavam o que tinham
para vender, não comunicavam quando os
produtos estavam em falta, nem quando eles
eram lançados.

O jornal moscovita concluiu
informando que as filas produziam varizes nas
donas de casa, atrasavam as refeições e eram a

5ª causa alegada para
os divórcios na então
nação soviética.

David Ogilvy, um dos papas
da comunicação de todos os
tempos, assina embaixo, ao dizer que
a publicidade é um meio de
informação.

Para o espanhol Jaime Compmany, a
publicidade comercial é apenas a
conseqüência necessária da liberdade, o
maior bem que o homem possui.

Por falar em liberdade, como
sobreviveriam os meios de comunicação sem
publicidade comercial, especialmente o rádio e
a televisão aberta, que você recebe de graça?
Publicidade rima com liberdade.

A boa e velha liberdade de você se informar,
de produtos e serviços a plataformas políticas.

Liberdade de defender uma causa ou contestar
uma idéia.

É o que falta nos regimes totalitários, como na
extinta União Soviética das imensas e demoradas filas
de cidadãos irritados, cansados e punidos pelas varizes
e pelos divórcios.

Viva a publicidade!
Viva a liberdade!

4 de Dezembro. Dia Mundial da Propaganda.

Mendes
Agência comprometida com a boa publicidade.

* Nossos agradecimentos a Jaime Compmany pela informação.

creative firm
Mendes Publicidade
Belém, (Pará) Brazil
creatives
Oswaldo Mendes, Marcel Chaves,
Cássio Tavernard
client
Mendes Publicidade

58

Griffo. The agency from the North most awarded in the 2004 North/Northeast Columnists event.

GRIFFO

It wasn't any miracle, but we think it's nice to say thanks.

creative firm
Griffo
Belém, (Pará) Brazil
creatives
Antônio Natsuo, Edgar Cardosa,
Sergio Bastos
client
Griffo

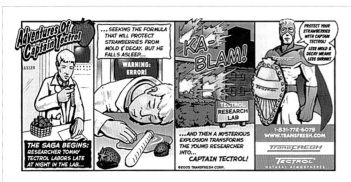

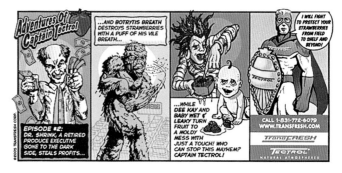

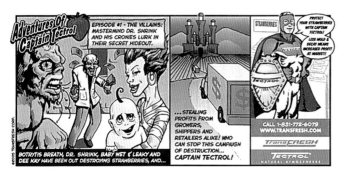

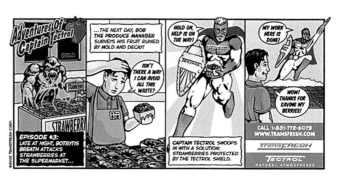

creative firm
Full Steam Marketing & Design
Salinas, (California) USA
creatives
Craig Kauffman, Karen Nardozza
client
Transfresh

creative firm
Griffo
Belém, (Pará) Brazil
creatives
António Natsuo, Edgar Cardosa,
Sergio Bastos, Vera Souza
client
Griffo

59

creative firm
Mendes Publicidade
Belém, (Pará) Brazil
creatives
Oswaldo Mendes, Emanuelle Conde,
Maria Alice Penna, Paula Sampaio
client
Instituto Criança Vida

60

HOW ONE JACKSONVILLE MAN AND 3 BUCKETS ARE SAVING THE WORLD

creative firm
Empire Communications Group
Jacksonville, (Florida) USA
creatives
Chris Alcantara, Fred Page,
Susan Kiernan-Lewis, Pete Helow,
Les Loggins, Paul Figura
client
Florida Times Union

Amazonia Newspaper, 4 years.

We give you the information that helps you decide. Democratically.

creative firm
Griffo
Belém, (Pará) Brazil
creatives
Antônio Natsuo, Beth Mendes,
Vera Souza
client
Assembléia Legislativa

creative firm
Acart Communications Inc.
Ottawa, (Ontario) Canada
creatives
John Staresinic, Tom Megginson, Javier Frutos,
Kerry Cavlovic, Stephen Fenn, Colin Pates,
Sue McKinney, Al Albania
client
Government of Canada—Department of Justice

61

creative firm
Planet Ads and Design Pte Ltd
Singapore
creatives
Hal Suzuki, Kitano Tomoya,
Michelle Lauridsen
client
MOS Foods Singapore Pte Ltd

creative firm
Equals Three Communications, Inc.
Bethesda, (Maryland) USA
creatives
Bruce Campbell, Tim Brown,
Alisa Weinstein, Eugene Faison
client
Girl Scout Council of the Nation's Capital

Childhood

This is Joe Jr.

This is Mike Jr.

Joe Jr's dad made a decision to move to the big city so he could make more money. Unfortunately, it isn't the greatest place to raise a kid. Bad choice, Joe, Sr.

Mike Jr's dad decided to stay in the Northern Tier to raise his family. Nothing better than camping and spending time in the great outdoors!

Joe and Mike were both born and raised in the Northern Tier. Joe was offered a big salary to move to the "big city". He jumped at the chance without taking into consideration the downfalls . . . high cost of living, lots of concrete, and the outside influences of city living! Mike, on the other hand, stayed in his home town, went to work for a local business and has just bought his own home complete with a view of the Endless Mountains. Could there be a better place to raise YOUR kids!

PENNSYLVANIA | come invent the future™

www.stayinnortherntier.com

Pay Day

Joe's Family.

Mike's Family.

Big city money – big city prices. Joe and his family can afford a tiny apartment but the neighborhood isn't the greatest. So on a nice day like today – here they sit. One big happy family.

This is Mike and his family. Mike can afford a new home with a big back yard so his daughters have plenty of room to play. It is a beautiful day in the Northern Tier. Life doesn't get any better than this.

Joe and Mike were both born and raised in the Northern Tier. Joe was offered a big salary to move to the "big city". He jumped at the chance without taking into consideration the downfalls . . . high cost of living, lots of concrete, and the SMELL! Mike, on the other hand, stayed in his home town, went to work for a local business and has just bought his own home complete with swing. The Northern Tier – the best place on earth. Why would you ever want to leave such a place?

PENNSYLVANIA | come invent the future™

www.stayinnortherntier.com

creative firm
Impact Advertising
Williamsport, (Pennsylvania) USA
creatives
Daniel Wodrig, Amy Jo Rieck,
Matthew Gartner, Christopher Johnson
client
**Northern Tier Regional Planning
& Development Commission**

62

She doesn't look like a drunk, does she?

Peer pressure begins early. One-third of 4th graders and more than half of 6th graders say they have been pressured by friends to drink alcohol.

But friends aren't the only problem. Alcohol is the drug of choice for most children because it is so easily accessible, the majority of whom find and begin using it in their own homes.

Underage Drinking
WAKE UP!
Know the Truth

For more information visit www.wakeupclintoncounty.org
Alcohol is a drug. Sponsored by District Attorney Ted McKnight's Task Force Against Drugs Impacting Our Youth.

Your 9th Grader's Favorite Drink?

Do you know what your child's favorite drink really is? **Would you believe that it is beer?** 37% of our tenth graders and half of our seniors drink to get drunk on a regular basis. One in three sixth graders is already drinking. Half of our 8th graders are drinking. Clinton County . . . these are **OUR children.** These statistics came from surveys taken right here in **OUR county.** Don't you think it's about time we **wake up** and do something to **stop underage drinking?**

Underage Drinking
WAKE UP!
Know the Truth

For more information, visit us on-line at
www.wakeupclintoncounty.org

"Alcohol is a drug"

Sponsored by **District Attorney Ted McKnight's Task Force Against Drugs Impacting Our Youth.**

creative firm
Impact Advertising
Williamsport, (Pennsylvania) USA
creatives
Christopher Johnson, Daniel Wodrig,
Amy Jo Rieck, Matthew Gartner
client
District Attorney Ted McKnight

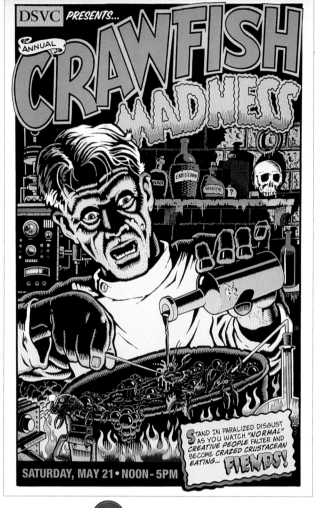

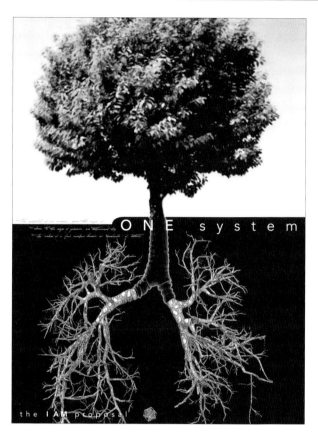

creative firm
Peterson & Company
Dallas, (Texas) USA
creatives
Scott Ray, George Toomer
client
**Dallas Society of
Visual Communication**

creative firm
Bohan Advertising/Marketing
Nashville, (Tennessee) USA
creatives
Kerry Oliver, Kevin Hinson,
Andy Anderson, Darrell Soloman
client
**Boy Scouts of America
Middle Tennessee Council**

creative firm
Portfolio Center
Atlanta, (Georgia) USA
creatives
Hart Armstrong
client
The I Am Proposal

creative firm
Rienzi & Rienzi Communications
Montville, (New Jersey) USA
creatives
Mary Gayle Scheper, Edward Horvath,
Frank Aiello, Kim Langley
client
Mylan Pharmaceuticals Inc.

63

HEAR WHAT YOU MISSED BY BEING **TOO YOUNG** AND **TOO WHITE.**

FRI AND SAT.

COUNTRY MUSIC HALL OF FAME MUSEUM NASHVILLE

NIGHT TRAIN TO NASHVILLE: MUSIC CITY RHYTHM & BLUES 1945-1970

creative firm
Bohan Advertising/Marketing
Nashville, (Tennessee) USA
creatives
Kerry Oliver, Gregg Boling
client
**Country Music Hall
of Fame and Museum**

SPONSORED BY THE DEPARTMENTS OF HISTORY AND CREATIVE WRITING

Susquehanna

OCT. 7, 2004 AT 7:30   ISAACS AUDITORIUM

2 MINUTES OF HISTORY

DAVID MARGOLICK

Contributing editor to *Vanity Fair* magazine,
Four-time Pulitzer Prize Nominee

creative firm
MFDI
Selinsgrove, (Pennsylvania) USA
creatives
Mark Fertig
client
Susquehanna University

64

THINKINGXXX

PREMIERES THURSDAY, OCTOBER 28, 11PM/10c
PERFECT DAY FILMS PRESENTS A FILM BY TIMOTHY GREENFIELD-SANDERS "THINKING XXX"
DIRECTED AND PRODUCED BY TIMOTHY GREENFIELD-SANDERS EDITOR LUKAS HAUSER

HBO

creative firm
HBO
New York, (New York) USA
creatives
Carlos Tejeda, Mary Tchorbajian,
Venus Dennison
client
HBO

THE TROJAN WOMEN

BY EURIPIDES

creative firm
**The Design Studio of
Kean University**
Union, (New Jersey) USA
creatives
Steven Brower,
Jason Washer
client
**Theater Department of
Kean University**

creative firm
Sommese Design
Port Matilda,
(Pennsylvania) USA
creatives
Lanny Sommese,
Ryan Russell,
John Heinrich
client
Central Pennsylvania
Festival of the Arts

creative firm
Tom Fowler, Inc.
Norwalk, (Connecticut)
USA
creatives
Thomas G. Fowler
client
Connecticut Grand
Opera & Orchestra

creative firm
Nassar Design
Brookline, (Massachusetts) USA
creatives
Nelida Nassar

65

creative firm
Sagon-Phior
Los Angeles, (California) USA
creatives
Sagon-Phior
client
McCormick Distilling Co.

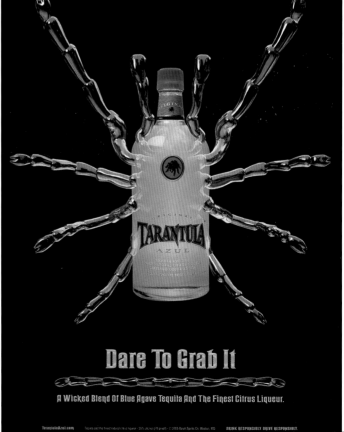

66

creative firm
Alexander Isley Inc.
Redding, (Connecticut) USA
creatives
Alexander Isley
client
**College of Saint Rose
Graphic Design Program**

creative firm
021 Comunicaciones
Mexico City, Mexico
creatives
Gabriel Flores, Dahian Rau, Paco Gutierrez,
Mariana Ortiz, Vladimir Nabor, Gabriel Flores,
Veronica Trujillo, Angel Martinez
client
Hyatt

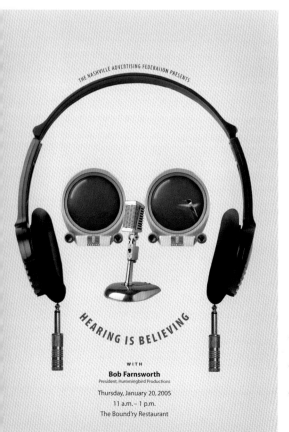

creative firm
Ventress Design Group
Franklin, (Tennessee) USA
creatives
Tom Ventress, Jane Finley,
David Williams
client
Nashville Advertising Federation

creative firm
Rodgers Townsend
St. Louis, (Missouri) USA
creatives
Tom Hudder, Luke Partridge,
Mike McCormick, Evan Willnow
client
Humane Society of Missouri

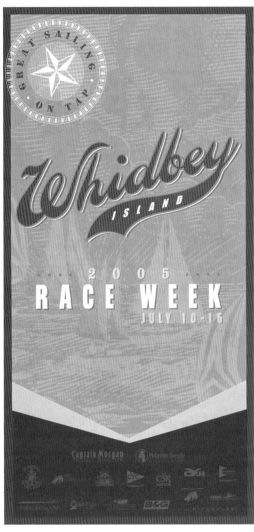

creative firm
Rodgers Townsend
St. Louis, (Missouri) USA
creatives
Tom Hudder, Tom Townsend,
Evan Willnow
client
Sievers Retrievers

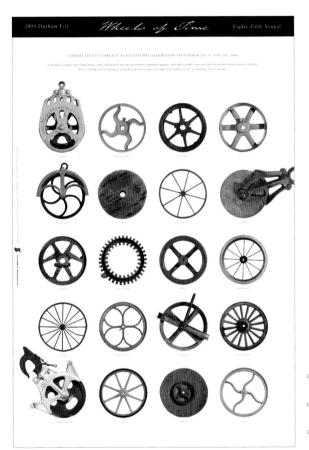

67

creative firm
Pivot + Levy
Seattle, (Washington) USA
creatives
Andy Lueck,
Terry Stoeser
client
Sail Northwest

creative firm
Bertz Design Group
Middletown, (Connecticut) USA
creatives
Richard Uccello, Ted Bertz,
Jody Dole
client
Maggie Peterson

creative firm
Rodgers Townsend
St. Louis, (Missouri) USA
creatives
Tom Hudder, Luke Partridge,
Mike McCormick, Evan Willnow
client
AD Club of St. Louis

LET'S PUT AWAY
THE INDEX FINGER.

Let's stop pointing fingers.
Let's pause for just one
night. Let's open our
borders. Let's fraternize
with the enemy. Heck, let's
yuk it up. Let's backslap
and act interested until
someone more important
comes along.

LET'S ADDY.

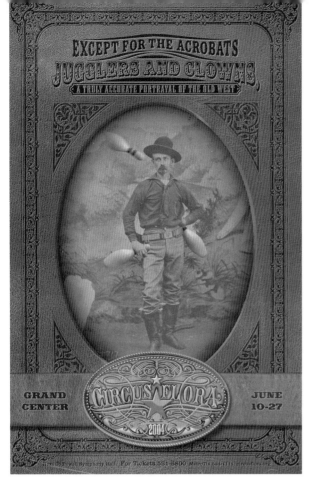

creative firm
Rodgers Townsend
St. Louis, (Missouri) USA
creatives
Tom Hudder,
Tim Varner,
Mike Dillon
client
Circus Flora

creative firm
Portfolio Center
Atlanta, (Georgia) USA
creatives
Patricio Juarez
client
Raydr Drama Society

68

creative firm
Kiku Obata & Company
St. Louis, (Missouri) USA
creatives
Rich Nelson
client
The Shakespeare Festival of St. Louis

creative firm
KO Design Institute
Tokyo, Japan
client
Fugu Corporation

WHILE EVERY CHEF BRINGS SOMETHING DIFFERENT TO THE TABLE ONLY THE GREAT ONES LEAVE A LITTLE OF THEMSELVES BEHIND.

FLAVORS OF PITTSBURGH · AN EVENING WITH CULINARY MASTERS · SEPTEMBER 19TH 2004

creative firm
MARC USA
Pittsburgh, (Pennsylvania) USA
creatives
Ron Sullivan, Laurie Habeeb, Dena Mosti, Jason Fotter
client
Western Pennsylvania Chapter Liver Foundation

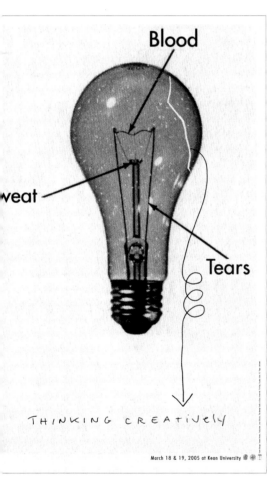

creative firm
The Design Studio of Kean University
Union, (New Jersey) USA
creatives
Steven Brower
client
Art Directors Club, NJ
Kean University

69

creative firm
Island Oasis
Walpole, (Massachusetts) USA
creatives
Jenny Keech

creative firm
Walt Denson
Sausalito, (California) USA
creatives
Walt Denson
client
Walt Denson

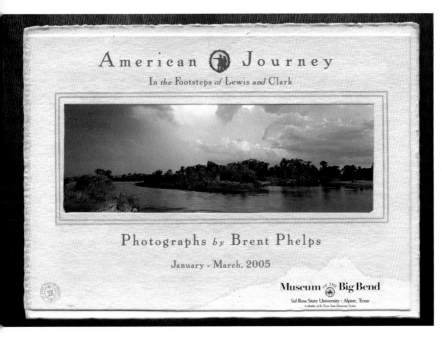

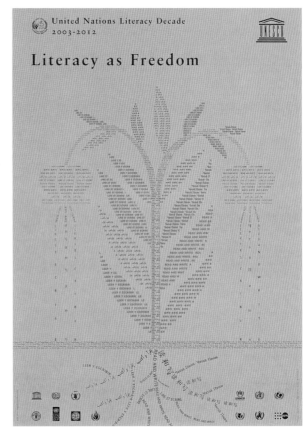

creative firm
VanPelt Creative
Garland, (Texas) USA
creatives
Chip VanPelt, Brent Phelps
client
Museum of the Big Bend

creative firm
Nassar Design
Brookline, (Massachusetts) USA
creatives
Nelida Nassar, Margarita Encomienda
client
UNESCO

creative firm
Desbrow
*Pittsburgh,
(Pennsylvania) USA*
creatives
Gabrielle Lane,
Kimberly Miller
client
Read!365

creative firm
Chase Creative
St. Pete Beach, (Florida) USA
creatives
George Chase
client
Bamboozle Ltd.

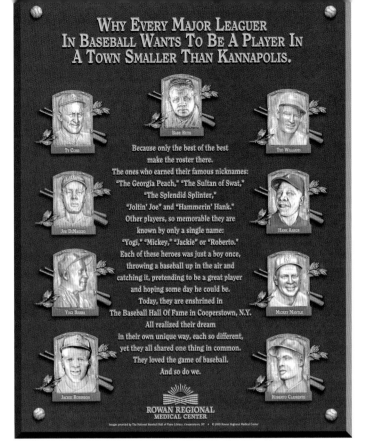

creative firm
Lee Stewart's Creative Works!
Charlotte, (North Carolina) USA
creatives
Lee Stewart, Adam Lingle
client
Rowan Regional Medical Center

creative firm
The Design Studio of Kean University
Union, (New Jersey) USA
creatives
Seymour Chwast
client
Kean University, ADCNJ

creative firm
Walls Art & Design
Tokyo, Japan
creatives
Pepii Watanabe
client
Graphic Arts Printing, Inc.

71

creative firm
VSA Partners, Inc.
*Chicago, (Illinois)
USA*
creatives
Tim Guy,
Claire Williams
client
Harley-Davidson

72

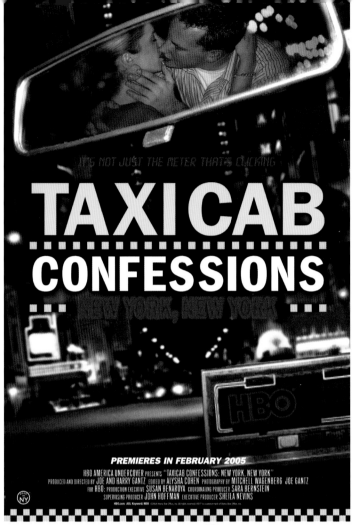

74

creative firm
Tom Fowler, Inc.
Norwalk, (Connecticut) USA
creatives
Thomas G. Fowler
client
**Connecticut Grand
Opera & Orchestra**

creative firm
Rodgers Townsend
St. Louis, (Missouri) USA
creatives
Tom Hudder, Chris Taurisano,
Allison Hammer
client
Arts and Education Council

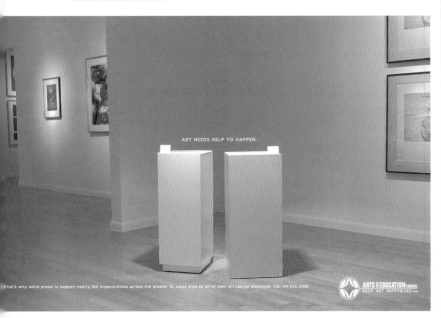

creative firm
021 Comunicaciones
Mexico City, Mexico
creatives
Gabriel Flores, Dahian Rau, Paco Gutierrez,
Mariana Ortiz, Vladimir Nabor, Gabriel Flores,
Veronica Trujillo, Angel Martinez
client
Hyatt

creative firm
Ventress Design Group
Franklin, (Tennessee) USA
creatives
Tom Ventress
client
Nashville Advertising Federation

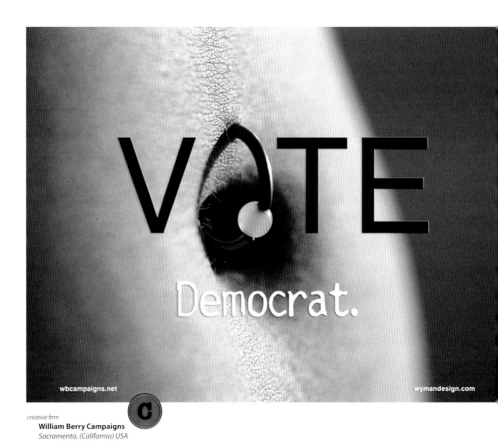

wbcampaigns.net

wymandesign.com

75

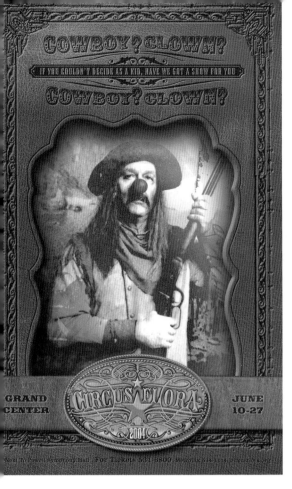

76

creative firm
**Empire Communications
Group**
Jacksonville, (Florida) USA
creatives
Chris Alcantara, Pete Helow,
Susan Kiernan-Lewis, Paul Figura
client
International Spirits

creative firm
MFDI
Selinsgrove, (Pennsylvania) USA
creatives
Mark Fertig
client
Susquehanna University

creative firm
HBO Creative Services
New York, (New York) USA
creatives
Jose Mendez,
Venus Dennison
client
HBO

creative firm
Rodgers Townsend
St. Louis, (Missouri) USA
creatives
Tom Hudder, Luke Partridge,
Mike McCormick, Gary Nolton,
Evan Willnow
client
Humane Society of Missouri

creative firm
McCabe Neill Jaggers
Oakville, (Ontario) Canada
creatives
John Neill, Egon Springer,
Rob Jaggers, Joe Bellaera
client
Holsten

78

creative firm
Revolución
New York, (New York) USA
creatives
Alberto Rodriguez, Roberto Pedroso,
Abby Lee
client
Palm Bay Imports

creative firm
Qualcomm
San Diego, (California) USA
creatives
Christopher Lee,
Allison Bridges
client
**Bastille Day,
Southern Caregiver**

creative firm
Rodgers Townsend
St. Louis, (Missouri) USA
creatives
Tom Hudder, Scott Lawson,
Mike Dillon, Evan Willnow
client
Memphis Rock-n-Soul Museum

creative firm
Rodgers Townsend
St. Louis, (Missouri) USA
creatives
Tom Hudder, Scott Lawson,
Kay Cochran
client
Arts and Education Council

creative firm
Tom Fowler, Inc.
Norwalk, (Connecticut) USA
creatives
Elizabeth P. Ball
client
Norwalk Emergency Shelter, Inc.

creative firm
DirectLine
Wilmington, (Delaware) USA
creatives
Steve Strohm
client
Tri-State Bird Rescue

creative firm
Rodgers Townsend
St. Louis, (Missouri) USA
creatives
Tom Hudder, Ron Copeland
Ryan McMichael, Evan Willnow
client
Soulard Mardi Gras of St. Louis

Just a drink. slight drink...Another drink! wake up! wake up!...

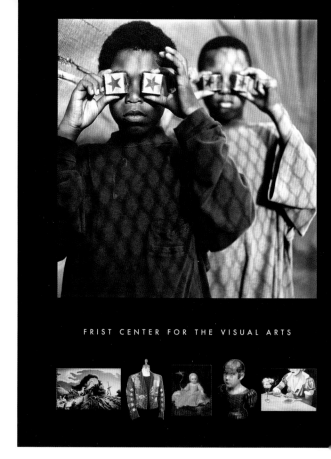

FRIST CENTER FOR THE VISUAL ARTS

80

NOTHING CAPS OFF A LONG DAY OF HOLDING UP TRAINS LIKE A TALL COLD ONE.

"Any god-damned son of a bitch with that name ought be shot." Such were the feelings of the James Gang toward John Lincoln, a passenger they encountered on the ill-fated train bound to Little Rock from St. Louis.

But no doubt Mr. Lincoln was expecting that, or worse, when he heard that it was Jesse James who had stopped the train. You might say Jesse had a chip on his shoulder ever since the Civil War ended less than ten years before.

John and Merriam Lincoln were not shot, however. The wealthy Yankees from Minnesota handed over $200 each. As the gang went passenger to passenger, they seemed as motivated by personal ideals as money. They would take nothing from any "working man" with calluses on his hands, and actually inspected the hands of each man, one by one. Nor from women, although when they discovered that Mrs. Scott of Pennsylvania had $400 in cash, they found a way to bend the rules.

They took the gold watch of the conductor, Chauncey Alford, but then returned it. They were respectful to a preacher on board, engaging in conversation about prayers that the gang might make it safely home to "the good country." They patted the heads of the children.

After they rummaged through the parcels of money and registered letters on board, the Express Manager, Mr. Wilson, said to one of the robbers surrounded by a sea of torn paper, envelopes, bags, and boxes, "I have always been in the habit of having people sign a receipt when I deliver them packages." One of them responded, "Fine. Hand me your book." He apparently signed, and added the words "Robbed at Gads Hill."

The boys even had a prepared press release for their captors, which advised the world that "There's a hell of a lot of excitement in this part of the country."

But even though they retained some sense of decorum, the work was heavy, the job was hard. They were carrying several large, heavy pistols each, all day long. Their faces were covered by bandanas, through which they breathed heavily, causing stains of black coal dust around their mouths.

But the Gads Hill Pub & Grill would be about 130 years late. So the gang couldn't stop before heading back out, put their feet up in the beer garden, or play some pool.

But you can. And get out for considerably less than the passengers on the Little Rock Express.
Highway K at Gads Hill 573-223-3687

Gads Hill Pub & Grill

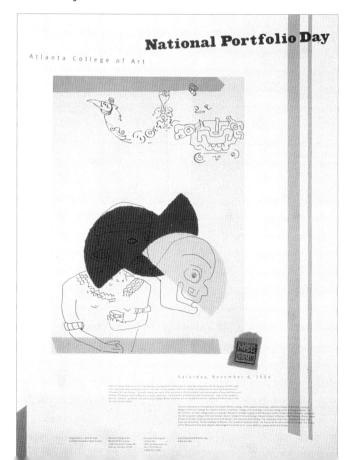

National Portfolio Day

Atlanta College of Art

Saturday, November 6, 2004

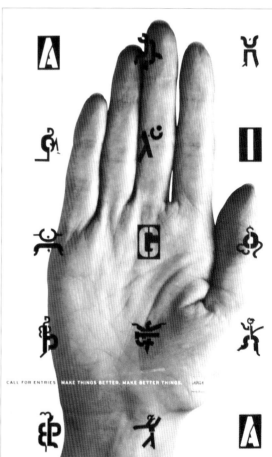

creative firm
Walls Art & Design
Tokyo, Japan
creatives
Pepii Watanabe
client
Graphic Arts Printing, Inc.

creative firm
BBK Studio
Grand Rapids, (Michigan) USA
creatives
Kevin Budelmann, Brian Hauch,
Jason Murray, Julie Ridl,
Sarah Calianan
client
AIGA Detroit

81

creative firm
Portfolio Center
Atlanta, (Georgia) USA
creatives
Mary Francis Hansford
client
The Royal Theater

creative firm
Rodgers Townsend
St. Louis, (Missouri) USA
creatives
Tom Hudder, Scott Lawson,
Kay Cochran
client
Arts and Education Council

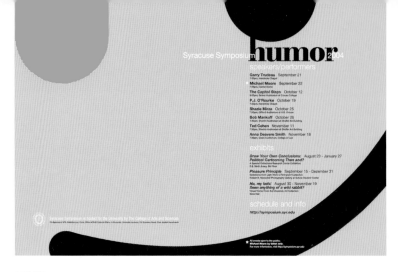

creative firm
stressdesign
Syracuse, (New York) USA
creatives
Marc Stress
client
Syracuse University College of Arts and Sciences

Sometimes what you really need is a
night out with the girls.

creative firm
Equals Three Communications, Inc.
Bethesda, (Maryland) USA
creatives
Bruce Campbell, Tim Brown, Alisa Weinstein, Eugene Faison
client
Girl Scout Council of the Nation's Capital

creative firm
Coda Creative, Inc.
Oakland, (California) USA
creatives
Paola Coda, Adolfo Garcia Cardo,
Leo Kundas
client
RSA Conferences

creative firm
Rodgers Townsend
St. Louis, (Missouri) USA
creatives
Tom Hudder, Luke Partridge,
Mike McCormick, Evan Willnow
client
AD Club of St. Louis

LET'S GUZZLE, NOT SIP.

Let's get some cool
eyeglasses and grow
a little facial hair. Let's
untuck our shirts and press
some flesh. Let's hobnob
like Hollywood hipsters.
Let's blow smoke. Let's
schmooze. Let's bask in
the refracted light of mini
Lucite monoliths.

LET'S ADDY.

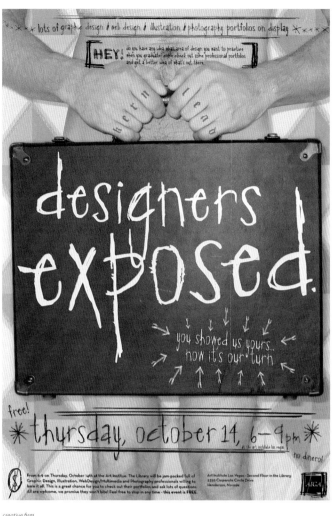

THE RIGHT ACCESSORIES CAN COMPLETE ANY OUTFIT

LAND ROVER

84

Tonight, poultry.

Sievers Retrievers
Labradors and Goldens. Stud dogs and
puppies. For hunting, show, and pets.
Nason, Illinois 618-705-2454

creative firm
Rodgers Townsend
St. Louis, (Missouri) USA
creatives
Tom Hudder, Tom Townsend,
Evan Willnow
client
Sievers Retrievers

creative firm
GOLD & Associates
Ponte Vedra Beach, (Florida) USA
creatives
Brian Gold, Keith Gold,
Jan Hanak
client
GOLD & Associates

creative firm
Barry Rayner Associates
Oakville, (Ontario) Canada
creatives
Egon Springer, Joe Bellaera,
McCabe Neill Jaggers
client
Land Rover Canada

creative firm
Rodgers Townsend
St. Louis, (Missouri) USA
creatives
Tom Hudder, Mike McCormick,
Evan Willnow
client
Impala Amusements

FOOTBALL. LET'S JUST HOPE NO ONE TAKES HIS SHIRT OFF IN CELEBRATION.
© 2004 IMPALA AMUSEMENTS OF SAN ANTONIO. COIN OPERATED BAR GAMES SINCE 1989. 210-415-8708

IMPALA AMUSEMENTS

Reach Higher

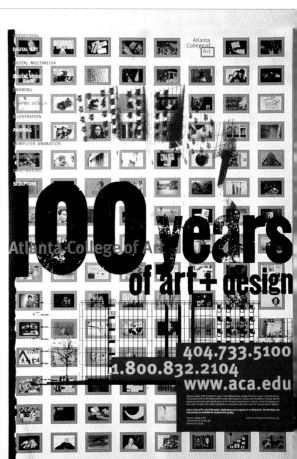

creative firm
Ravenhouse Design Practice
Tacoma, (Washington) USA
creatives
Lance Kagey, Jay Hember,
Tom Llewellyn
client
Wintergrass Music Festival

creative firm
Rodgers Townsend
St. Louis, (Missouri) USA
creatives
Erik Mathre, Martha Koenig,
Bill Eckloff
client
Pleats

creative firm
Atlanta College of Art/Communication Design Department
Atlanta, (Georgia) USA
creatives
Peter Wong, Amin Mohandesi, Andrew Ericson
client
Atlanta College of Art

85

creative firm
Rodgers Townsend
St. Louis, (Missouri) USA
creatives
Tom Hudder, Tom Townsend,
Evan Willnow
client
Gads Hill

creative firm
Rodgers Townsend
St. Louis, (Missouri) USA
creatives
Tom Hudder, Scott Lawson,
Mike Dillon, Evan Willnow
client
Memphis Rock-N-Soul Museum

creative firm
Design Club
Tokyo, Japan
creatives
Akihiko Tsukamoto, Masami Ouchi,
Masayuki Minoda, Radical Suzuki
client
Sea Road International Corporation

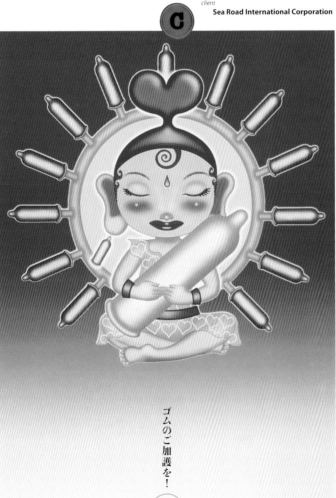

ゴムのご加護を！

creative firm
Maribeth Kradel-Weitzel
Pottstown, (Pennsylvania) USA
creatives
Maribeth Kradel-Weitzel
client
Philadelphia University

creative firm
Rodgers Townsend
St. Louis, (Missouri) USA
creatives
Erik Mathre, Martha Koenig,
Bill Eckloff
client
Pleats

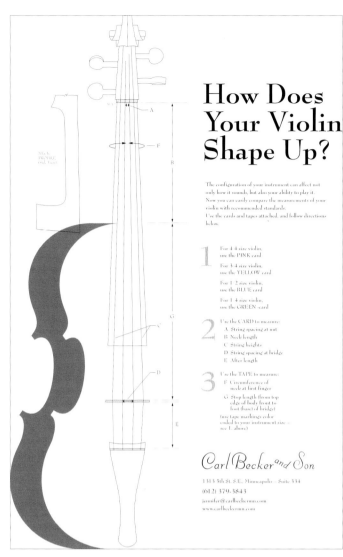

How Does Your Violin Shape Up?

The configuration of your instrument can affect not only how it sounds, but also your ability to play it. Now you can easily compare the measurements of your violin with recommended standards. Use the cards and tapes attached, and follow directions below.

1 For 4/4 size violin, use the PINK card.
For 3/4 size violin, use the YELLOW card.
For 1/2 size violin, use the BLUE card.
For 1/4 size violin, use the GREEN card.

2 Use the CARD to measure:
A String spacing at nut
B Neck length
C String heights
D String spacing at bridge
E After length

3 Use the TAPE to measure:
F Circumference of neck at first finger
G Stop length (from top edge of body front to foot (base) of bridge)

(use tape markings color coded to your instrument size – see 1, above)

Carl Becker and Son

1313 5th St. S.E., Minneapolis – Suite 334
(612) 379-3843
jennifer@carlbeckermn.com
www.carlbeckermn.com

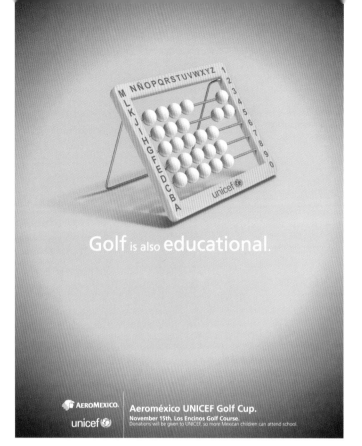

Golf is also educational.

AEROMEXICO. | **Aeroméxico UNICEF Golf Cup.**
unicef | November 15th. Los Encinos Golf Course.
Donations will be given to UNICEF, so more Mexican children can attend school.

87

ART NEEDS HELP TO HAPPEN.

...why we're proud to support nearly 100 organizations across the greater St. Louis area so all of their art can be heard. Call 314.535.3600.

ARTS AND EDUCATION COUNCIL
KEEP ART HAPPENING...

Fleurs de Fete 2005

Please join us for an afternoon in the park
Sunday, May 22, 1pm - 4pm
At Carillon Historical Park • Dayton, Ohio

Proceeds benefit the
Heart & Cancer
Wellness Foundation.

For Ticket Information
Please Call: (937) 223-4117 ext. 107

Sponsored by:

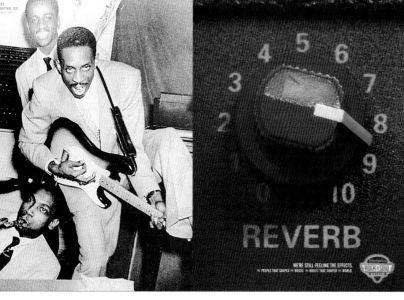

88

senger who arrives on a
flight from Grenada in a
most unusual mode of
transport. (1:00)

Lee C. Wilkins

(NIK) **Full House**—Comedy 255285
7:05 (SHO) **Making of 'Sky Captain and the World
of Tomorrow'** 30838662
7:15 (12) **Mystery!** 16856556
7:30 (OCT) (20) 2004 **Campaigns and Conscience:
The ethics and craft of News Coverage
of the 2004 Presidential Election**
Edward S. and A. Rita Schmidt Lectureship in
Ethics presents Professor Lee C. Wilkins, Joint
appointment: Missouri School of Journalism,
Harry S. Truman School of Public Affairs, University of Missouri. Wednesday, October 20, 7:30-
9:00 PM. Lecture and Q&A, Stretansky Hall *NEW*
(5) (9) (11) (29) (43) **News** 1:00 36594/63662/
58730/41020/65662
Mystery! 1:30 56556
"Inspector Lynley Mysteries": Lynley and Hav-
ers (Nathaniel Parker, Sharon Small) are
assigned a kidnapping case in which the vic-
tim—the secret love child of a leftist politician
and a conservative tabloid editor—is found
dead days before the ransom deadline. Also
odd is that the demand wasn't for money but
for a public admission of paternity by the girl's
father, a friend of Lady Helen Clyde.

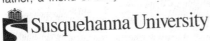

Susquehanna University

(15) **King of Queens**—Comedy 92551

You really need a vacation.

HYATT
HOTELS & RESORTS
MEXICO

For reservations, call 9138 1234

creative firm
021 Comunicaciones
Mexico City, Mexico
creatives
Gabriel Flores, Dahian Rau, Paco Gutierrez, Mariana Ortiz,
Vladimir Nabor, Gabriel Flores, Veronica Trujillo, Angel Martinez
client
Hyatt

www.artanddesign.tcu.edu | art@tcu.edu | 817.257.7697

creative firm
Atomic Design
Crowley, (Texas) USA
creatives
Lewis Glaser
client
TCU Art Department

LET'S BURN THE STRATEGY.
Let's not just think out
of the box. Let's jump
out of the box and
streak around the office.
Let's concept willy-nilly.
Let's borrow interest.
Let's bury the USP.
Let's tickle ourselves
today and rewrite
the brief tomorrow.
LET'S ADDY.

> 2004 ADDY Show > Thursday, February 19th 7-11, Busch Student Center, 20 North Grand Blvd, St. Louis University > Members $40 > Non-members $50 > Ticket orders, including names of guests along with checks or credit card info, can be sent to Ron c/o Ad Club of St. Louis, PO Box 25800, St. Louis MO 63136. For questions call 231.4185 > ADDY Invitation Creation: Rodgers Townsend > Printing courtesy of Swift Print Communications

creative firm
Rodgers Townsend
St. Louis, (Missouri) USA
creatives
Tom Hudder, Luke Partridge,
Mike McCormick, Evan Willnow
client
AD Club of St. Louis

creative firm
Cisco Brand Strategy
San Jose, (California) USA
creatives
Bob Jones,
Gary McCavitt
client
Cisco Systems

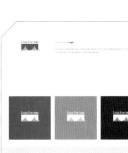

The Cisco Brand Identity System

creative firm
Rodgers Townsend
St. Louis, (Missouri) USA
creatives
Tom Hudder, Scott Lawson,
Mike Dillon, Evan Willnow
client
Memphis Rock-N-Soul Museum

creative firm
Tom Fowler, Inc.
Norwalk, (Connecticut) USA
creatives
Thomas G. Fowler
client
**Connecticut Grand
Opera & Orchestra**

90

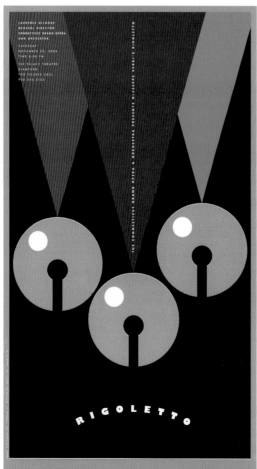

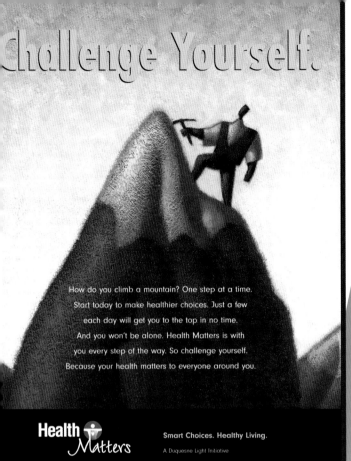

challenge Yourself.

How do you climb a mountain? One step at a time.
Start today to make healthier choices. Just a few
each day will get you to the top in no time.
And you won't be alone. Health Matters is with
you every step of the way. So challenge yourself.
Because your health matters to everyone around you.

Health Matters

Smart Choices. Healthy Living.

A Duquesne Light Initiative

NUTRITION   SMART HABITS   EXERCISE

Your Good Health. It's the **Heart** of the Matter.

Someone once said, "If you have health, you have everything."
Don't test the theory; make healthier choices now. Duquesne Light's
Health Matters is your support network for eating right, exercising
and making better choices for healthy living. Because your health is
at the heart of everything we do. Smart Choices. Healthy Living.

Health Matters

A Duquesne Light Initiative

91

creative firm
VH1
New York, (New York) USA
creatives
Nigel Cox-Hagan, Phil Delbourgo,
Nancy Mazzei, Julie Ruiz, Traci Terrill,
Nicole Morgese, Richard Lufrano, Allison Geldart
client
VH1

creative firm
Desbrow
Pittsburgh, (Pennsylvania) USA
creatives
Kimberly Miller, Brian Lee Campbell
client
Duquesne Light Company

GOLDEN TEE HAIL THE LATE NIGHT DUFFER POWERED BY B
© 2004 IMPALA AMUSEMENTS OF SAN ANTONIO. COIN-OPERATED BAR GAMES SINCE

AIR HOCKEY HE WHO STAYS ON THE BARSTOOL NEVER DRINKS FROM THE CUP. IMPALA AMUSEMENT
© 2004 IMPALA AMUSEMENTS OF SAN ANTONIO. COIN-OPERATED BAR GAMES SINCE 1993. 210-415-8708

creative firm
Rodgers Townsend
St. Louis, (Missouri) USA
creatives
Tom Hudder, Mike McCormick,
Evan Willnow
client
Impala Amusements

92

creative firm
Ad Planet Group
Singapore
creatives
Alfred Teo, Anthony Siow,
Leo Teck Chong, Kim Tan,
Eddie Eng, James Tan
client
Pesterminator Pte Ltd

WASHINGTON, DC
YEAH, WE KNOW HOCKEY.
OUR CITY'S FULL OF LEFT AND RIGHT
WINGERS.

2009, 2010 & 2011 NCAA MEN'S FROZEN F

WASHINGTON, DC
YEAH, WE KNOW HOCKEY.
AFTER ALL, WE DID INVENT THE
FACE-OFF.

2009, 2010 & 2011 NCAA MEN'S FROZEN FOUR

WASHINGTON, DC
YEAH, WE KNOW HOCKEY.
WE'RE PERFECT FOR THE NCAA,
HONEST.

NCAA MEN'S FROZEN FOUR

creative firm
Fixation Marketing
Washington, (D.C.) USA
creatives
Bruce E. Morgan,
Rick Brady
client
Greater Washington Sports Alliance

93

OUR APOLOGIES
TO THE
REGULAR
INHABITANTS.

MAY 15TH, 8 A.M. - 1 P.M.
TO REGISTER,

BARK
IN THE
PARK

QUEENY PARK

APOLOGIES
E REGULAR
ABITANTS.

MAY 15TH, 8 A.M. - 1 P.M.
TO REGISTER,
CALL 314.951.1505 OR

BARK
IN THE
PARK

QUEENY PARK

creative firm
Rodgers Townsend
St. Louis, (Missouri) USA
creatives
Tom Hudder, Luke Partridge,
Mike McCormick
client
Humane Society of Missouri

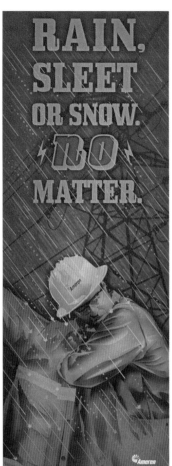

creative firm
Rodgers Townsend
St. Louis, (Missouri) USA
creatives
Tom Hudder, Luke Partridge,
Kris Wright, Mike McCormick
client
Ameren UE

94

creative firm
30sixty advertising+design
St. Louis, (California) USA
creatives
Henry Vizcarra, David Fuscellero,
Glenn Harrington, Yasushi Ono
client
Kings Seafood Company

creative firm
Rodgers Townsend
St. Louis, (Missouri) USA
creatives
Tom Hudder, Ron Copeland,
Ryan McMichael, Evan Willnow
client
Soulard Mardi Gras of St. Louis

95

creative firm
Rodgers Townsend
St. Louis, (Missouri) USA
creatives
Tom Hudder, Mike Dillon,
Evan Willnow
client
Ad Club of St. Louis

creative firm
**Hornall Anderson
Design Works**
Seattle, (Washington) USA
creatives
Jack Anderson, James Tee,
Sonja Max
client
TerraVida Coffee

96

creative firm
FCB/ESPA OY
Helsinki, Finland
creatives
Ove Tammela, Pekka Ruokolainen,
Markku Vierula, Jussi Liimatainen,
Riikka Ranta, K. Tirkkonen, S. Seppilä,
J. Laakso, T. Hokkanen
client
Finnish Tourist Board

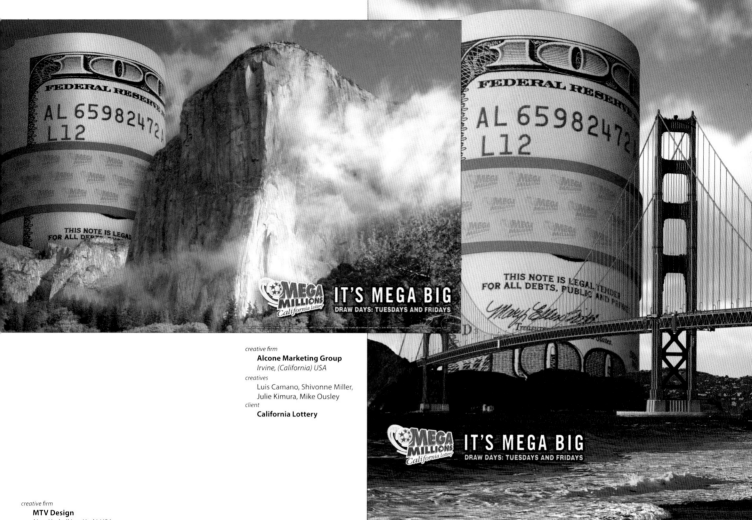

IT'S MEGA BIG
DRAW DAYS: TUESDAYS AND FRIDAYS

creative firm
Alcone Marketing Group
Irvine, (California) USA
creatives
Luis Camano, Shivonne Miller,
Julie Kimura, Mike Ousley
client
California Lottery

creative firm
MTV Design
New York, (New York) USA
client
MTV

G OES CO
MM AN DO

THE2HEADEDDOG.COM

PL AYS DI
RT Y

THE2HEADEDDOG.COM

NE W TR
I CK S

MTV2.COM

creative firm
Michael Patrick Partners
Palo Alto, (California) USA
creatives
Duane Maidens, Dan O'Brien,
Eko Tjoek
client
Michael Patrick Partners, Inc.

98

creative firm
Fry Hammond Barr
Orlando, (Florida) USA
creatives
Tim Fisher, Sean Brunson,
Lara Mann, Stephania Ruelke,
John Deeb
client
The Enzian Theater

creative firm
Rodgers Townsend
St. Louis, (Missouri)
USA
creatives
Tom Hudder,
Luke Partridge,
Kris Wright,
Mike McCormick
client
Lusso

99

creative firm
Heye&Partner GmbH
Unterhaching, (Bavaria) Germany
creatives
Ralph Taubenberger, Joerg Jahn,
Andreas Stenzel, Rene Wentzel
client
Tierpark Hellabrunn München

ART NEEDS HELP TO HAPPEN.

That's why we're proud to support nearly 100 organizations across the greater St. Louis area so all of their art can be seen. Call 314.535.3600.

ART NEEDS HELP TO HAPPEN.

That's why we're proud to support nearly 100 organizations across the greater St. Louis area so all of their art can be heard. Call 314.535.3600.

ARTS AND EDUCATI
KEEP ART HAPP

creative firm
Rodgers Townsend
St. Louis, (Missouri) USA
creatives
Tom Hudder, Chris Taurisano,
Allison Hammer
client
Arts and Education Council

creative firm
021 Comunicaciones
Mexico City, Mexico
creatives
Gabriel Flores, Dahian Rau, Paco Gutierrez,
Mariana Ortiz, Vladimir Nabor, Gabriel Flores,
Veronica Trujillo, Angel Martinez
client
Hyatt

100

You really need a vacation.

You really need a vacation.

HYATT
HOTELS & RESORTS
MEXICO

For reservations, call 9138 1234

HYATT
HOTELS & RESORTS
MEXICO

For reservations, call

101

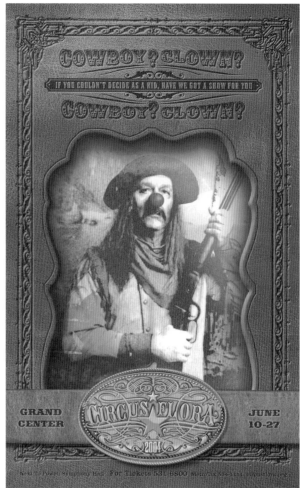

creative firm
Rodgers Townsend
St. Louis, (Missouri)
USA
creatives
Tom Hudder,
Tim Varner,
Mike Dillon
client
Circus Flora

102

creative firm
Fry Hammond Barr
Orlando, (Florida) USA
creatives
Tim Fisher, Sean Brunson,
Lara Mann, Melissa Cooney
client
McDonalds-Central Florida Co-op

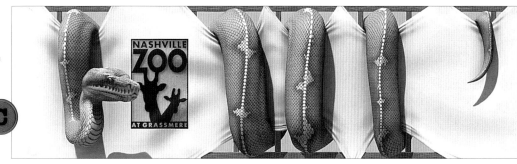

creative firm
Bohan Advertising/Marketing
Nashville, (Tennessee) USA
creatives
Kerry Oliver, Kevin Hinson,
Rainey Kirk
client
Nashville Zoo

creative firm
Brooks Marketing Resources
Ontario, Canada
creatives
Mark Falkins, Rob Doda
client
Atlas Auto Parts

creative firm
Sagon-Phior
Los Angeles, (California) USA
creatives
Sagon-Phior
client
McCormick Distilling Co.

103

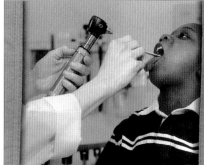

creative firm
Rodgers Townsend
St. Louis, (Missouri) USA
creatives
Tom Hudder, Luke Partridge,
Mike McCormick
client
Children's Hospital St. Louis

creative firm
Hoffman/Lewis
San Francisco, (California) USA
creatives
Sharon Krinsky, Chris Toffoli,
Anne Lewis
client
Northern California Toyota Dealers

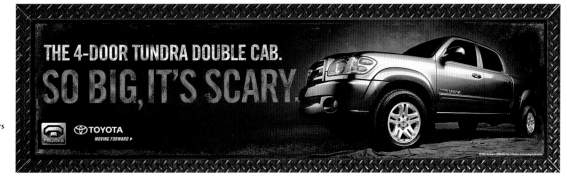

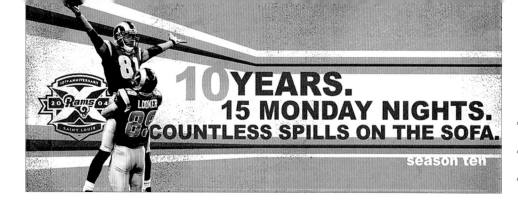

creative firm
Rodgers Townsend
St. Louis, (Missouri) USA
creatives
Tom Hudder, Luke Partridge,
Mike McCormick, Evan Willnow
client
St. Louis Rams

creative firm
Bald & Beautiful
Venice, (California) USA
creatives
Luis Camano,
Cameron Young
client
Aspen Dental

104

creative firm
Bohan Advertising/Marketing
Nashville, (Tennessee) USA
creatives
Kerry Oliver, Gregg Boling,
Darrell Soloman
client
Frist Center for the Visual Arts

creative firm
Fitting Group
Pittsburgh, (Pennsylvania) USA
creatives
Michael Henry
client
KidsVoice

creative firm
Rodgers Townsend
St. Louis, (Missouri) USA
creatives
Tom Hudder, Luke Partridge,
Mike McCormick
client
Children's Hospital St. Louis

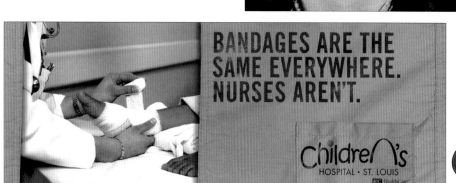

MANISM#23

ONE PLACE YOU NEVER NEED TO PUT THE SEAT DOWN.

Spike TV

HENRY'S FARMERS MARKET

FARM FRESH. DIRT CHEAP.™

105

FIND OUT THE *TRUE* COST OF THAT PUPPY

www.PuppyMillTruth.org

THE HUMANE SOCIETY OF THE UNITED STATES

CELEBRATING 10 YEARS OF A WHOLE LOT OF THIS

season ten

AH, SUMMER. BIKINIS AND POWERBALL.

delottery.com

POWERBALL POWERPLAY®

Delaware Lottery Games

Wanna Play?

creative firm
Campbell-Ewald Advertising
Warren, (Michigan) USA
creatives
Bill Ludwig, Brent Bouchez,
Robin Todd, Nathan O'Brien
client
Chevrolet

creative firm
McCann-Erickson NY
New York, (New York) USA
creatives
Craig Markus, Shalom Auslander
client
USA Today

creative firm
Hoffman/Lewis
San Francisco, (California) USA
creatives
Sharon Krinsy, James Cabral,
Anne Lewis
client
Henry's Farmers Market

106

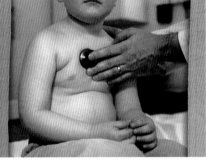

creative firm
Rodgers Townsend
St. Louis, (Missouri) USA
creatives
Tom Hudder, Luke Partridge,
Mike McCormick
client
Children's Hospital St. Louis

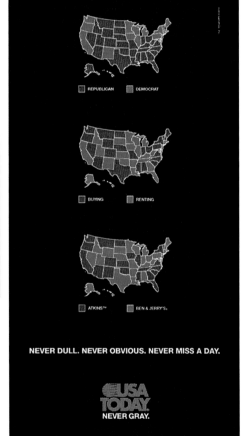

creative firm
PHP Communications
Birmingham, (Alabama) USA
creatives
Joan Perry,
Lynn Smith
client
Bradford Health Services

107

$\mathcal{B}$illboards, campaign

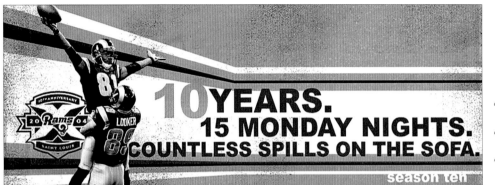

creative firm
Rodgers Townsend
St. Louis, (Missouri) USA
creatives
Tom Hudder, Luke Partridge,
Mike McCormick, Evan Willnow
client
St. Louis Rams

108

creative firm
Bohan Advertising/Marketing
Nashville, (Tennessee) USA
creatives
Kerry Oliver, Gregg Boling,
Chris Gower, Amy Liz Riddick
client
Frist Center for the Visual Arts

creative firm
Publicis Dialog
San Francisco, (California) USA
creatives
Alex Grossman, Lotus Child,
Tom Kavanaugh
client
Shanti

50 years of grilling innovation, in the shape of a football.

The new Weber® Q™ portable gas grill. 280 square-inches of real Weber power and technology, in a package big enough to cook 18 burgers or brats at the same time. It's a tailgater's dream. Check it out at www.weber.com/Q.

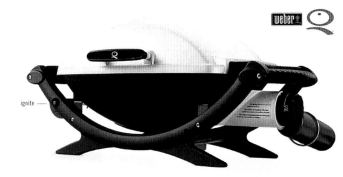

any more power, and you'd need a license.

The new Weber® Q™ portable gas grill. It's barely street legal. This is 280 square-inches and 12,000 BTUs of real Weber power in a compact package to go. Easily cooks 18 burgers or brats at the same time. Wanna take it for a spin? www.weber.com/Q.

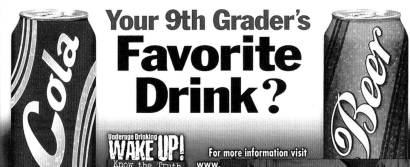

Your 9th Grader's Favorite Drink?

WAKE UP! Underage Drinking — Know the Truth

For more information visit www.

Alcohol is a drug. Sponsored by District Attorney Ted McKni

109

IS YOUR KID THE ONE?

For more information visit www.wakeupclintoncounty.org

WAKE UP! Underage Drinking — Know the Truth

Alcohol is a drug. Sponsored by District Attorney Ted McKnight's Task Force Against Drugs Impacting Our Youth.

Be pro-antioxidant.

KAISER PERMA

SINCE YOU CAN'T TAKE IT WITH YOU,
STAY LONGER.

KAISER PERMANENTE® **thrive**

BANDAGES ARE THE SAME EVERYWHERE. NURSES AREN'T.

Children's HOSPITAL · ST. LOUIS
BJC HealthCare

creative firm
Rodgers Townsend
St. Louis, (Missouri) USA
creatives
Tom Hudder, Luke Partridge,
Mike McCormick
client
Children's Hospital St. Louis

STETHOSCOPES ARE THE SAME EVERYWHERE. DOCTORS AREN'T.

Children's HOSPITAL · ST. LOUIS
BJC HealthCare

Me, quit? Never.

RISING ABOVE

Pass It On.

THE FOUNDATION FOR A BETTER LIFE

ALEX'S LEMONADE STAND

Raised $1M to fight cancer. Including hers.

INSPIRATION

Pass It On.

THE FOUNDATION FOR A BETTER LIFE

creative firm
The Foundation for a Better Life
Denver, (Colorado) USA
creatives
Hammed Zaidi,
Jay Schulberg
client
The Foundation for a Better Life

precyzyjnie realizowana obsługa

www.cityboard.pl

precisely executed service

indywidualnie dopasowana ekspozycja

www.cityboard.pl

cityboard media

individually crafted exposition

creative firm
Moby Dick Warszawa
Warsaw, Poland
creatives
Marcin Bobroliicz,
Marcin Kosiorowski
client
Cityboard Media

creative firm
Rassman Design
Denver, (Colorado) USA
creatives
John Rassman,
Anne Worsley
client
Porter Adventist Hospital

111

Begin.

Porter
Women's Center
&Birthplace

www.porterhospital.org

Porter Adventist Hospital
Centura Health

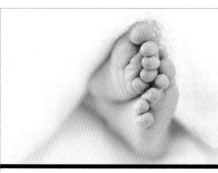

Cradle.

Porter
Women's Center
&Birthplace

www.porterhospital.org

Porter Adventist Hospital
Centura Health

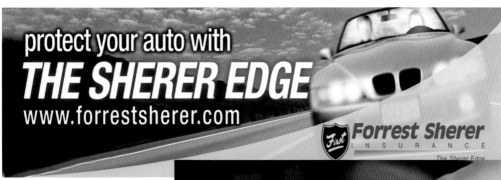

creative firm
Miller White, LLC
Terre Haute, (Indiana) USA
creatives
Lori Lucas
client
Forrest Sherer Insurance

112

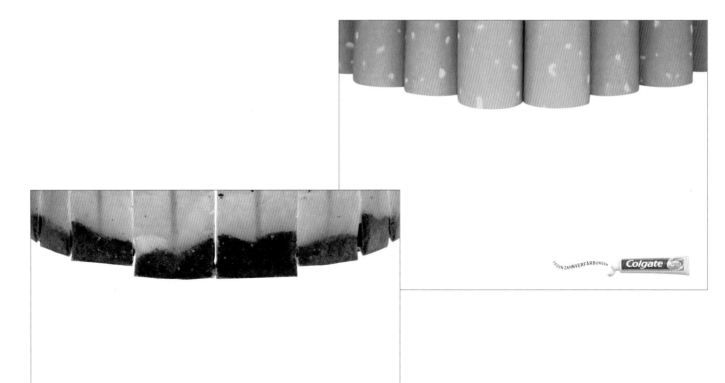

creative firm
Y&R Germany
Frankfurt, Germany
creatives
Christian Daul, Uwe Marquardt,
Monika Spirkl, Michael Meisen
client
Colgate Palmolive Germany

creative firm
Rodgers Townsend
St. Louis, (Missouri) USA
creatives
Tom Hudder,
Luke Partridge,
Mike McCormick,
Evan Willnow
client
St. Louis Rams

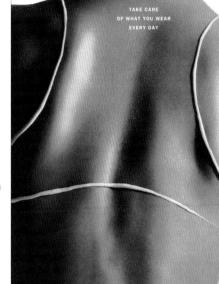

creative firm
Taxi Canada Inc.
*Montréal, (Québec)
Canada*
creatives
Stephane Charier,
Patrick Chaubet,
Maxime Patenaude
client
**KAO Brand Canada
(Jergens)**

113

creative firm
Janet Hughes and Associates
Wilmington, (Delaware) USA
creatives
Wendy Wolfinger, Sara Thurston,
Felice Croul
client
Delaware Division of Public Health

creative firm
Hoffman/Lewis
San Francisco, (California) USA
creatives
Sharon Krinsky, Chris Toffoli,
David Swope, Jeff Billig,
Scott Leeper
client
Wild Oats Natural Marketplace

Never confuse your dinner table with the periodic table.

WILD OATS
NATURAL MARKETPLACE

CELEBRATING 10 YEARS OF A WHOLE LOT OF THIS.

season ten

114

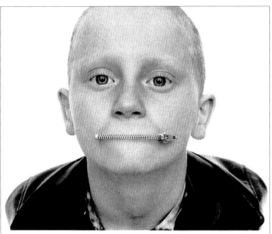

Don't let KidsVoice fall silent

April is National Child Abuse Prevention Month

KidsVoice
Protecting Children's Rights

ONE DOWN, 10 PINS LEFT.

stlouisrams.com

season ten

THE 10TH ANNIVERSARY OF THE LAST DULL SUNDAY IN ST. LOUIS.

stlouisrams.com

season ten

TAKING 4 DOWNS
TO MOVE 10 YARDS
NEVER MOVED ANYONE.

stlouisrams.com

season ten

FOR THE VACATION OF A LIFETIME

IRELAND BRITAIN

C·I·E TOURS International
EXPERIENCE · QUALITY · RELIABILITY

USTOA

SEE YOUR TRAVEL AGENT OR CALL 1-800-CIE TOURS VISIT US ON THE WEB AT WWW.CIETOURS.COM

Like a regular grocery store.
Only with real food.

WILD OATS.
NATURAL MARKETPLACE

115

10 YEARS.
15 MONDAY NIGHTS.
COUNTLESS SPILLS ON THE SOFA.

stlouisrams.com

season ten

season ten

300 POUNDS
OF ILL WILL IN T MINUS 10, 9, 8

stlouisrams.com

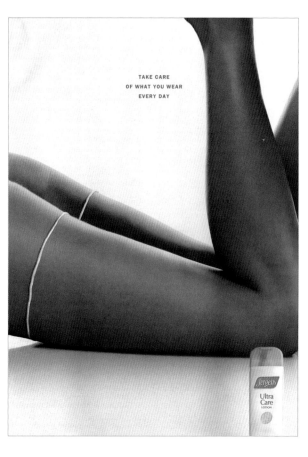

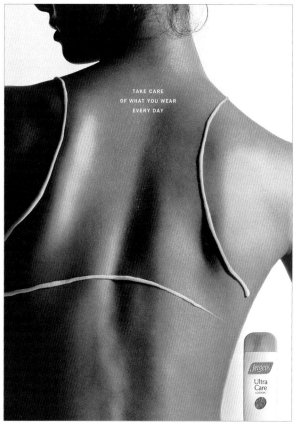

TAKE CARE
OF WHAT YOU WEAR
EVERY DAY

creative firm
Taxi Canada Inc.
*Montréal, (Québec)
Canada*
creatives
Stephane Charier,
Patrick Chaubet,
Maxime Patenaude
client
**KAO Brand Canada
(Jergens)**

creative firm
Rodgers Townsend
St. Louis, (Missouri) USA
creatives
Tom Hudder, Luke Partridge,
Mike McCormick, Evan Willnow
client
St. Louis Rams

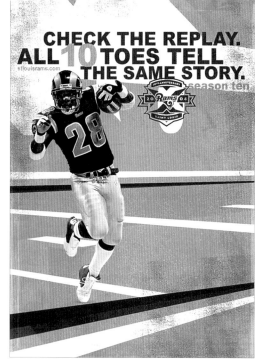
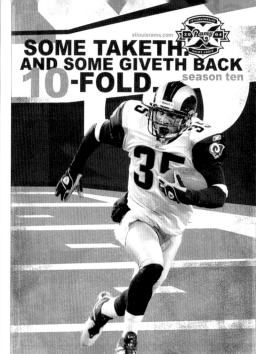

creative firm
Rodgers Townsend
St. Louis, (Missouri) USA
creatives
Tom Hudder, Luke Partridge,
Mike McCormick, Evan Willnow
client
St. Louis Rams

Like a regular grocery store.
Only with real food.

WILD OATS
NATURAL MARKETPLACE

117

creative firm
Hoffman/Lewis
San Francisco, (California) USA
creatives
Sharon Krinsky, Chris Toffoli,
David Swope, Jeff Billig,
Scott Leeper
client
Wild Oats Natural Marketplace

Sure, you could buy food somewhere else.
But then you'd have to eat it.

WILD OATS
NATURAL MARKETPLACE

Never confuse your dinner table
with the periodic table.

WILD OATS
NATURAL MARKETPLACE

creative firm
RT&E Integrated Communications
Wilmington, (Delaware) USA
creatives
Randall Jones
client
WHYY

Know that person next to you on the platform with the earphones and the briefcase and how they somehow seem a little more OK with the fact that they are standing there waiting for the train, while everyone else is treating it like this big waste of time, making funny "I'm so bored." faces and wishing they could get the whole thing over with? Oh...you're that person. Then you know WHYY 91FM.

WHYY 91FM
For 50 years, radio worth your time.

WHYY 91FM • NEWS & PUBLIC AFFAIRS • ARTS & CULTURE

Know that person listening with the earphones and the sunglasses who seems to take the whole commuting thing in stride like it's no big deal really, like the time that funny guy with the FERRET! parked himself real close saying "Ivan likes you." and everyone else was squirming to make an exit stage left while the earphones person just kinda grinned? Oh...you're that person. Then you know WHYY 91FM.

WHYY 91FM
For 50 years, radio worth your time.

WHYY 91FM • NEWS & PUBLIC AFFAIRS • ARTS & CULTURE

creative firm
Pisarkiewicz Mazur & Co.
New York, (New York) USA
creatives
Mary Pisarkiewicz,
Allie Delgado
client
White Plains Public Library

118

creative firm
Rodgers Townsend
St. Louis, (Missouri) USA
creatives
Tom Hudder, Luke Partridge,
Mike McCormick, Evan Willnow
client
St. Louis Rams

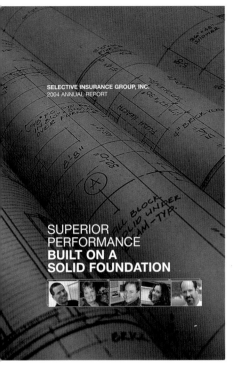

Sadržaj

creative firm
Taylor & Ives Incorporated
New York, (New York) USA
creatives
Alisa Zamir, Trevor Paccione
client
Selective Insurance Group, Inc.

creative firm
Bruketa & Zinic
Zagreb, Croatia
creatives
Maja Bagic
client
Adris Group d.d. **119**

creative firm
Bohan Advertising/Marketing
Nashville, (Tennessee) USA
creatives
Kerry Oliver, Kevin Hinson,
Andy Anderson, Darrell Soloman
client
Boy Scouts of America Middle TN Council

creative firm
1919 Studio
New York, (New York) USA
creatives
Peter Klueger,
Gili Bar-shay Boneh
client
ImClone Systems Incorporated

creative firm
Bruketa & Zinic
Zagreb, Croatia
creatives
Maja Bagic, Marin Topic
client
Podravka d.d.

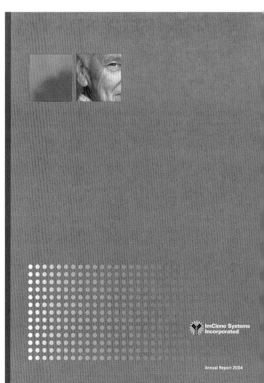

CISCO SYSTEMS, INC. 2004 ANNUAL REPORT
BUILDING TOMORROW'S NETWORKS

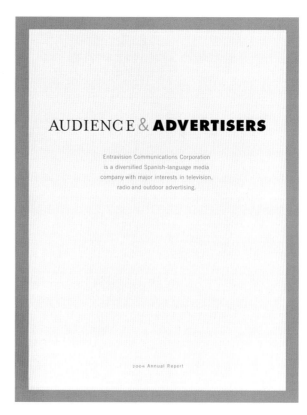

creative firm
Cisco Brand Strategy
San Jose, (California) USA
creatives
Art Kihinski, Gary McCavitt,
Jeff Brand, Gary Ferguson,
Monique Mulbry, Linda Mayer
client
Cisco Systems

120

creatives
David Kohler,
Rick Slusher
client
The McGraw-Hill Companies, Inc.

creative firm
Douglas Joseph Partners
Los Angeles, (California) USA
creatives
Doug Joseph, Scott Lambert,
Frederik Broden
client
Entravision Communications

creative firm
Corporate Reports, Inc.
Atlanta, (Georgia) USA
client
Russell Corporation

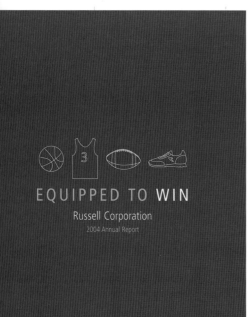

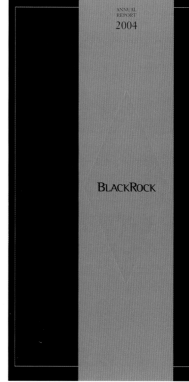

creative firm
Taylor & Ives Incorporated
New York, (New York) USA
creatives
Alisa Zamir, Daniel Caspescha
client
Blackrock, Inc.

seeing it through →

creative firm
karacters design group
Vancouver, (British Columbia) Canada
creatives
James Bateman, Deborah Kieselbach
client
Finning International

creative firm
Arnold Saks Associates
New York, (New York) USA
creatives
Arnold Saks, Lisa Corcoran
client
Hospital for Special Surgery

creative firm
**Five Visual
Communication & Design**
*West Chester, (Ohio)
USA*
creatives
Rondi Tschopp
client
Miami University

creative firm
Erwin Zinger Graphic Design
Groningen, The Netherlands
creatives
Erwin Zinger
client
N.V. Nederlandse Gasunie

HOSPITAL
FOR SPECIAL
SURGERY:
SPECIALISTS
IN MOBILITY

SPRING
2005

2004 ANNUAL
REPORT

Horizon

A Lifetime of Mobility

creative firm
**Emerson, Wajdowicz
Studios**
*New York, (New York)
USA*
creatives
Jurek Wajdowicz,
Lisa LaRochelle,
Yoko Yoshida
client
**Médecins Sans
Frontières USA**

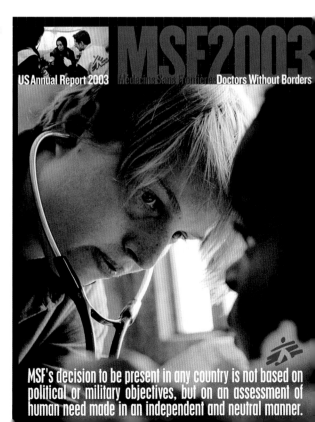

MSF's decision to be present in any country is not based on
political or military objectives, but on an assessment of
human need made in an independent and neutral manner.

advancing

Hospira

creative firm
VSA Partners, Inc.
Chicago, (Illinois) USA
creatives
Dana Arnett,
Dave Ritter,
Renee Schultz,
Lindsay Gallcup,
Mike Noble,
Dolly Chen
client
**First Data
Corporation**

6:30AM

FIRST DATA CORPORATION
2004 ANNUAL REPORT

FIRST DATA

creative firm
Paragraphs Design
Chicago, (Illinois) USA
creatives
Robin Zvonek,
Sue Mitsikonch
client
Hospira

creative firm
Design Objectives Pte Ltd
Singapore
creatives
Ronnie S. C. Tan,
Lawrence Tong
client
**Singapore Economic
Development Board**

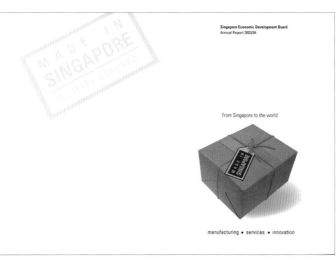

MADE IN SINGAPORE

Singapore Economic Development Board
Annual Report 2003/04

From Singapore to the world

manufacturing • services • innovation

creatives
David Kohler, Craig Dobie,
Miho Nishimaniwa
client
The Mills Corporation

BOL2004

Global Opportunities

Bausch&Lomb

creative firm
Bertz Design Group
*Middletown, (Connecticut)
USA*
creatives
Andrew Wessels,
John Gibson,
Paul Horton
client
Bausch & Lomb

EXCEPTIONAL LEADERSHIP
UNMATCHED VISION
DYNAMIC GROWTH

The Mills Corporation Annual Report 2004

creative firm
KBDA
*Los Angeles, (California)
USA*
creatives
Kim Baer,
Allison Bloss,
Michael D'Ambrosia
client
**Prostate Cancer
Foundation**

creative firm
Graphicat Limited
Hong Kong, China
creatives
Colin Tillyer
client
Noble Group Limited

Great people building great brands

Summary Annual Report 2004

creative firm
Taylor & Ives Incorporated
New York, (New York) USA
creatives
Alisa Zamir,
Pamela Brooks
client
Hershey Foods Corporation

creative firm
BCN Communications
Chicago, (Illinois) USA
creatives
Michael Neu, Harri Boller,
Ted Stoik, Ron Gordon Photography,
Roth & Ramberg Photography
client
CN

MOLSON *Coors*

Adolph Coors Company 2004 Annual Report

creative firm
Coates and Coates
Naperville, (Illinois) USA
creatives
Jim Brophy, Ron Coates,
Carolin Coates
client
Adolph Coors Company

2004 Annual Report

This is excellence.

creative firm
KROG
Ljubljana, Slovenia
creatives
Dragan Arrigler,
Edi Berk
client
Probanka, Maribor

creative firm
Epigram
Singapore
creatives
Edmund Wee,
Zann Wan
client
**National Arts
Council**

creative firm
Finger Design Associates
Oakland, (California) USA
creatives
Arlene Finger,
Greg Nelson,
Joe Curley,
Brenda Kahn
client
**Metropolitan
Transportation
Commission**

creative firm
**Michael Patrick
Partners**
*Palo Alto,
(California) USA*
creatives
Eko Tjoek,
Dan O'Brien
client
**Pacific Sunwear of
California**

creative firm
Lexicon Design
Singapore
client
**NTUC Fairprice
Co-Operative Ltd**

creative firm
Karakter
London, England
creatives
Clive Rohald, Kam Devsi,
Nei Wing Chan, Martin Watkins
client
Norsk Hydro

creative firm
Arnold Saks Associates
New York, (New York) USA
creatives
Arnold Saks, Robert Yasharian
client
Xerox

creative firm
Taylor & Ives Incorporated
New York, (New York) USA
creatives
Alisa Zamir, Pamela Brooks
client
**The Depository Trust &
Clearing Corporation**

creative firm
Nesnadny + Schwartz
Cleveland, (Ohio) USA
creatives
Mark Schwartz, Stacie
Ross, Lois Conner
client
Vassar College

creative firm
Davidoff Associates, Inc.
New York, (New York) USA
creatives
Patrina Marino, Roge Davidoff
client
The Pepsi Bottling Group Inc.

creatives
Richard Colbourne,
Christina Antonopoulos
client
iStar Financial Inc.

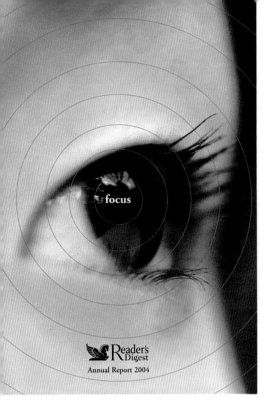

nothing is impossible.

Umpqua Holdings Corporation / Annual Report 2004

ANNUAL REPORT 2004

ANNUAL REPORT 2004

Is Strategic

The California Wellness Foundation
Grantmaking for a Healthier California

creative firm
Hershey Associates
Santa Monica, (California)
USA
creatives
R. Christine Hershey,
Joanna Lee,
Kristin Bright
client
The California
Wellness Foundation

Goldman Sachs
2004 ANNUAL REPORT

Goldman Sachs

creative firm
VSA Partners, Inc.
Chicago, (Illinois) USA
creatives
Jeff Walker, Grey Sylvester,
Amanda Gentry, Anne Marie Rosser
client
Goldman Sachs Group, Inc.

creative firm
Taylor & Ives Incorporated
New York, (New York) USA
creatives
Alisa Zamir,
Trevor Paccione
client
LaBranche & Co. Inc.

Exelon.

realizing the promise
Exelon Corporation 04 Summary Annual Report

127

creative firm
Paragraphs Design
Chicago, (Illinois) USA
creatives
Robin Zvonek,
Meow Vatanatumrak
client
Exelon Corporation

LaBranche & Co Inc.

ANNUAL REPORT 2004

creative firm
Suka Design
New York, (New York) USA
creatives
Brian Wong
client
GLSEN
(Gay, Lesbian and
Straight Education
Network)

READING/WRITING/RESPECT
THE FIRST TEN YEARS

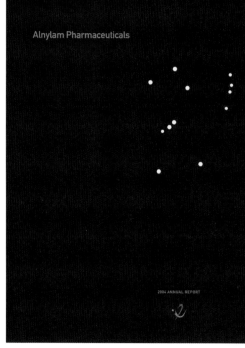

creative firm
Nolin Branding & Design
Montreal, (Quebec) Canada
creatives
Elisabeth Côté, Jacqueline Otis,
Yves Lacombe
client
Alcan

creative firm
Gill Fishman Associates
Cambridge, (Massachusetts) USA
creatives
Tammy Torrey, John Earle
client
Alnylam Pharmaceuticals

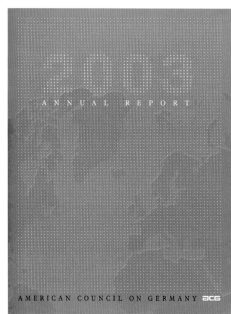

creative firm
WestGroup Creative
New York, (New York)
USA
creatives
Chip Tolaney,
Marvin Berk
client
**American Council on
Germany**

128

creative firm
March of Dimes
White Plains, (New York) USA
creatives
Kathy D'Aloise, Barbara Jones,
William Masto, Linda Simone

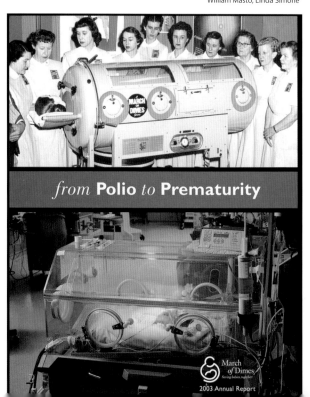

creative firm
Nesnadny + Schwartz
Cleveland, (Ohio) USA
creatives
Mark Schwartz,
Joyce Nesnadny,
Michelle Moehler,
Keith Pishnery
client
**The Progressive
Corporation**

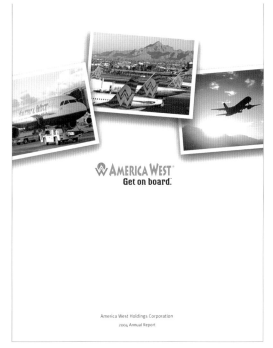

WHAT DO YOU SEE?

AGL RESOURCES INC.   2004 ANNUAL REPORT

America West Holdings Corporation
2004 Annual Report

creative firm
RWI
New York, (New York) USA
creatives
Linda Toh Chen
client
America West

creative firm
Thinkhouse Creative
Atlanta, (Georgia)) USA
creatives
Randy Allison, Linda Baird,
Loraine Fick, Susan Lindsay
client
AGL Resources

"We ride
with you."

HARLEY-DAVIDSON, INC. 2004 ANNUAL REPORT

creative firm
VSA Partners, Inc.
Chicago, (Illinois) USA
creatives
Jason Jones,
Dana Arnett,
Adam Dines,
Charlie Simokaitis,
Bob Klein
client
Harley-Davidson

129

creatives
Richard Colbourne,
Eunice Woo
client
Avery Dennison Corporation

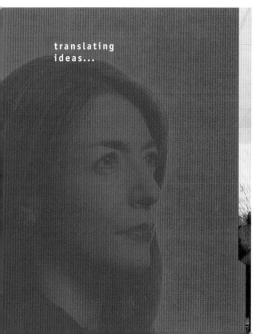

translating
ideas...

beautychina
Annual Report 2004

eyeonbeauty

creative firm
Design Objectives Pte Ltd
Singapore
creatives
Ronnie S.C. Tan, Lawrence Tong,
Teo See Kim, Lawrence Chong
client
Beauty China Holdings, Ltd.

Wyeth

Annual Report 2004

Building on Our Strengths

Investing in Our Future

Expanding Opportunity

The Rockefeller Foundation

2003 Annual Report

Hands on the
wheel.

Eyes on the
road.

creative firm
BCN Communications
Chicago, (Illinois) USA
creatives
Michael Neu, Mike O'Brien,
Ted Stoik, James Schnepf Photography,
Sandro Photography
client
General Motors Corporation

130

creative firm
Arnold Saks Associates
New York, (New York) USA
creatives
Arnold Saks, Robert Yasharian
client
Wyeth

creative firm
Nolin Branding & Design
Montreal, (Quebec) Canada
creatives
Isabel Beaudry, Pascal Roux,
Martin Tremblay
client
Société des Alcools du Québec

creative firm
Emerson, Wajdowicz Studios
New York, (New York) USA
creatives
Jurek Wajdowicz, Lisa LaRochelle,
Jonas Bendiksen, Yoko Yoshida
client
The Rockefeller Foundation

creative firm
Anjaro
San Francisco, (California) USA
creatives
Jacques Rossouw, Annria Rossouw,
Susan Sharpe, Mark Tuschman
client
Palo Alto Medical Foundation

POUR NOUS, LA SAQ C'EST LE DÉBUT
D'UNE AVENTURE GUSTATIVE ET LE PLAISIR
DE DÉCOUVRIR AVEC DES GENS PASSIONNÉS
NICOLAS SANTANGELIS ET ÉLISE DENAULT, clients

SAQ
RAPPORT
ANNUEL

PALO ALTO MEDICAL FOUNDATION   ANNUAL REPORT

COMMON GROUND

2003   2004

creative firm
Lewis Moberly
London, England
creatives
Mary Lewis,
Paul Cilia La Corte
client
NABS

商機無限 合作無間
Collaborating *for* Growth

二零零四年年報
Annual Report 2004

creative firm
Graphicat Limited
Hong Kong, China
creatives
Colin Tillyer
client
**CITIC International Financial
Holdings Limited**

131

creative firm
Paragraphs Design
Chicago, (Illinois) USA
creatives
Meow Vatanatumrak, Rachel Radtke,
Robin Zvonek
client
Coca-Cola Femsa

SOLUTIONS

UNIVERSAL AMERICAN FINANCIAL CORP.
2004 Annual Report

creative firm
Taylor & Ives Incorporated
New York, (New York) USA
creatives
Alisa Zamir,
Trevor Paccione
client
**Universal American
Financial Corp.**

THE COCA-COLA FEMSA

ROUTE TO
SUCCESS

COCA-COLA FEMSA 2004 ANNUAL REPORT

creative firm
Ruder Finn Design
New York, (New York) USA
creatives
Lisa Gabbay, Sal Catania,
Kaven Lam
client
New York Theatre Workshop

Altria Group, Inc. 2004 Annual Report

creative firm
RWI
New York, (New York) USA
creatives
Robert Webster,
Alexandra Hoffman
client
Altria Group, Inc.

Eaton Corporation
2004 Annual Report

everywhere

creative firm
Nesnadny + Schwartz
Cleveland, (Ohio) USA
creatives
Mark Schwartz, Gregory Oznowich,
Dana Anderson
client
Eaton Corporation

The right place...

The right moment...

The right company

GEO 2004 ANNUAL REPORT

creative firm
Signi
Mexico City, Mexico
creatives
Felipe Salas
client
Casas Geo

creative firm
Suka Design
New York, (New York) USA
creatives
Maria Belfiore
client
**American Foundation
for the Blind**

132

creatives
Richard Colbourne,
Jason Miller
client
ITT Industries, Inc.

IN A PERFECT WORLD...

ITT Industries
Engineered for life
2004 Annual Report

access

American Foundation for the Blind
2004 Annual Report

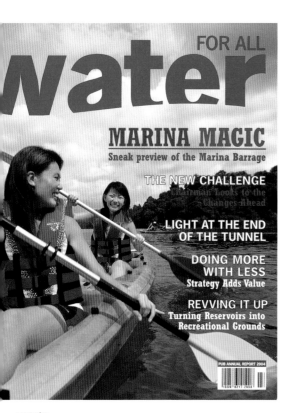

Raise the bar.

Bradley Arant
BRADLEY ARANT ROSE & WHITE LLP

creative firm
Greenfield/Belser Ltd.
Washington, (D.C.) USA
creatives
Burkey Belser,
Charlyne Fabi,
Jennifer Myers,
Alan Sciulli
client
**Bradley Arant
Rose & White LLP**

creative firm
Epigram
Singapore
creatives
Edmund Wee, Jennifer Jordan
client
Public Utilities Board

TODAY. FOR
TOMORROW.

Annual report
Year ended
January 31, 2005

BOMBARDIER

creative firm
Nolin Branding & Design
Montreal, (Quebec) Canada
creatives
Caroline Blanchette, Pascal Roux,
Monic Richard, Etienne Magny
client
Bombardier Inc.

133

creative firm
Paragraphs Design
Chicago, (Illinois) USA
creatives
Meow Vatanatumrak,
Rachel Radtke
client
DiamondCluster

GESCHÄFTSBERICHT 2004
– DIE LETZTE KLAPPE

creative firm
Q
Wiesbaden, Germany
creatives
Thilo von Debschitz,
Christoph Dahinten,
Matthias Frey
client
VKE

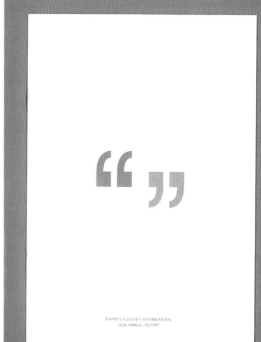

DIAMONDCLUSTER INTERNATIONAL
2004 ANNUAL REPORT

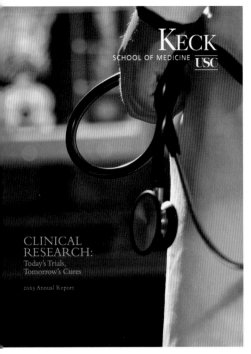

creative firm
The Jeffries Association
Los Angeles, (California) USA
creatives
Ron Jeffries, Hau Chee Chung
client
USC-Keck School of Medicine

creatives
Richard Colbourne,
Craig Dobie
client
Diebold Incorporated

134

creative firm
Paragraphs Design
Chicago, (Illinois) USA
creatives
Jim Chilcutt,
Robin Zvonek
client
Baxter International Inc.

creative firm
RWI
New York, (New York) USA
creatives
Michael DeVourney
client
Foot Locker, Inc.

creative firm
Q-Plus Design Pte Ltd
Singapore
creatives
Dillon. J,
Mark Sidwell
client
**Singapore Airport
Terminal Services**

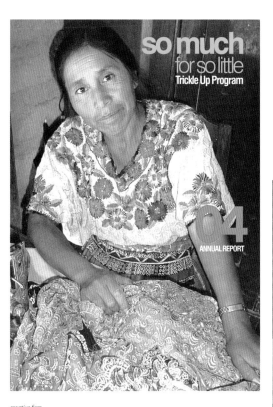

creative firm
Emerson, Wajdowicz Studios
New York, (New York) USA
creatives
Lisa LaRochelle, Jurek Wajdowicz,
Jill Simonsen, Yoko Yoshida,
Trickle Up Program Photographers
client
Trickle Up Program

creative firm
Q
Wiesbaden, Germany
creatives
Laurenz Nielbock,
Christoph Dahinten
client
Soka-Bau

creative firm
Design Objectives Pte Ltd
Singapore
creatives
Ronnie S.C. Tan, Lawrence Tong,
Lawrence Chong, Giselle Lam
client
Pearl Energy Ltd.

creative firm
RTS Rieger Team GmbH
*Leinfelden-Echterdingen,
Germany*
creatives
Michaela Müller,
Ulrich Gielisch
client
ThyssenKrupp Elevator

"If we are to prevent the meaning of marriage from being changed forever, our nation must enact a constitutional amendment to protect marriage in America." — *George W. Bush*

protect it from whom?

the Human Rights Campaign and the Human Rights Campaign Foundation 2004 Annual Report

creative firm
Suka Design
*New York, (New York)
USA*
creatives
Brian Wong
client
**The Human
Rights Campaign**

PAXAR

The right company...

Annual Report 2004

creative firm
Taylor & Ives Incorporated
New York, (New York) USA
creatives
Alisa Zamir, Pamela Brooks
client
Paxar Corporation

Colgate-Palmolive Company 2004 Annual Report

Investing Strategically For Profitable Growth

▶ Strengthening Global Brands
▶ Accelerating Innovation
▶ Driving Greater Efficiency
▶ Developing Colgate People

Possibilities Imagined...

Genworth Financial, Inc. 2004 ANNUAL REPORT

creatives
David Kohler,
Christina Antonopoulas
client
Genworth Financial

creative firm
RWI
New York, (New York) USA
creatives
Robert Webster, Sophia Cheung,
Alexandra Hoffman
client
Colgate-Palmolive Company

136

creative firm
Signi
Mexico City, Mexico
creatives
Rene Galindo, Odette Edwards,
Nora Shwadski
client
Televisa

creative firm
Q-Plus Design Pte Ltd
Singapore
creatives
Dillon. J, Thomas Teo
client
Tat Hong Holdings Ltd

creative firm
VSA Partners, Inc.
Chicago, (Illinois) USA
creatives
Jeff Walker, Thomas Wolf, David Harbarger,
Glenn Chan, Claudia Alberts, Anne Marie Rosser
client
General Electric Company

Televisa

reaching beyond ...

Annual Report 2004

TAT HONG HOLDINGS LTD
annual report 2005

Our Time

GE 2004 Annual Report

creative firm
Futura DDB
Ljubljana, Slovenia
creatives
Marko Vičič, Žare Kerin,
Andraž Filač, Marko Cmahen
client
Futura DDB

creative firm
Time Creative Services
New York, (New York) USA
creatives
Andrea Costa, Liza Greene
client
Time Magazine

creative firm
Salterbaxter
London, England
client
Provident Financial

creative firm
Salterbaxter
London, England
client
Salterbaxter in-house

creative firm
Group T Design
Washington, (D.C.) USA
creatives
Tom Klinedinst
client
"The President's Own"
United States Marine Band

The University Lectures 2004 - 2005

CELEBRATING THE INAUGURATION OF NANCY CANTOR AS
SYRACUSE UNIVERSITY'S ELEVENTH CHANCELLOR AND PRESIDENT.

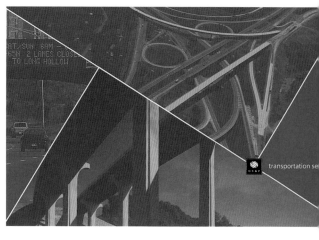

transportation se

creative firm
stressdesign
Syracuse, (New York) USA
creatives
Marc Stress
client
**Syracuse University Office
of Academic Affairs**

creative firm
Gresham, Smith and Partners
Hendersonville, (Tennessee) USA
creatives
Joy Blankenship, Chip Jordan,
Ben Bahil, Ellie Jones, Rebecca Campbell
client
Gresham, Smith and Partners

2:

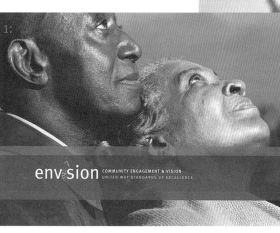

ze IMPACT STRATEGIES, RESOURCES & RESULTS
UNITED WAY STANDARDS OF EXCELLENCE

138

1:

env•sion COMMUNITY ENGAGEMENT & VISION
UNITED WAY STANDARDS OF EXCELLENCE

creative firm
Grafik
Alexandria, (Virginia) USA
creatives
Gregg Glaviano, Mila Arrisueno,
Regina Esposito, Ivan Hooker
client
United Way

ADVANCED MEDICAL CARE CLOSE TO HOME   MERC

creative firm
Five Visual Communication & Design
West Chester, (Ohio) USA
creatives
Rondi Tschopp
client
Mercy Health Partners

M MMA
FINANCIAL

INTEGRITY. INNOVATION. SERVICE.

438%
INCREASE IN
ASSETS UNDER
MANAGEMENT IN THE
LAST 4 YEARS

"...IN COMPARISON TO
OTHER EQUITY/DEBT
SOURCES WE'VE USED,
MMA WAS RESPONSIVE
TO OUR NEEDS..."

A MUNIMAE COMPANY

the company for 10 years or more. Our senior management
team has an average of 18 years' industry expertise.

Supported by excellent information and a strong organization,
our employees have the tools to help clients meet their needs.
We have both the data and experience to make good decisions

about investments, loans and market conditions, and to
manage client portfolios to the highest performance.

Most importantly, our employees understand client needs.
We listen to our customers. We innovate our products and
services as needs change. We know that our success follows
from our client's success.

Great people focused on our partnership with you, the client.
That's MMA Financial.

each client and each transaction.

Our employees have been working together for a long
time, building the trust and teamwork that creates seamless
service for clients. Over 22% of our employees have been with

experience

creative firm
Gill Fishman Associates
Cambridge, (Massachusetts) USA
creatives
Tammy Torrey
client
MMA Financial

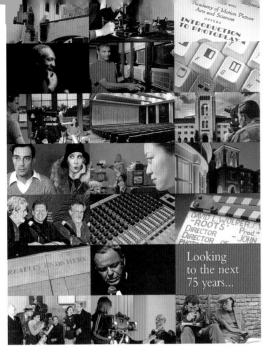

FROM RESEARCH TO REALITY

The Campaign to *accelerate*
the Cure for Diabetes

JDRF Juvenile Diabetes Research Foundation International

In this chamber,

In this hall,

the world community
could try again to
condemn Israel.

Will it succeed?

SPACE TO LEARN

Creating Great Places to Teach, Learn, and Grow

HermanMiller

HermanMiller

creative firm
Revolución
New York, (New York) USA
creatives
Alberto Rodríguez,
Roberto Pedroso,
Abby Lee
client
Revolución

creative firm
Cahan & Associates
Zeeland, (Michigan) USA
creatives
Todd Richards, Steve Frykholm,
Clark Malcolm
client
Herman Miller Inc.

creative firm
Gill Fishman Associates
Cambridge,
(Massachusetts) USA
creatives
Alicia Ozyjowski
client
Schneider Associates

creative firm
Karakter
London, England
creatives
Clive Rohald, Kam Devsi,
Mei Wing Chan, Martin Watkins
client
Norsk Hydro

HYDRO
Progress of a different nature

creative firm
Firefly Studio Pte Ltd
Singapore
creatives
Terry Lee,
Azhar Talib
client
**Mindef Scholarship
Centre**

creative firm
Alcone Marketing Group
Irvine, (California) USA
creatives
Luis Camano, Catherine Lorenzo,
Julie Kimura, Shivonne Miller
client
California Housing Finance Agency

Celebrating 30 Years of Affordable Housing

California Housing Finance Agency

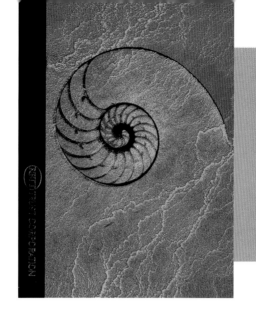

RBTT FINANCIAL GROUP

creative firm
**All Media Projects Ltd
(Ample)**
Port of Spain, (Trinidad) West Indies
creatives
Cathleen Jones,
Josiane Khan,
Caribbean Paper &
Printed Products Ltd.
client
RBTT Trust Corporation

creative firm
Group T Design
Washington, (D.C.) USA
creatives
Tom Klinedinst
client
Whole Foods Market

creative firm
CSC-P2 Communications Services
Falls Church, (Virginia) USA
creatives
Mark Richards, Aaron Kobilis,
John Farquhar
client
CSC

141

creative firm
**The McGraw-Hill Companies
Corporate Creative Services Department**
New York, (New York) USA
creatives
Marianne Johnston,
Paul Biedermann
client
McGraw-Hill Construction

creative firm
Thinkhouse Creative
Atlanta, (Georgia) USA
creatives
Randy Allison,
Susan Lindsay
client
Atlanta Girls' School

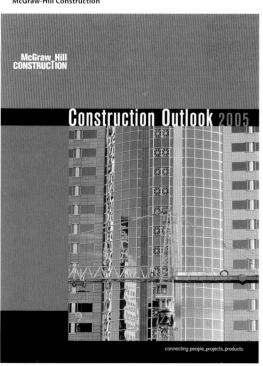

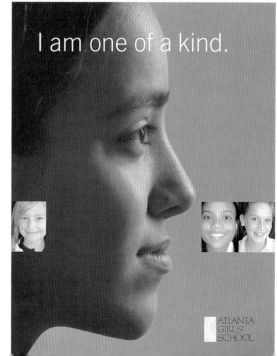

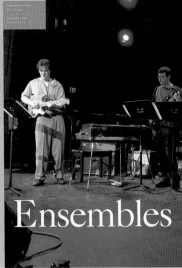

creative firm
kor group
Boston,
(Massachusetts) USA
creatives
Jim Gibson,
Libretto,
Bill Gallery
client
Berklee College of Music

creative firm
Salterbaxter
London, England
client
Context

creative firm
Michael Patrick Partners
Palo Alto, (California) USA
creatives
Duane Maidens
client
Dehen, Inc.

142

creative firm
Design Nut
Washington, (D.C.) USA
creatives
Brent M. Almond, Jimmy Learned,
Pablo Izquierdo, Alexander Dobert
client
Elevation/Democratic National Committee

creative firm
McGaughy Design
Centreville, (Virginia) USA
creatives
Malcolm McGaughy
client
National Postal Forum

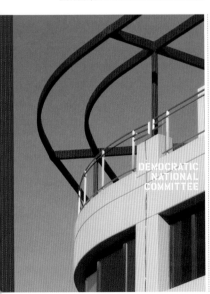

creative firm
Greenfield/Belser Ltd.
Washington, (D.C.) USA
creatives
Burkey Belser,
Jonathan Bruns,
Siobhan Davis,
Patrice Gilbert,
Jennifer Myers,
Alan Sciulli,
Brett Mannes
client
**Sutherland Asbill
& Brennan LLP**

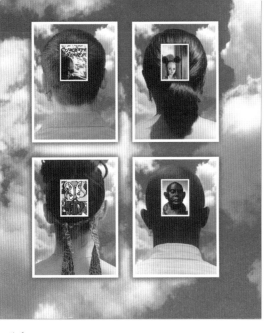

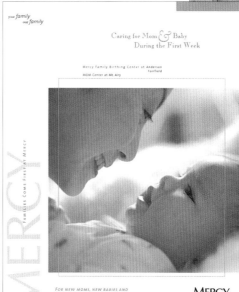

creative firm
The College of Saint Rose Office of Public Relations
Albany, (New York) USA
creatives
Mark Hamilton, Chris Parody, Paul Castle, Lisa Haley
client
The College of Saint Rose

creative firm
Five Visual Communication & Design
West Chester, (Ohio) USA
creatives
Rondi Tschopp
client
Mercy Health Partners

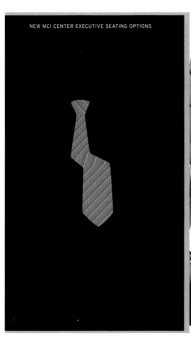

creative firm
Beth Singer Design, LLC
Arlington, (Virginia) USA
creatives
Sucha Snidvongs
client
American Israel Public Affairs Committee

creative firm
Hornall Anderson Design Works
Seattle, (Washington) USA
creatives
Jack Anderson, Elmer dela Cruz,
Henry Yiu, Kathy Saito,
Hayden Schoen, Michael Brugman,
Alan Copeland
client
Washington Wizards

creative firm
Mortensen Design, Inc.
Mountain View, (California) USA
creatives
Gordon Mortensen,
Patricia Margaret,
Timothy Cook
client
CPP. Inc

creative firm
Firefly Studio Pte Ltd
Singapore
creatives
Terry Lee, Azhar Talib,
Brice Li
client
Mindef Scholarship Centre

144

creative firm
CSC-P2 Communications Services
Falls Church, (Virginia) USA
creatives
Jennifer Voltaggio, Aaron Robilis,
John Farquhar
client
CSC

creative firm
kor group
Boston, (Massachusetts)
USA
creatives
James Grady,
Peter Howard,
Dorene Dzuiba
client
Emerson College

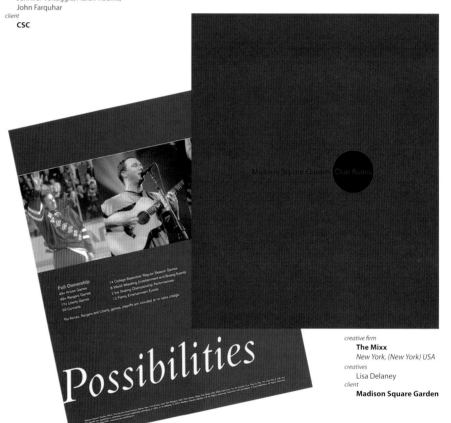

creative firm
The Mixx
New York, (New York) USA
creatives
Lisa Delaney
client
Madison Square Garden

creative firm
Moby Dick Warszawa
Warsaw, Poland
creatives
Matgorzata
Cuepielak,
Wiktor Jaroszynski,
Marcin Kosiorowski
client
**The Polish Security
Printing Works**

creative firm
stressdesign
Syracuse, (New York) USA
creatives
Christine Walker
client
CNY MedTech

A viable society. A need. An idea. 36,000 professionals. Energy. Cooperation. Aluminium. Determination. Pushing boundaries. Respect. Nature. Courage. 100 years. Thinking ahead.

Progress of a different nature.

HYDRO

Celebrating the Hydro Centennial

10

creative firm
Karakter
London, England
creatives
Clive Rohald,
Kam Devsi,
Mei Wing Chan,
Martin Watkins
client
Norsk Hydro

SCHOOL of THEATRE

USC
SCHOOL OF
THEATRE

2005
2006

creative firm
IE Design & Communications
Hermosa Beach, (California) USA
creatives
Marcie Carson
client
USC School of Theatre

145

creative firm
Herman Miller Inc.
Zeeland, (Michigan) USA
creatives
Andrew Dull, Clark Malcolm,
Marlene Capotosto
client
Herman Miller Inc.

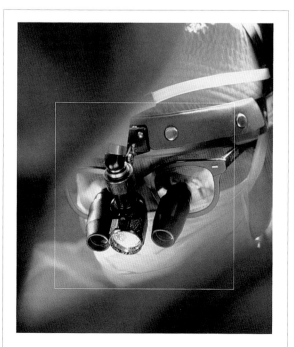

Department of Surgery
translating discoveries

STANFORD
UNIVERSITY
MEDICAL CENTER

creative firm
Michael Patrick Partners
*Palo Alto,
(California) USA*
creatives
Eko Tjoek,
Dan O'Brrien
client
**Stanford Univ.
Medical Center**

HermanMiller

ENVIRONMENTAL ADVOCACY

AT THE ROOT OF IT ALL
How Human Resources Supports Our Growth

Field of Dreams
The Place Where Future All-Stars Are Born

BACKSTAGE PASS
Increasing Associate Access

CONSTRUCTION ZONE
Redesigning Divisions and Departments

THE SECRET RECIPE
Getting the Best Value for the Long Term

THE TIE THAT BINDS
Building Positive Relationships

creative firm
Buck Consultants, an ACS Co.
St. Louis, (Missouri) USA
creatives
Elizabeth Lohmeyer, Jennifer Whitlow,
Aime Laurent, Melissa Kramper
client
Albertsons

146

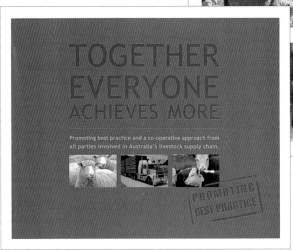

creative firm
E-lift Media
Millicent, Australia
creatives
Heather Burdon,
Simone Burdon
client
**Australian Livestock
Transporters Association**

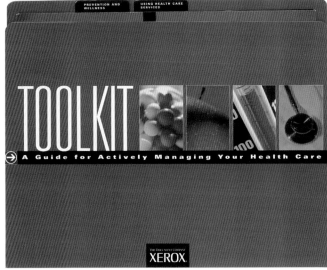

creative firm
Tom Fowler, Inc.
*Norwalk, (Connecticut)
USA*
creatives
Thomas G. Fowler,
Brien O'Reilly
client
Xerox

creative firm
Pensaré Design Group, Ltd
Washington, (D.C.) USA
creatives
Mary Ellen Vehlow,
Amy Billingham
client
Navy League

We take the time to find out what your needs
are so we can be sure that we are giving you the
information or assistance you require.

creative firm
Phoenix Creative Group
Potomac Falls, (Virginia) USA
creatives
Nicole Kassolis, Kathleen Rush,
Matthew Borkoski, Barbara Reed,
Nick Lutkins
client
Homestead Funds

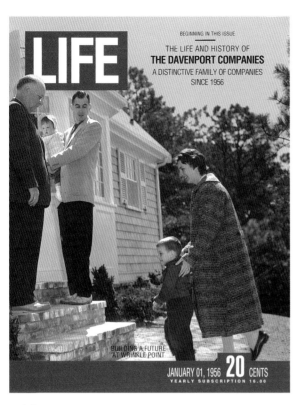

BEGINNING IN THIS ISSUE

LIFE

THE LIFE AND HISTORY OF
THE DAVENPORT COMPANIES
A DISTINCTIVE FAMILY OF COMPANIES
SINCE 1956

BUILDING A FUTURE
AT WRINKLE POINT

JANUARY 01, 1956 **20** CENTS
YEARLY SUBSCRIPTION 16.00

creative firm
Fleming & Roskelly
Newport, (Rhode Island) USA
creatives
Tom Roskelly
client
The Davenport Companies

creative firm
John Wingard Design
Honolulu, (Hawaii) USA
creatives
John Wingard
client
Hawaii Prince Hotel Waikiki

SIMPLE
ELEGANCE

Happily ever after begins with a wedding at the Prince. Celebrate the start of your life together at one of the most romantic locations in the world, where special touches ensure that the memory of your special day will last forever.

HAWAII PRINCE HOTEL WAIKIKI
AND GOLF CLUB

bp
Trinidad and Tobago

bpTT Community Review 2003/2004

creative firm
**All Media Projects Ltd
(Ample)**
Port of Spain, (Trinidad) West Indies
creatives
Cathleen Jones, Charmaine Daisley,
Astra Da Costa, Kay Baldeosingh
client
BP Trinidad and Tobago (bptt)

The Ferring Report
Dreams Fulfilled in 2004

FERRING
PHARMACEUTICALS

FOR SALES REPRESENTATIVE USE ONLY
NOT TO BE LEFT WITH PHYSICIAN.
PLEASE PROVIDE PHYSICIAN WITH FULL
PRESCRIBING INFORMATION.

147

creative firm
Natrel Communications
Parsippany, (New Jersey) USA
creatives
Lorraine Hinck, Susan Roher
client
Ferring Pharmaceuticals

creative firm
Firefly Studio Pte Ltd
Singapore
creatives
Terry Lee, Muhammad Yazidm,
Norman Lai, Irene Wong
client
Public Service Commission

THE SINGAPORE ADMINISTRATIVE SERVICE
This is the scheme of the Civil Service that deals with the broader policy issues and lets you have a direct hand in shaping the many facets of our nation. You will be rotated around the different ministries to deal with a wide range of issues, and be involved in formulating and implementing policies for the success of our nation.

PROFESSIONAL SERVICE
There are many professional schemes of service in the Civil Service. They include being Engineers, Economists, Teachers and so forth. Each Profession has its own proud traditions and significant contributions to Singapore.

OTHERS
Depending on your interest and performance and our nation's needs, you may well find yourself in any of the Statutory Boards or GLCs. You can be assured that the job purview and responsibilities in these organisations will be just as interesting and challenging!

Even if you decide to leave for the private sector after your scholarship bond, you will find that your MA skills will have prepared you for top positions in any organisation and stand you in good stead wherever you may wish to contribute after the civil service.

copyright © PUBLIC SERVICE COMMISSION
mapping minds, mapping the future

TOP

148

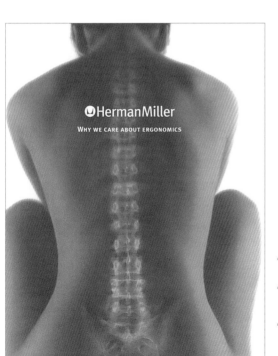

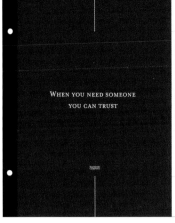

creative firm
Hornall Anderson Design Works
Seattle, (Washington) USA
creatives
Jack Anderson, Andrew Wicklund,
Leo Raymundo
client
Koehler Group

creative firm
Firefly Studio Pte Ltd
Singapore
creatives
Terry Lee,
Norman Lai,
Adrian Lim
client
Public Service Commission

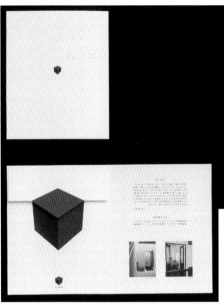

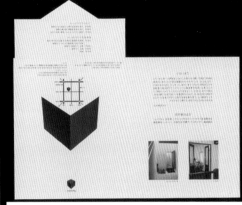

creative firm
Design Club
Tokyo, Japan
creatives
Akihiko Tsukamoto,
Mitsuko Wakabayashi
client
Photon Co., Ltd.

THIS BROCHURE CONTAINS 13 RECYCLED TETRA PAK CARTONS*

Recycling of used beverage cartons in Europe

149

creative firm
Salterbaxter
London, England
client
Tetra Pak

creative firm
Fleming & Roskelly
Newport, (Rhode Island) USA
creatives
Tom Roskelly,
Andrea Carneiro
client
Preservation Society of Newport County

creative firm
Herman Miller Inc.
Zeeland, (Michigan) USA
creatives
Todd Richards,
Steve Frykholm,
Clark Malcolm
client
Herman Miller Inc.

creative firm
Atlanta College of Art
Communication Design Department
Atlanta, (Georgia) USA
creatives
Peter Wong, Shanika Ballard,
Andrew Ericson, Amin Mohandesi,
Julie Yee
client
Atlanta College of Art

creative firm
Epigram
Singapore
creatives
Edmund Wee

creative firm
VSA Partners
Chicago, (Illinois) USA
creatives
Curt Schreiber,
Ashley Lippard,
Wendy Belt
client
IBM

creative firm
Howard Hanna Smythe Cramer
Seven Hills, (Ohio) USA
creatives
Aimee Campbell
client
The Coral Company

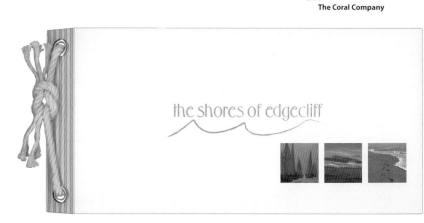

creative firm
Sherman Advertising/Mermaid, Inc.
New York, (New York) USA
creatives
Sharon Lloyd McLaughlin,
William Touchet,
Stephen Morse
client
120 Riverside Boulevard

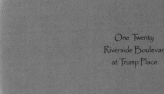

One Twenty
Riverside Boulevard
at Trump Place

creative firm
Avenue
Chicago, (Illinois) USA
creatives
Geoffrey Mark,
Alisa Wolfson
client
The Joffrey Ballet

SUBSCRIBE NOW
FOR THE BEST SEATS,
YOURS TO
RENEW EVERY YEAR.

creative firm
Ventress
Design Group
Franklin, (Tennessee)
USA
creatives
Tom Ventress,
Katherine Seigenthaler
client
DigiScript

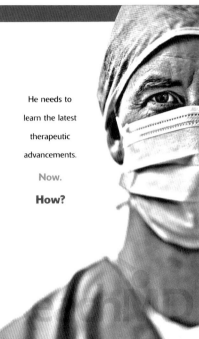

He needs to
learn the latest
therapeutic
advancements.

Now.

How?

151

creative firm
Catalyst
Klarwick,
(Rhode Island)
USA
creatives
Cindi Emery,
Mike Morphy,
John Beaupre
client
Signature
Design Studio

Let your ideas flow.

FANTASIA JEWEL

ADDENDA

creative firm
Pivot Design, Inc.
Chicago, (Illinois)
USA
creatives
Brock Haldeman, Don Emery,
Steve Graziano, David Altholz
client
Weyerhaeuser

ROYAL PARK HOTEL

ROYAL PARK HOTEL

Magical

Extraordinary

creative firm
Premier Communications Group
Royal Oak, (Michigan) USA
creatives
Doug Konen, Kate Pultz
client
Royal Park Hotel

SEATING INSPIRED BY

Sundance Spas

EVERY DAY.

creative firm
Kevershan Testerman
San Diego, (California) USA
creatives
Patty Kevershan, Patti Testerman,
Lynn Fleschutz
client
Sundance Spas

About the Artist

The fact that Fred Johnson has opened for both Aretha Franklin and Dr. Deepak Chopra points to his versatility as an artist. An acclaimed jazz musician and performer, Fred is a graduate of the National Academy of the Performing Arts as well as the Master Performers School of the National Mime Theater. He has recorded and toured worldwide with Chick Corea, Richard Elliot, George Benson, David Sanborn, B.B. King, Ramsey Lewis, Patti LaBelle, Herbie Mann, and the great Miles Davis. Currently the Director of Education and Outreach at The Center for Creative Resources in New York, Fred was for many years affiliated with the Tampa Bay Performing Arts Center in Florida where he served as both Vice President of Education and Humanities and Artist-in-Residence.

During that time he produced the Center's American Music Festival and the Art and Spirituality Festival. He is recognized globally for his work in the health and wellness community. His presentations on the healing power of music have caught the attention of internationally renowned holistic health practitioners. Mentored by masters of the African oral and percussion legacy, Fred has been hailed as one of the true guardians of an oral tradition transplanted and nurtured to create a fusion of cultural heritage that is uniquely American and inherently African.

creative firm
WestGroup Creative
New York, (New York) USA
creatives
Chip Tolaney, Marvin Berk,
Carol Rosegg
client
Fred Johnson

152

creative firm
Datagraf
Auning, Denmark
creatives
Anne Marie Nordlyng
client
DTU

MYSTIC

helikon

creative firm
Jones Studio Limited
Staten Island, (New York) USA
creatives
Pui-Pui Li, Eric Jones,
Amos Chan
client
Helikon

DYNAMO

TEMA: NANOTEKNOLOGI

UDDANNELSE AF INDUSTRIENS LEDERE

creative firm
Sherman Advertising/Mermaid, Inc.
New York, (New York) USA
creatives
Sharon Lloyd McLaughlin, William Touchet,
Stephen Morse
client
The St. Clair

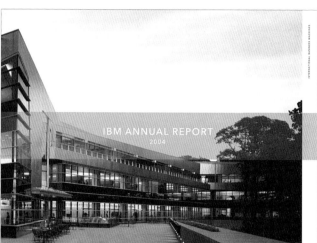

creative firm
VSA Partners
Chicago, (Illinois) USA
creatives
Curt Schreiber,
Steve Ryan,
Ashley Lippard,
Wendy Belt,
Silas Munro,
Amy Glaiberman
client
IBM

153

creative firm
KARAKTER Ltd
London, England
creatives
Clive Rohald,
Kam Devsi,
Rei Wing Chan,
Martin Watkins
client
Nice Systems

creative firm
Q
Wiesbaden, Germany
creatives
Thilo von Debschitz,
Matthias Frey
client
Arjo Wiggins

creative firm
Gill Fishman Associates
*Cambridge, (Massachusetts)
USA*
creatives
Michael Persons
client
**Spaulding Rehabilitation
Center**

154

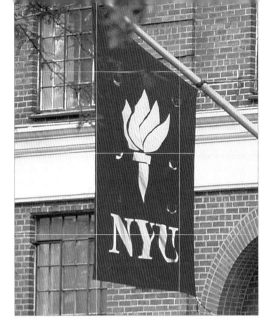

appealing
orange

Orange is a high arousal color invariably associated with autumn's burnished foliage or the radiant shadings of sunset. Growing and yellow, has shown to exert a measurable affect on the autonomic nervous system, which stimulates the appetite. Fast food restaurants have used warm colors to entice people in for instant appetite appeasement.

the process:

MeadWestvaco Signature Press Set 80lb cover

creative firm
Pantone, Inc.
Carlstadt, (New Jersey) USA
creatives
Yolanda Lamourt,
Tom Gladwell
client
Pantone, Inc.

creative firm
Suka Design
New York, (New York) USA
creatives
Brian Wong
client
New York University

creative firm
Torre Lazur McCann
Parsippany, (New Jersey) USA
creatives
Marianne Rivello, Juliet Martinez,
Sandra Golbicki, Jodi Smith
client
Ortho-McNeil

CompuChicks, Inc. enjoyed beautiful makeover results, with a 188% increase in revenue.

Take this booklet to any Sprint Store before your discount expires.

20% off on all Sprint PCS Phones and Accessories with a total retail price of $99.99 or more

and

$150 instant savings for every Best value Sprint PCS Advantage Agreement you sign

Get unique wireless solutions for your business at a price that fits all budgets.
Hurry in for an exclusive discount that ends April 8, 2006.

> With Sprint, CompuChicks, Inc. is beautiful.

> Call 1-800-209-274
Or visit www.spri
to locate a store

Sprint.

155

creative firm
Publicis Dialog
San Francisco, (California) USA
creatives
Blair Cerny, Brandie Uno,
Katie Hopkins, Jonathan Butts,
Brian Tyler, Martin Kojnok
client
Sprint

OPAMAX—the first new medicine r migraine prevention in 8 years

fewer migraines

PAMAX can help **prevent** migraine attacks, you get **fewer** of them. Its effectiveness has en proven in the largest well-controlled clinical als to date for migraine prevention.

like medicine you take when you feel migraine eadache pain, TOPAMAX is **clinically proven** to prevent attacks before they happen, so you fewer of them.

PAMAX is approved for migraine prevention adults only. The usefulness of TOPAMAX in acute treatment of migraine headache has been studied.

OPAMAX
(topiramato)

creative firm
**Creaxis Design
Pte Ltd**
Singapore
creatives
Lester Lim,
Yang Qiao'e
client
**CityHub Business
Services**

Unprecedented support

If it's **migraine**, it's personal

Personal perspectives about migraine and migraine prevention

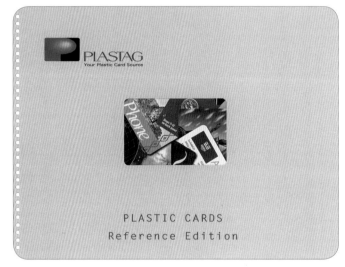

PLASTIC CARDS
Reference Edition

156

creative firm
Decker Design, Inc.
Brooklyn, (New York) USA
creatives
Lynda Decker, Jan Sabach,
James Turner, Boris Brever
client
Vesta Group

PIER VILLAGE
LONG BRANCH

creative firm
Sherman Advertising/Mermaid, Inc.
New York, (New York) USA
creatives
Sharon Lloyd McLaughlin, William Touchet,
Stephen Morse
client
Pier Village

157

creative firm
Sterling Group
New York, (New York) USA
creatives
Marcus Hewitt, Kim Berlin,
Kelly Stewart, Alan McNear
client
Lockes Diamantaires

LOCKES

creative firm
Subplot Design Inc.
Vancouver, (British Columbia) Canada
creatives
Matthew Clark, Roy White
client
Martha Sturdy Furniture

creative firm
Empire Communications Group
Jacksonville, (Florida) USA
creatives
Chris Alcantara, Susan Kiernan-Lewis,
Fred Page
client
Mello Trading

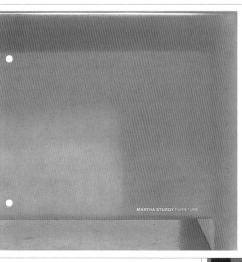

MARTHA STURDY FURNITURE

BOLCHOJ
BLACK LABEL

creative firm
Vince Rini Design
Huntington Beach,
(California) USA
creatives
Vince Rini
client
Orange County
Performing Arts Center

creative firm
Ventress Design Group
Franklin, (Tennessee)
USA
creatives
Tom Ventress,
Hunter Hodge
client
DigiScript

158

creative firm
VSA Partners
Chicago, (Illinois) USA
creatives
Dana Arnett, Jason Jones,
Tim Guy, Jake Gardner,
Ron Berkheimer, Richard Weaver,
Mid Coast Studio, Reid Armbruster
client
Harley-Davidson

creative firm
Portfolio Center
Atlanta, (Georgia) USA
creatives
Zelda Devon

creative firm
Haase & Knels
Bremen, Germany
creatives
Sibylle Haase,
Hans Hansen,
Katja Hirschfelder
client
B.T. Dibbern
GmbH & C0. KG

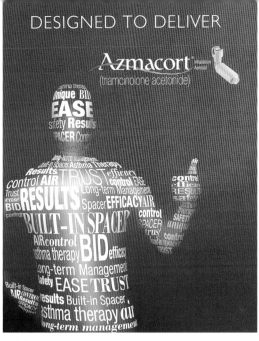

DESIGNED TO DELIVER

creative firm
KPR
New York, (New York) USA
creatives
Bernard Steinman, Scott Frank,
Jeff Stevenson, Kari Tortorello
client
Kos Pharmaceuticals

Our Key Strengths

creative firm
Riordon Design
Oakville, (Ontario) Canada
creatives
Ric Riordon, Shirley Riordon
client
McKellar Group

With billions of dollars invested and not a penny lost,
The McKellar Structured Settlement™
provides tax-free financial security to injured people every day.

We guarantee it.

159

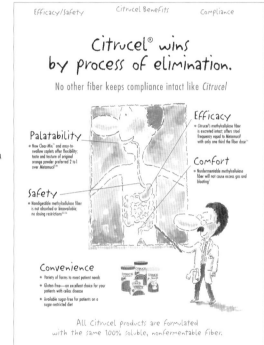

Efficacy/Safety   Citrucel Benefits   Compliance

Citrucel® wins
by process of elimination.

No other fiber keeps compliance intact like *Citrucel*

creative firm
Torre Lazur McCann
Parisippany, (New Jersey) USA
creatives
Gail Berlose,
Maureen O'Rourke
client
GlaxoSmithKline

creative firm
Ventress Design Group
Franklin, (Tennessee) USA
creatives
Tom Ventress, Vicki Schauer
client
DigiScript

creative firm
True North
Mississauga, (Ontario) Canada
creatives
Kyle McKenna
client
Oxford Properties

Your Latest Clinical Trial.
Hundreds of Investigators and CRAs.
How Do You Ensure Consistent Trial Training?

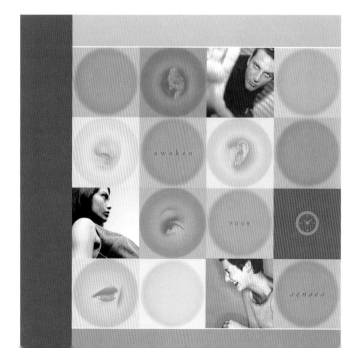

awaken

YOUR

senses

MAINTAIN YOUR IDENTITY COAST TO COAST.
Turn up Your Sales Volume with XM.

160

Style
FOR YOUR
STANDARDS

AWARDCOLLECTIONS

05 Beaver
SUMMER PROGRAMS

THE EXCLUSIVELY MISOOK
COLLECTION OFFERS A
BALANCE OF CASUAL AND
FORMAL DESIGNS FOR A
TRULY VERSATILE WARDROBE.
THE LINE OF COLORFUL
VARIATIONS ON A BLACK
FOUNDATION. **A CLASSIC,
SOPHISTICATED LOOK.**

EXCLUSIVELY misook

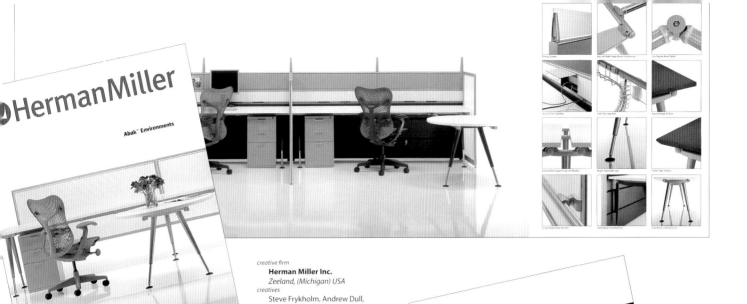

creative firm
Herman Miller Inc.
Zeeland, (Michigan) USA
creatives
Steve Frykholm, Andrew Dull,
Marlene Capotosto
client
Herman Miller Inc.

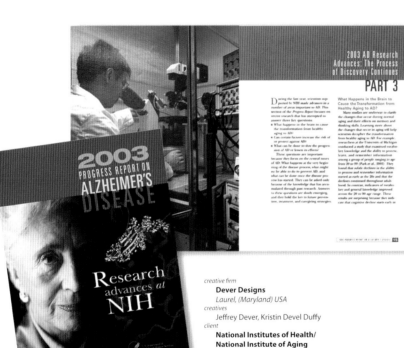

creative firm
Dever Designs
Laurel, (Maryland) USA
creatives
Jeffrey Dever, Kristin Devel Duffy
client
**National Institutes of Health/
National Institute of Aging**

56
PINE

creative firm
Liska + Associates, Inc.
Chicago, (Illinois) USA
creatives
Tanya Quick, Fernando Munoz,
Pete Margonelli, Don Pietache,
Francesco Gianesini
client
Rosen Partners

At Burnham Square, you are part of something more.

creative firm
Scott Adams Design Associates
Columbus, (Ohio) USA
creatives
Scott Adams, Tom Griffin,
Rick Carey
client
Nationwide Realty Investors

airdivision.net

The PLANK Collection

creative firm
Dezainwerkz
Singapore
creatives
Xavier Sanjiman, Kristal Melson,
Flux Fotography
client
Air Division

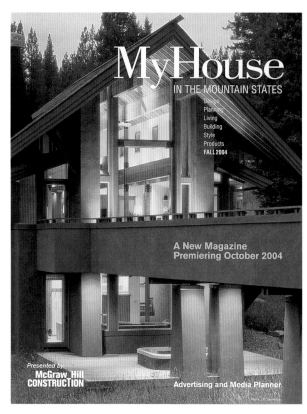

MyHouse
IN THE MOUNTAIN STATES

Design
Planning
Living
Building
Style
Products
FALL 2004

A New Magazine
Premiering October 2004

Presented by
McGraw_Hill
CONSTRUCTION   Advertising and Media Planner

creative firm
The McGraw-Hill Companies
Corporate Creative Services Department
New York, (New York) USA
creatives
Marianne Johnston, Paul Biedermann
client
McGraw-Hill Construction

162

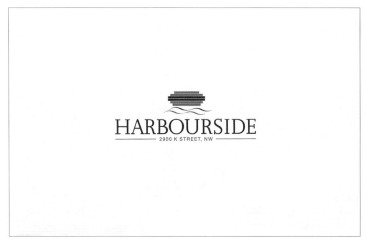

HARBOURSIDE
2900 K STREET, NW

creative firm
ds&f
Washington, (D.C.) USA
creatives
Don Schaaf,
Ami Barker
client
Lano Armada HarbourSide, LLC

creative firm
Noevir USA, Inc.
Irvine, (California) USA
creatives
Joseph Gaydos, Rene Armenta
client
Noevir USA, Inc.

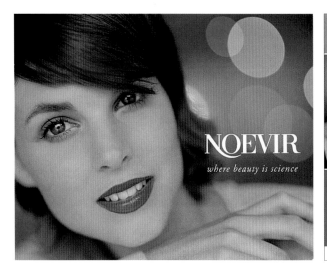

NOEVIR
where beauty is science

EXTRA
CLEANSING FOAM

6 • Noevir Extra Skincare

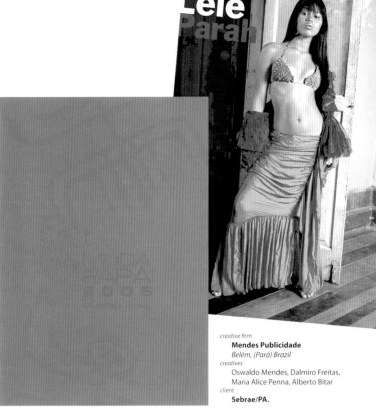

TY FAVORITES FROM GENUINE MOTOR PARTS AND ACCESSORIES

creative firm
VSA Partners, Inc.
Chicago, (Illinois) USA
creatives
Dana Arnett, Jason Jones,
Tim Guy, Claire Williams,
Richard Weaver, Mid Coast Studio,
John Furr
client
Harley-Davidson

creative firm
Mendes Publicidade
Belém, (Pará) Brazil
creatives
Oswaldo Mendes, Dalmiro Freitas,
Maria Alice Penna, Alberto Bitar
client
Sebrae/PA.

creative firm
Campbell-Ewald
Warren, (Illinois) USA
creatives
Bill Ludwig, Susan Logar Brody,
Raymond Allston, Ed Davis,
Lizz Behler, Sue Podgorski,
Janine Benedict, Ben Haynes
client
XM Satellite Radio

163

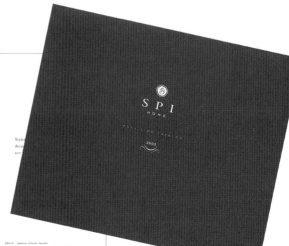

creative firm
Helena Seo Design
Sunnyvale, (California) USA
creatives
Helena Seo
client
SPI

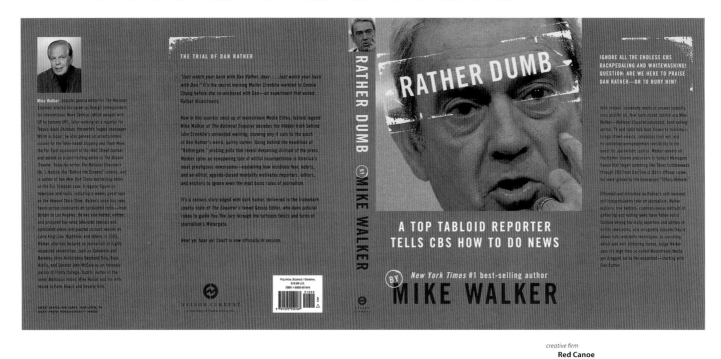

creative firm
Red Canoe
Deer Lodge, (Tennessee) USA
creatives
Deb Koch, Caroline Kavanagh,
Mike Walker, Honda/AFP/Getty Images
client
Thomas Nelson Publishers, Nelson Current

creative firm
Wendell Minor Design
Washington, (Connecticut) USA
creatives
Wendell Minor
client
Simon & Schuster

creative firm
Portfolio Center
Atlanta, (Georgia) USA
creatives
Kurt Huggins

creative firm
Mendes Publicidade
Belém, (Pará) Brazil
creatives
Oswaldo Mendes,
Maria Alice Penna
client
Banco da Amazônia

creative firm
Design Club
Minato-ku, (Tokyo) Japan
creatives
Akihiko Tsukamoto
client
PIE Co., Ltd.

165

creative firm
Scott Adams Design Associates
Columbus, (Ohio) USA
creatives
Scott Adams,
Wilma Bulkin Siegel
client
Museum of Art//Fort Lauderdale

SURVIVORS *and* LIBERATORS:

PORTRAITS *by* WILMA BULKIN SIEGEL

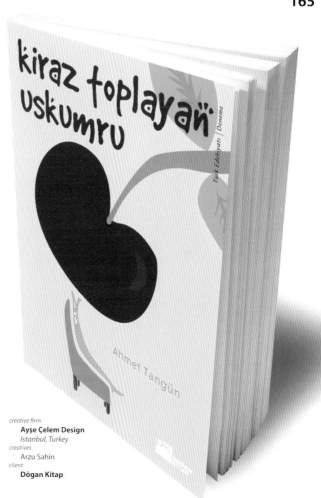

creative firm
Ayşe Çelem Design
Istanbul, Turkey
creatives
Arzu Sahin
client
Dôgan Kitap

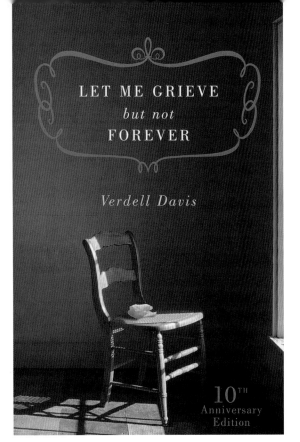

creative firm
Red Canoe
Deer Lodge, (Tennessee) USA
creatives
Deb Koch, Caroline Kavanagh,
Robin Jones Gunn, Bob Skinner
client
Thomas Nelson Publishers, W Publishing Group

creative firm
Ayşe Çelem Design
Istanbul, Turkey
creatives
Arzu Sahin
client
Dôgan Kitap

creative firm
Nassar Design
Brookline, (Massachusetts) USA
creatives
Nelida Nassar,
Margarita Encomienda
client
Harvard Design School

creative firm
Red Canoe
Deer Lodge, (Tennessee) USA
creatives
Deb Koch, Caroline Kavanagh,
Constantine C. Menges, Andrew Garn
client
Thomas Nelson Publishers, Nelson Current

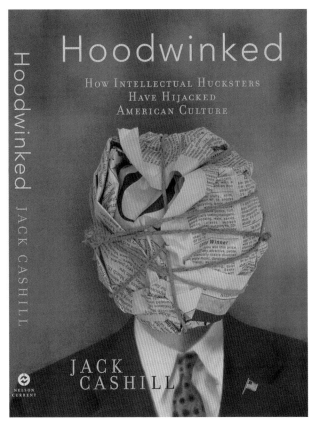

creative firm
Red Canoe
Deer Lodge, (Tennessee) USA
creatives
Deb Koch, Caroline Kavanagh,
Jack Cashill, Malcolm Tarlofsky
client
Thomas Nelson Publishers, Nelson Current

creative firm
Ayşe Çelem Design
Istanbul, Turkey
creatives
Ayşe Çelem
client
Dôgan Kitap

167

creative firm
Portfolio Center
Atlanta, (Georgia) USA
creatives
Jeff Jarvis

creative firm
Red Canoe
Deer Lodge, (Tennessee) USA
creatives
Deb Koch, Caroline Kavanagh,
Phil Valentine, Kevin Bapp
client
Thomas Nelson Publishers, Nelson Current

168

creative firm
Epigram
Singapore
creatives
Edmund Wee,
Zann Wan
client
**National Trades
Union Congress**

creative firm
Visual Arts Press
New York, (New York) USA
creatives
Genevieve Williams, Ha Do,
Lenny Naar, Ana Pavlović,
Lisa Sobczynski,
Chris Spooner,
David Miao, Kanako Sasaki,
Dorothy Hong, Tanja Diklić,
Ralph Piper
client
School of Visual Arts

creative firm
Pivot Design, Inc.
Chicago, (Illinois) USA
creatives
Brock Haldeman,
Don Emery
client
Fitz Gerald's

169

creative firm
KBDA
Los Angeles, (California) USA
creatives
Kim Baer, Keith Knueven,
Dave Lauridsen, Jill Vacarra
client
ColorNet Press

creative firm
Carin Goldberg Design
New York, (New York) USA
creatives
Carin Goldberg, Richard Wilde,
Akiko Busch, Adam Wahler
client
School of Visual Arts

creative firm
Erwin Zinger Graphic Design
Groningen, The Netherlands
creatives
Erwin Zinger, Wim Vander Haegen,
Rudy De Doncker, Guidovan Damme,
Pascal Meulenberg, Ronald Den Dekker
client
Aventura Entertainment

When you're scared, you will get through,
But this is what you have to do:
When asked to go and your parents don't know,
Shout "No!" Shout "No!"

Hooty Knows

Child Find

170

creative firm
Greenfield/Belser Ltd.
Washington, (D.C.) USA
creatives
Burkey Belser,
Donna Greenfield,
Brett Mannes
client
Greenfield/Belser Ltd.

25 YEARS
OF LEGAL
BRANDING

A LOPSIDED VIEW FROM GREENFIELD/BELSER OF THE HISTORY OF LEGAL MARKETING

BY BURKEY BELSER AND DONNA GREENFIELD

creative firm
Velocity Design Works
Winnipeg, (Manitoba) Canada
creatives
Lasha Orzechowski, Eric Peters
client
Child Find Manitoba

creative firm
CS Design
San Diego, (California) USA
creatives
Christopher Lee, Steve Lim,
Ken Hansen, Eric Myer
client
CS Design

creative firm
Ruder Finn Design
New York, (New York) USA
creatives
Lisa Gabbay, Sal Catania,
Winnie Chang
client
Zabriskie Gallery

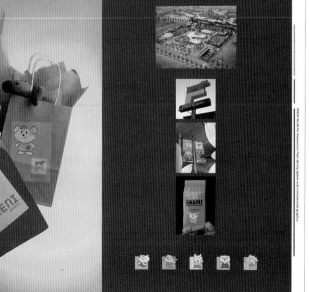

ZABRISKIE
FIFTY YEARS

TITLE: Spring 2005; strapless, horizontal, and striped patchwork gown in silk and rayon
FIRM: Petro Zillia
DESIGNER: Nony Tochterman, Designer/Owner

TITLE: Spring 2005; Silk, multi-layered evening gown featuring an in-house designer Orchid print
FIRM: Petro Zillia
DESIGNER: Nony Tochterman, Designer/Owner

ALIFORNIA
ESIGN 05

PASADENA MUSEUM OF CALIFORNIA ART

TITLE: Green Jacob Crochet Dress
FIRM: Olga Troyan
DESIGNER: Kristopher Enake

creative firm
Picnic Design
Santa Monica, (California) USA
creatives
Vesna Petrovic, Marci Boudreau
client
**Pasadena Museum of
California Art**

creative firm
Design Club
Tokyo, Japan
creatives
Akihiko Tsukamoto, Nobuya Hoki
client
**Daiwa Radiator Factory Co., Ltd.
and Taro Nasu Gallery**

ART & CULTURE

Embodying Andersen

TROUBLEYN / JAN FABRE

creative firm
Lund & Co
Esbjerg, Denmark
creatives
Peter Lund,
Jakob Gad
client
World Pictures

chapter two
where do you want to go?

HANS CHRISTIAN ANDERSEN
2005

FAIRY TALES

OFFICIAL PROGRAMME

COMMUNICATIONS TOOLKIT

A guide to navigating communications for the nonprofit world

creative firm
Cause Communications
Santa Monica, (California) USA
creatives
R. Christine Hershey,
Joanna Lee,
Kristin Bright
client
**The Annenberg Foundation,
The California Endowment,
The James Irvine Foundations,
Marguerite Casey Foundation**

WILDERNESS WITHIN

WILDERNESS WITHOUT

A Personal Journey
Through Pressley Ridge Wilderness Camp at Ohiopyle

by Shannon Szwarc

Whenever Baxter Bunny goes somewhere,
He always remembers to be aware.

"He brings a buddy along!"

Baxter Bunny
Brings his Buddies

Child Find

creative firm
Velocity Design Works
Winnipeg, (Manitoba) Canada
creatives
Lasha Orzechowski, Eric Peters
client
Child Find Manitoba

172

creative firm
Kolbrener
Pittsburgh, (Pennsylvania) USA
creatives
Michael Kolbrener, Shannon Szwarc,
Abby Mendelson
client
Pressley Ridge

creative firm
Datagraf
Auning, Denmark
creatives
Rikke Thorsen
client
Pressalit

pressalit group

1954-2004
Pressalit

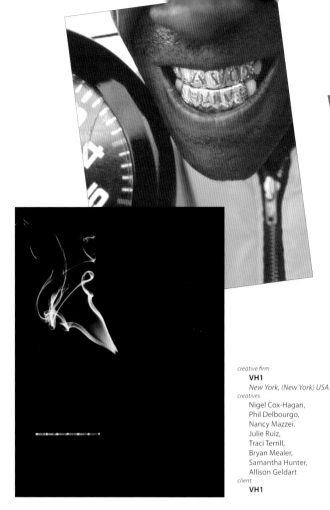

creative firm
VH1
New York, (New York) USA
creatives
Nigel Cox-Hagan,
Phil Delbourgo,
Nancy Mazzei,
Julie Ruiz,
Traci Terrill,
Bryan Mealer,
Samantha Hunter,
Allison Geldart
client
VH1

creative firm
Mendes Publicidade
Belém, (Pará) Brazil
creatives
Oswaldo Mendes, Maria Alice Penna,
Luiz Braga, InterFoto, Geraldo Ramos,
Walda Marques
client
Sebrae/PA.

creative firm
Ruder Finn Design
New York, (New York) USA
creatives
Lisa Gabbay, Sal Catania,
Laura Vinchesi
client
Bill Baker

Lighthouse Island
OUR FAMILY ESCAPE BILL BAKER

creative firm
Futura DDB
Ljubljana, Slovenia
creatives
Zare Kerin, Stojan Pelko,
Janez Pukšič, Marko O'Mahen
client
KRKA

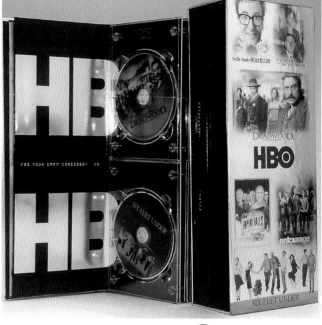

creative firm
Epos, Inc.
Santa Monica, (California) USA
creatives
Gabrielle Raumberger,
Eric Martinez
client
Spiral Subwave Records, Inc.

creative firm
HBO Creative Services
New York, (New York) USA
creatives
Gary Dueno, Tony Viola,
Venus Dennison
client
HBO

174

creative firm
Riordon Design
Oakville, (Ontario)
Canada
creatives
Dan Wheaton,
Tim Warnock,
Sharon Pece
client
Empty Heart

creative firm
30sixty advertising & design
Los Angeles, (California) USA
creatives
Henry Vizcarra, Duy Nguyen,
Richard Hilary
client
Universal Home Entertainment

creative firm
Studioerin
Jupiter, (Florida) USA
creatives
Erin Starks
client
Tom Alexander

creative firm
Spike TV
New York, (New York) USA
creatives
Pam Schecter, Niels Schuurmans,
Milinda Zumpano, Junichi Nakane,
Jenny Jameson, Ian Kahn
client
Spike TV

creative firm
Anjaro
San Francisco, (California) USA
creatives
Jacques Rossouw,
Francoise Bourzat,
Annria Rossouw
client
Francoise Bourzat & Jacques Rossouw

creative firm
**The Humane Society
of the United States**
Washington, (D.C.) USA
creatives
Paula Jaworski,
Elizabeth McNulty
client
**The Humane Society
of the United States**

175

creative firm
Cisco Brand Strategy
San Jose, (California) USA
creatives
Jeff Brand, Chris Sereno
client
Cisco Systems

creative firm
Empire Communications Group
Jacksonville, (Florida) USA
creatives
Chris Alcantara, Susan Kiernan-Lewis
client
Shands Jacksonville

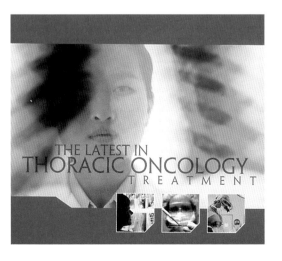

𝒫ackage Design

creative firm
Portfolio Center
Atlanta, (Georgia) USA
creatives
Dread Madison

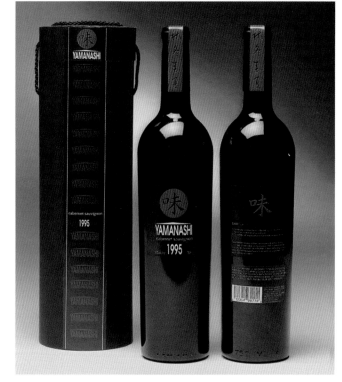

creative firm
www.karmasavage.com
Anaheim, (California) USA
creatives
Karma Savage,
Mayuko Ishikawa

176

creative firm
MetaDesign
San Francisco, (California) USA
creatives
Brett Wickens, Conor Mangat,
Hui-Ling Chen, Nick Veasey,
Jim Wehtje, Jamie Welsh, Jeff Allison
client
Adobe Systems Inc.

creative firm
Lewis Moberly
London, England
creatives
Mary Lewis, Christian Stacey,
Ann Marshal
client
Waitrose PLC

creative firm
Lipson Alport Glass & Assoc.
Northbrook, (Illinois) USA
creatives
Scotty Hardy, Vince Bowman
client
Jim Beam Brands

creative firm
Futura DDB
Ljubljana, Slovenia
creatives
Marko Vičić, Žare Kerin,
Marko Piškur
client
Dana

177

creative firm
Lewis Moberly
London, England
creatives
Mary Lewis,
Joann Smith
client
William Grant & Sons

creative firm
Turner Duckworth
London & San Francisco
London, England
creatives
David Turner, Bruce Duckworth
client
The Steel Brewing Company

creative firm
Optima Group
Highland Park, (Illinois) USA
creatives
Sara Belskis
client
Coca-Cola Company

creative firm
Arcanna, Inc.
Peekskill, (New York) USA
creatives
Robert Frissora, Sondra Greenspan
client
Bonjour La Parisienne

creative firm
Semmer Group
Minneapolis, (Minnesota) USA
creatives
Emily Oberg,
Joan Semmer
client
Hormel

creative firm
Rienzi & Rienzi Communications
Montville, (New Jersey) USA
creatives
Mary Gayle Scheper, Ramona Thukral,
Kim Langley, CNS News
client
Mylan Bertek Pharmaceuticals Inc.

creative firm
Clorox Creative Services
Oakland, (California) USA
creatives
Chris Twilling, Tim Ferdun
client
The Clorox Company

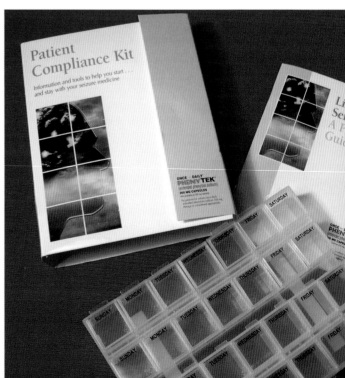

creative firm
Mind & Media
Alexandria, (Virginia) USA
creatives
Chris Ammon, Troy Thompson,
Jason Hunter
client
Army National Guard

creative firm
Lipson Alport Glass & Assoc.
Northbrook, (Illinois) USA
creatives
Lisa Adams, Bob Pauly
client
Sara Lee Corporation

creative firm
Lewis Moberly
London, England
creatives
Mary Lewis
client
Waitrose PLC

WHOLEGRAIN MUSTARD

ENGLISH MUSTARD

FRENCH MUSTARD

creative firm
Clorox Creative Services
Oakland, (California) USA
creatives
Liliana Barbieri, Anthony Luk,
Robert Evans
client
The Glad Products Company

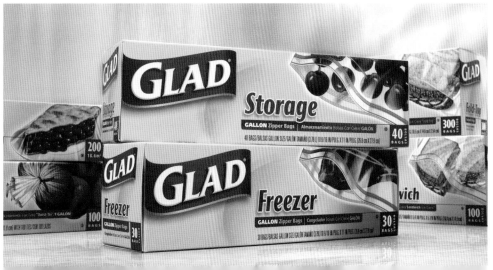

creative firm
Semmer Group
Minneapolis, (Minnesota) USA
creatives
Emily Oberg, Heidi Miller
client
Target

creative firm
Lipson Alport Glass & Assoc.
Northbrook, (Illinois) USA
creatives
Scott Hardy
client
Ahold USA

180

creative firm
Portfolio Center
Atlanta, (Georgia) USA
creatives
Marcel Cabrera
client
Pock T

creative firm
Rassman Design
Denver, (Colorado) USA
creatives
Lyn D'Amato
client
**Certified Financial Planner
Board of Standards**

creative firm
Octavo Designs
Frederick, (Maryland) USA
creatives
Sue Hough
client
Citrus Scent

creative firm
Hornall Anderson Design Works
Seattle, (Washington) USA
creatives
John Anicker, Jack Anderson,
Leo Raymundo, Sonja Max,
Andrew Wicklund
client
Clearwire

creative firm
S2 Design Group
*New York, (New York)
USA*
creatives
Eileen Strauss,
Lauretta Worm
client
Schering-Plough

creative firm
Tom Fowler, Inc.
Norwalk, (Connecticut) USA
creatives
Elizabeth P. Ball
client
**Unilever Home &
Personal Care USA**

181

creative firm
Pinnacle Graphics
Addison, (Texas) USA
creatives
Wendy Hanson
client
Stonewick

creative firm
North American Packaging
New York, (New York) USA
creatives
Francoise Olivas,
John De Stefano, Warren Beishir
client
Nanette Lepore

creative firm
Wallace Church, Inc.
New York, (New York) USA
creatives
Stan Church,
Wendy Church
client
Ocean Spray Cranberries, Inc.

creative firm
**Scott Vision
Communication Co., Ltd**
Taipei, Taiwan
creatives
Scott Lee, Phoenix
client
7-Eleven

182

creative firm
Cassata & Associates
Schaumburg, (Illinois) USA
creatives
Mary Holzer,
Suzanne Skoczynski
client
Fannie May Confections

creative firm
Portfolio Center
Atlanta, (Georgia) USA
creatives
Brian Stokes
client
Vespertine

creative firm
Lipson Alport Glass & Assoc.
Northbrook, (Illinois) USA
creatives
Christie McMearty
client
Well's Dairy

creative firm
Design Resource Center
Naperville, (Illinois) USA
creatives
John Norman, Melanie Gibb,
Marc Rumaner
client
Kehe Food Distributors, Inc.

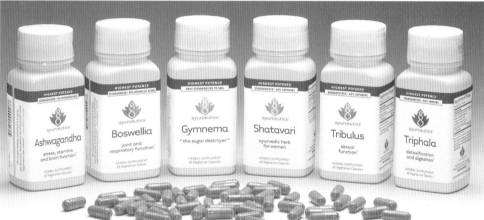

creative firm
Pure Design Co. LLC
Leverett, (Massachusetts) USA
creatives
Dan Mishkind,
Graeme Ritchie
client
Renaissance Herbs, Inc.

183

creative firm
Di Donato Associates
Chicago, (Illinois) USA
creatives
Peter Di Donato,
Doug Miller
client
Barton Brands Ltd.

creative firm
Cornerstone
New York, (New York) USA
creatives
Keith Steimel
client
Coca-Cola Co.

creative firm
Creative Link
San Antonio, (Texas) USA
creatives
Mark Broderick, Lawrence Sahulka,
John A. Wilson
client
Montealegre & Associates

creative firm
Launch Creative Marketing
Chicago, (Illinois) USA
creatives
Michelle Morales
client
Ford Gum

184

creative firm
Semmer Group
Minneapolis, (Minnesota) USA
creatives
Emily Oberg, Heidi Miller
client
Target

creative firm
MackeySzar
*Plymouth,
(Minnesota) USA*
client
Ecolab

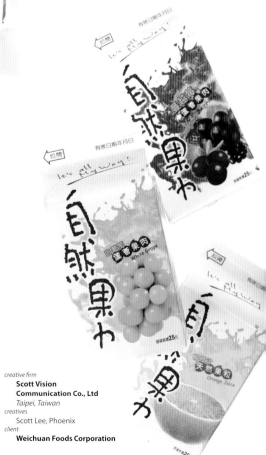

creative firm
**Scott Vision
Communication Co., Ltd**
Taipei, Taiwan
creatives
Scott Lee, Phoenix
client
Weichuan Foods Corporation

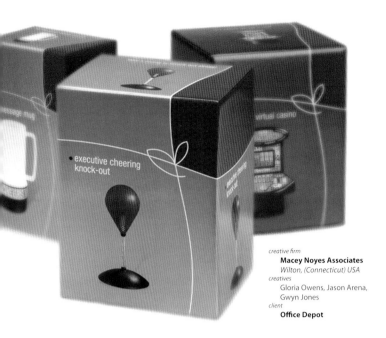

creative firm
Macey Noyes Associates
Wilton, (Connecticut) USA
creatives
Gloria Owens, Jason Arena,
Gwyn Jones
client
Office Depot

creative firm
Tom Fowler, Inc.
Norwalk, (Connecticut) USA
creatives
Mary Ellen Butkus,
Lael Porcelli,
Jeff Fowler
client
**Honeywell Consumer
Products**

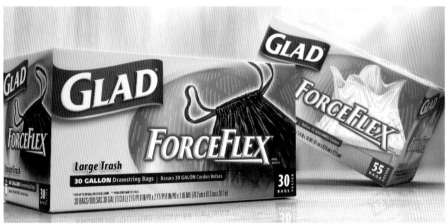

creative firm
Clorox Creative Services
Oakland, (California) USA
creatives
Liliana Barbieri,
Anthony Luk,
Marc Ericksen
client
**The Glad Products
Company**

creative firm
Cassata & Associates
Schaumburg, (Illinois) USA
creatives
James Wolfe
client
Wm Wrigley Jr. Co.

creative firm
Libby Perszyk Kathman
Cincinnati, (Ohio) USA
creatives
Liz Grubow
client
Procter & Gamble

creative firm
**McElveney & Palozzi
Design Group**
Rochester, (New York) USA
creatives
Steve Palozzi,
Lisa Gates,
Mike Johnson
client
Wagner Vineyards

creative firm
Deutsch Design Works
San Francisco, (California) USA
creatives
Barry Deutsch, Jess Giambroni,
Lori Wynn, Mike Kunisaki
client
Infinite Spirits

creative firm
Portfolio Center
Atlanta, (Georgia) USA
creatives
Curtis Jenkins

186

creative firm
Flowdesign, Inc.
Northville, (Michigan) USA
creatives
Dan Matauch
client
Philipsburg Liquor Store

creative firm
Deutsch Design Works
San Francisco, (California) USA
creatives
Barry Deutsch, John Marota,
Mike Kunisaki, Eric Pino
client
**Anheuser Busch
Image Development**

creative firm
**Hornall Anderson
Design Works**
*Seattle, (Washington)
USA*
creatives
Jack Anderson,
Larry Anderson,
Bruce Stigler,
Jay Hilburn,
Elmer dela Cruz,
Bruce Branson-Meyer
client
Widmer Brothers Brewery

creative firm
Wallace Church, Inc.
New York, (New York) USA
creatives
Stan Church, Camilla Kristiansen
client
Icon Brands

creative firm
**Turner Duckworth
London & San Francisco**
London, England
creatives
David Turner, Bruce Duckworth,
Sam Lachlan
client
Heavenly Wine

187

creative firm
**McElveney & Palozzi
Design Group**
Rochester, (New York) USA
creatives
Steve Palozzi,
Mike Johnson
client
Warm Lake Estate

creative firm
Spring Design Partners
New York, (New York) USA
creatives
Ron Wong,
Katarina Sjoholm,
Frank Castaldi
client
Bacardi

creative firm
Scott Vision Communication Co., Ltd
Taipei, Taiwan
creatives
Scott Lee, Phoenix
client
7-Eleven

creative firm
Tom Fowler, Inc.
Norwalk, (Connecticut) USA
creatives
Mary Ellen Butkus, Lael Porcelli,
Jeff Fowler
client
Honeywell Consumer Products

creative firm
Lipson Alport Glass & Assoc.
Northbrook, (Illinois) USA
creatives
Veronica Jung
client
Well's Dairy

188

creative firm
MackeySzar
Plymouth, (Minnesota) USA
client
Land O' Lakes Purina Feed LLC

creative firm
Semmer Group
Minneapolis, (Minnesota) USA
creatives
Emily Oberg, Heidi Miller
client
Target

creative firm
Flowdesign, Inc.
Northville, (Michigan) USA
creatives
Dan Matauch, Dennis Nalezyty
client
Honest Tea

creative firm
Deutsch Design Works
San Francisco, (California) USA
creatives
Barry Deutsch, Marion Schneider,
Sherry Voytek, Jacques Rossouw
client
Pepsi-Cola Design Group

creative firm
Axion Design Inc.
San Anselmo, (California) USA
client
Bewley's Tea/Java City

creative firm
Cornerstone
New York, (New York) USA
creatives
Keith Steimel
client
Coca-Cola Co.

creative firm
Lewis Moberly
London, England
creatives
Mary Lewis, Zoe Green,
Ann Marshall
client
Waitrose Ltd

creative firm
Libby Perszyk Kathman
Cincinnati, (Ohio) USA
creatives
Gina Tesnar
client
Procter & Gamble

creative firm
Lipson Alport Glass & Assoc.
Northbrook, (Illinois) USA
creatives
Tim Binzer,
Scott Smith
client
Sara Lee Corporation

creative firm
Spring Design Partners
New York, (New York) USA
creatives
Ron Wong,
Pete Novello
client
Nabisco

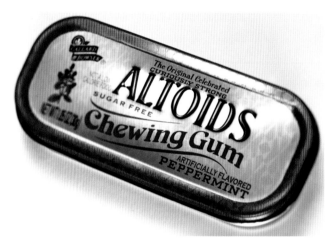

190

creative firm
Turner Duckworth
London & San Francisco
London, England
creatives
David Turner, Bruce Duckworth,
Sam Lachlan, Christian Eager,
Andy Grimshaw, Peter Ruane
client
Superdrug Stores PLC

creative firm
Scott Vision Communication Co., Ltd
Taipei, Taiwan
creatives
Scott Lee, Phoenix
client
7-Eleven

creative firm
Design Resource Center
Naperville, (Illinois) USA
creatives
John Norman, Melanie Gibb
client
Senario, LLC

creative firm
Wallace Church, Inc.
New York, (New York) USA
creatives
Stan Church, Lawrence Haggerty,
Clare Reece, Ray Bould
client
American Italian Pasta Co.

191

creative firm
Launch Creative Marketing
Chicago, (Illinois) USA
creatives
Alvin Wilcox
client
EAS

creative firm
Sagon-Phior
*Los Angeles,
(California) USA*
creatives
Sagon-Phior
client
**McCormick
Distilling Co.**

creative firm
Zunda Design Group
South Norwalk, (Connecticut) USA
creatives
Charles Zunda, Todd Nickel,
Danisha Devor-Mackesy,
Seymour Schachter
client
Unilever Bestfoods North America

creative firm
Clorox Creative Services
Oakland, (California) USA
creatives
Chris Twilling,
Tim Ferdun
client
The Clorox Company

creative firm
Octavo Designs
Frederick, (Maryland) USA
creatives
Sue Hough,
Mark Burrier
client
**National Association
of School Psychologists**

192

creative firm
Deutsch Design Works
San Francisco, (California) USA
creatives
Barry Deutsch, John Marota,
Mike Kunisaki, Erika Schoenhoff
client
**Anheuser-Busch
Image Development**

creative firm
Di Donato Associates
Chicago, (Illinois) USA
creatives
Peter Di Donato,
Amy Wybo
client
Season's Enterprises, Ltd.

creative firm
Qualcomm
*San Diego,
(California) USA*
creatives
Christopher Lee,
Allison Bridges
client
**Bastille Day,
Southern Care**

creative firm
Heye&Partner GmbH
Unterhaching, (Bavaria) Germany
creatives
Florian Drahorad,
Dominik Neubauer
client
Winery Kornell

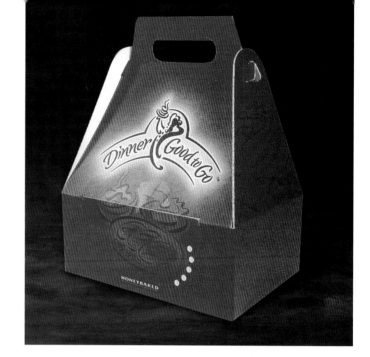

creative firm
Lipson Alport Glass & Assoc.
Northbrook, (Illinois) USA
creatives
Anna Shteerman, Mark Krukanis
client
The Honey Baked Ham Company

193

creative firm
Faine-Oller Productions, Inc.
Seattle, (Washington) USA
creatives
Catherine Oller,
Bruce Hale,
Ron Bomba
client
Neiman Marcus
Essential Baking Company

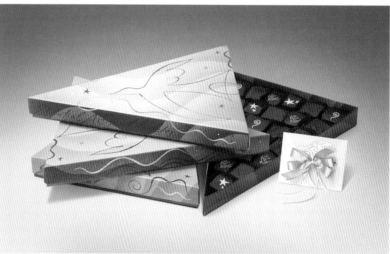

creative firm
North American Packaging
New York, (New York) USA
creatives
Vanessa Noel, John De Stefano,
Warren Beishir
client
Vanessa Noel

creative firm
Lewis Moberly
London, England
creatives
Mary Lewis,
Lucilla Lavender
client
Waitrose Ltd

creative firm
Zunda Design Group
South Norwalk, (Connecticut) USA
creatives
Charles Zunda,
Chris Seremetis
client
Dunkin' Brands, Inc.

creative firm
Lipson Alport Glass & Assoc.
Northbrook, (Illinois) USA
creatives
Marco Escalante, Rob Swan,
Luca Torregiain, Heather Allen
client
Schieffelin

creative firm
Brand Engine
Sausalito, (California) USA
creatives
Eric Read, Yusuke Asaka
Coralie Russo, Tyvan
client
Mighty Leaf Tea Company

194

creative firm
Launch Creative Marketing
Chicago, (Illinois) USA
creatives
Bruce Butcher
client
World's Finest

creative firm
Turner Duckworth
London & San Francisco
London, England
creatives
David Turner, Bruce Duckworth,
Mike Harris, Steve Baxter,
Matt Kay, Carol Kemp
client
Manor Bakeries

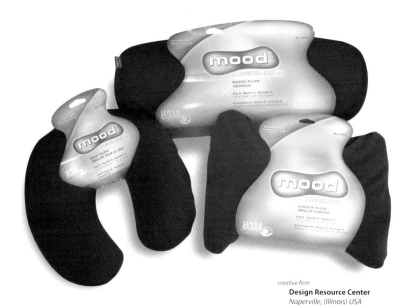

creative firm
Design Resource Center
Naperville, (Illinois) USA
creatives
John Norman, Melanie Gibb
client
L.C. Industries, LLC

creative firm
Mark Oliver, Inc.
Solvang, (California) USA
creatives
Mark Oliver, Patty Driskel,
Burke/Triolo Photography
client
Ocean Beauty Seafoods

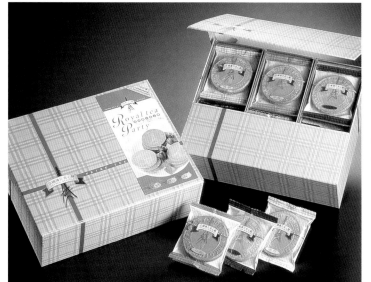

creative firm
Scott Vision Communication Co., Ltd
Taipei, Taiwan
creatives
Scott Lee, Phoenix
client
7-Eleven

195

creative firm
Launch Creative Marketing
Chicago, (Illinois) USA
creatives
Don Dzielinski
client
EAS

creative firm
Axion Design Inc.
San Anselmo, (California) USA
client
Mazola/ACH Foods

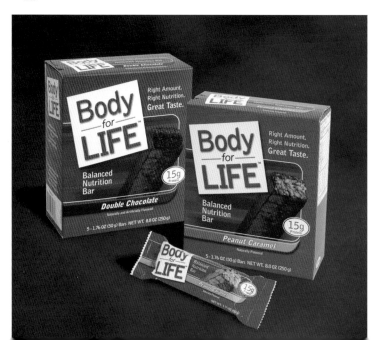

creative firm
Creative Link
San Antonio, (Texas) USA
creatives
Mark Broderick, Jason Little,
Jordan Merson
client
HEB Cooking Connection

creative firm
Eight in One Design Group
Hauppauge, (New York) USA
creatives
Nina Lombardo,
Jennifer Giannotti-Genes/JAG,
Russel Helfman
client
Target

196

creative firm
Tom Fowler, Inc.
Norwalk, (Connecticut) USA
creatives
Mary Ellen Butkus,
Lael Porcelli, Jeff Fowler
client
**Honeywell Consumer
Products**

creative firm
Subplot Design Inc.
Vancouver, (British Columbia)
Canada
creatives
Roy White,
Matthew Clark
client
Caffé Artigiano

creative firm
Jack Nadel, Inc.
Los Angeles, (California) USA
creatives
Scott Brown
client
KMB Foods, Inc.

creative firm
Optima Group
Highland Park, (Illinois) USA
creatives
Sara Belskis
client
National Beverage Co.

creative firm
Spring Design Partners
New York, (New York) USA
creatives
Ron Wong, Katarina Sjoholm
client
Bacardi

197

creative firm
Deutsch Design Works
San Francisco, (California) USA
creatives
Barry Deutsch,
Phillip Ting
client
Robert Mondavi Winery

creative firm
Cornerstone
New York, (New York) USA
creatives
Keith Steimel
client
Coca-Cola Co.

creative firm
Clorox Creative Services
Oakland, (California) USA
creatives
Chris Twilling, Tim Ferdun,
Kean Hiroshima
client
The Armor All/STP Products Company

creative firm
Pure Design Co. LLC
Leverett, (Massachusetts) USA
creatives
Dan Mishkind,
Graeme Ritchie
client
New Silk Road Marketing LLC

198

creative firm
Colemanbrandworx
New York, (New York) USA
creatives
Allison Koller
client
**Johnson & Johnson Consumer
Products Company**

creative firm
Mark Oliver, Inc.
Solvang, (California) USA
creatives
Mark Oliver, Patty Driskel,
Harry Bates
client
Ocean Beauty Seafoods

creative firm
S2 Design Group
New York, (New York) USA
creatives
Eileen Strauss, Lauretta Worm
client
Hasbro Inc.

creative firm
Libby Perszyk Kathman
Cincinnati, (Ohio) USA
creatives
Beth Malone, Jennifer Rippe,
Dave Umbenhour
client
Procter & Gamble

creative firm
Launch Creative Marketing
Chicago, (Illinois) USA
creatives
Don Dzielinski
client
Chef Solutions

APPLE SAUCE   MINT JELLY   SEAFOOD SAUCE

creative firm
Whitney Edwards Design
Easton, (Maryland) USA
creatives
Charlene Whitney Edwards,
Barbara J. Christopher
client
Maryland Plastics Inc.

creative firm
Lewis Moberly
London, England
creatives
Mary Lewis,
Fiona Verdon-Smith
client
Waitrose Ltd

creative firm
Lipson Alport Glass & Assoc.
Northbrook, (Illinois) USA
creatives
Christie McMearty
client
CIBA Vision

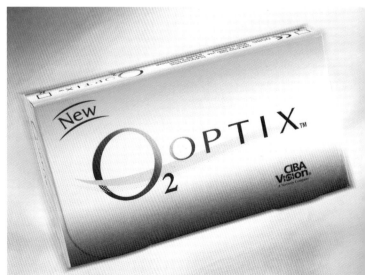

creative firm
JGA
Southfield, (Michigan) USA
creatives
Ken Nisch
client
Metropark USA

creative firm
Lipson Alport Glass & Assoc.
Northbrook, (Illinois) USA
creatives
Jamey Wagner,
Steve Ledar
client
Tractor Supply Company

creative firm
Turner Duckworth
London & San Francisco
London, England
creatives
David Turner, Bruce Duckworth,
Christian Eager, Steve Baxter,
Peter Ruane
client
Waitrose Stores PLC

200

creative firm
McGaughy Design
Centreville, (Virginia) USA
creatives
Malcolm McGaughy
client
Sappony

creative firm
Sterling Group
New York, (New York) USA
creatives
Marcus Hewitt,
Simon Lince,
James Grant
client
Island Nuts

creative firm
karacters design group
Vancouver, (British Columbia) Canada
creatives
Maria Kennedy, Lisa Nakamura
client
Shoppers Drug Mart

creative firm
Moby Dick Warszawa
Warsaw, Poland
creatives
Anna Bal,
Marcin Kosiorowski
client
Felix Polska

creative firm
Maddocks
Los Angeles, (California) USA
creatives
Jen Caughey, Ann Marie Siciliano
client
Herbalife

creative firm
Scott Vision Communication Co., Ltd
Taipei, Taiwan
creatives
Scott Lee, Phoenix
client
Weichaun Foods Corporation

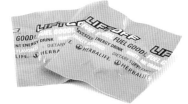

creative firm
Turner Duckworth
London & San Francisco
London, England
creatives
David Turner, Bruce Duckworth,
Matt Kay
client
Waitrose Stores PLC

creative firm
Marinelli Communications
New York, (New York) USA
creatives
Louis Manzone
client
NHS

creative firm
Deutsch Design Works
San Francisco, (California) USA
creatives
Barry Deutsch,
Mike Kunisaki,
Steffan Bergemann
client
Bronco Winery

creative firm
Snap Creative
St. Charles, (Missouri) USA
creatives
Snap Creative,
Stephanie Carter
client
O'Fallon Brewery

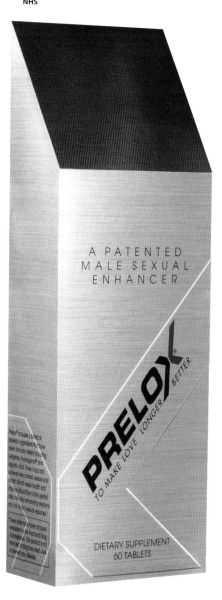

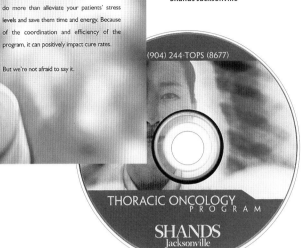

THE LATEST IN
THORACIC ONCOLOGY
T R E A T M E N T

CURE

Not an easy word to say.

The multidisciplinary approach of the Thoracic Oncology Program at Shands Jacksonville can do more than alleviate your patients' stress levels and save them time and energy. Because of the coordination and efficiency of the program, it can positively impact cure rates.

But we're not afraid to say it.

(904) 244-TOPS (8677)

THORACIC ONCOLOGY
P R O G R A M

SHANDS
Jacksonville

203

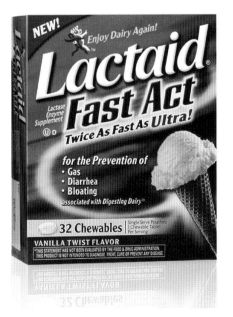

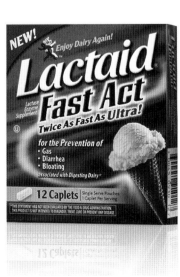

creative firm
Clorox Creative Services
Oakland, (California) USA
creatives
Chris Twilling, Anthony Luk,
Kevin Ng
client
The Clorox Company

creative firm
Spring Design Partners
New York, (New York) USA
creatives
Ron Wong, Tet Marti,
Ben Glotzer
client
**Coca-Cola
(Frederic Kahn)**

creative firm
**Hornall Anderson
Design Works**
Seattle, (Washington) USA
creatives
Jack Anderson, Bruce Stigler,
Elmer dela Cruz, Larry Anderson,
Bruce Branson-Meyer,
Jay Hilburn, Beckon Wyld
client
Redhook Brewery

204

creative firm
Scott Vision Communication Co., Ltd
Taipei, Taiwan
creatives
Scott Lee, Phoenix
client
Kinmen

creative firm
Lipson Alport Glass & Assoc.
Northbrook, (Illinois) USA
creatives
Don Childs, John Foley,
Kevin Wimmer
client
Proctor & Gamble

creative firm
Design Resource Center
Naperville, (Illinois) USA
creatives
John Norman, Melanie Gibb
client
Aquarium Products

creative firm
Spring Design Partners
New York, (New York) USA
creatives
Ron Wong, Frank Castaldi,
Katarina Sjoholm
client
Bacardi

creative firm
Hornall Anderson Design Works
Seattle, (Washington) USA
creatives
Lisa Cerveny, James Tee,
Mark Popich, Tiffany Place,
Jana Nishi, Leo Raymundo,
Yuri Shvets, Belinda Bowling,
Elmer dela Cruz
client
Tahitian Noni

creative firm
Pearlfisher
London, England
creatives
Shawn Bowen,
Mark Christon,
Kerry Bolt
client
Waitrose

creative firm
Clorox Creative Services
Oakland, (California) USA
creatives
Chris Twilling, Tim Ferdun,
Anthony Luk
client
**The Armor All
STP Products Company**

creative firm
Libby Perszyk Kathman
Cincinnati, (Ohio) USA
creatives
Libby Perszyk Kathman,
Geoff Reichel, Jason Phillips
client
Procter & Gamble

206

creative firm
Pearlfisher
London, England
creatives
Shawn Bowen, Kate Marlow,
Henry Leeson, Kerry Bolt,
Vicky Tate
client
Waitrose

creative firm
Addax Design
*Richmond Hill, (Ontario)
Canada*
creatives
Elena Kraynov
client
**Upper Canada Soap
& Candle Makers**

creative firm
Turner Duckworth
London & San Francisco
London, England
creatives
David Turner, Bruce Duckworth,
Sam Lachlan, Nathan Jurevicius
client
Superdrug Stores PLC

creative firm
Lipson Alport Glass & Assoc.
Northbrook, (Illinois) USA
creatives
Scott Smith, Jen Vorhees,
Doug Bennett
client
Williamson-Dickie Mfg Co.

creative firm
Portfolio Center
Atlanta, (Georgia) USA
creatives
Hart Armstrong
client
Philips

207

creative firm
Pearlfisher
London, England
creatives
Shaun Bowen, Natalie Chung,
Kerry Bolt
client
Waitrose

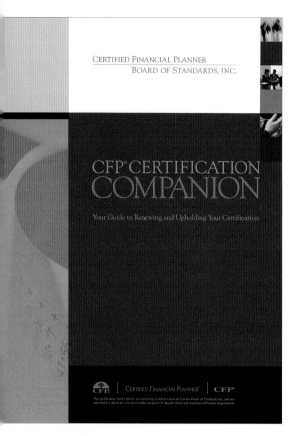

creative firm
Arcanna, Inc.
Peekskill, (New York) USA
creatives
Robert Frissora, Sondra Greenspan,
Lori Anzalone
client
American Quality Beverages

creative firm
Empire Communications Group
Jacksonville, (Florida) USA
creatives
Chris Alcantara, Susan Kleinan-Lewis
client
Mello Trading

creative firm
Rassman Design
Denver, (Colorado) USA
creatives
Lyn D'Amato
client
**Certified Financial Planner
Board of Standards**

208

creative firm
Clorox Creative Services
Oakland, (California) USA
creatives
Chris Twilling, Fabienne David,
Robert Evans
client
The Clorox Company

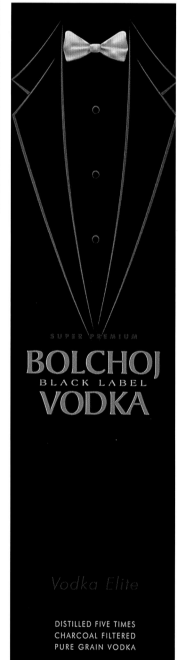

creative firm
Deutsch Design Works
San Francisco, (California) USA
creatives
Barry Deutsch, John Marota,
Mike Kunisaki, Eric Pino
client
Anheuser-Busch Image Development

creative firm
Zunda Design Group
*South Norwalk,
(Connecticut) USA*
creatives
Charles Zunda,
Todd Nickel,
Chris Seremetis
client
Dunkin' Brands, Inc.

creative firm
Optima Group
Highland Park, (Illinois) USA
creatives
Adam Ferguson
client
National Beverage Co.

209

creative firm
Brand Engine
Sausalito, (California) USA
creatives
Will Burke, Eric Read,
Coralie Russo, Tyvan
client
Mighty Leaf Tea Company

creative firm
Spring Design Partners
New York, (New York) USA
creatives
Ron Wong, Pete Novello,
May Wong
client
**Coca-Cola
(Frederic Kahn)**

creative firm
Emerson, Wajdowicz, Studios
New York, (New York) USA
creatives
Jurek Wajdowicz, Lisa LaRochelle,
Yoko Yoshida, Magnum Photos
client
Smart Papers

creative firm
Coates and Coates
Naperville, (Illinois) USA
creatives
Carolin Coates
client
HSBC-North America

creative firm
1 stop design shop
Woburn, (Massachusetts) USA
creatives
Christine Hennigan, Chris O'brien,
Julie Quinn, Rebecca Leonard,
Donna Blais
client
1 stop design shop

creative firm
Studio Universal
Rome, Italy
creatives
Luca Marcucci
client
**Universal Studios
Networks Italy**

creative firm
All Media Projects Ltd. (AMPLE)
Port of Spain, (Trinidad) West Indies
creatives
Cathleen Jones, Patti-Anne Ali,
Boscoe Holder, Images Studio,
Deborah Garraway; CPPPL
client
Clico (Trinidad) Limited

creative firm
House Of Design
Graz, Austria
creatives
André Stangc, Mischa Stangc
client
Fire Girls

211

creative firm
Maddocks
Los Angeles, (California) USA
creatives
Jen Caughey, Jonah Levine,
Dave Lauridsen, B&G Printing
client
Maddocks

creative firm
**Nickelodeon
Creative Resources**
New York, (New York) USA
creatives
Tim Blankley,
Rob LaQuinta,
Sandra Pieloch,
Jenn Simonds,
Annie Tao,
Piero Piluso,
Erin Hicks
client
**Nickelodeon/
Viacom Consumer Products**

sunday	monday	tuesday	wednesday	thursday	friday	saturday
1	2	3	4	5	6	7
8	9	10	11	12	13	14
15	16	17	18	19	20	21
22	23	24	25	26	27	28
29	30	31				

26 corpus christi
30 indian arrival day

may 2005

This shady retreat bridges river and
ocean at Manzanilla

bp
Trinidad and Tobago

...investing beyond petroleum

creative firm
Julia Tam Design
*Palos Verdes Estates,
(California) USA*
creatives
Julia Tam
client
Driven, Inc.

creative firm
All Media Projects Ltd. (AMPLE)
Port of Spain, (Trinidad) West Indies
creatives
Cathleen Jones, Glenn Forte,
Astra Da Costa, Josiane Khan,
Abigail Hadeed, Digital Photo Center,
Fazad Mohammed, Scrip-J Printers
client
BP Trinidad and Tobago (bptt)

212

THE MIRACLE WORKER

LA TRAGÉDIE DE CARMEN

Livskraft i 100 år

HYDRO

Jubileumskalender

2005

creative firm
Martin-Schaffer, Inc.
Bethesda, (Maryland) USA
creatives
Tina Martin, Steve Cohn,
Karen Falk
client
Olney Theatre Center

creative firm
KARAKTER Ltd
London, England
creatives
Clive Rohald, Kam Devsi,
Mei Wing Chan, Martin Watkins
client
Norsk Hydro

creative firm
Redpoint design
Midland, (Michigan) USA
creatives
Clark Most, Ty Smith
client
Central Michigan University

CALENDA

213

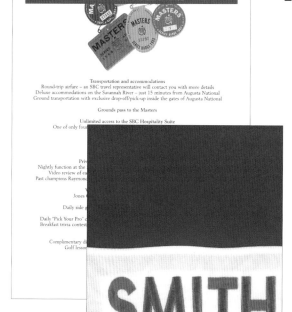

It's time to **Believe**
in magic again.

It's time to
Come Home.

again and again for a full year of magic you'll never forget!

Disneyland Annual Passport

NEXT SPRING, PLAYERS FROM EVERYWHERE WILL
CONVERGE ON AUGUSTA.

WE HOPE YOU'RE ONE OF THEM.

creative firm
KPR
New York, (New York) USA
creatives
Bernard Steinman, Scott Frank,
Sal Diana, Regina Regan,
Catherine Kanner, Austin Wei
client
Janssen Pharmaceutica

creative firm
Rodgers Townsend
St. Louis, (Missouri) USA
creatives
Tom Hudder, Kris Wright,
Tom Townsend, Evan Willnow
client
St. Louis Black Repertory Co.

214

creative firm
E-lift Media
Millicent, Australia
creatives
Simone Burdon
client
Tan in 10

creative firm
Alcone Marketing Group
Irvine, (California) USA
creatives
Luis Camano, Catherine Lorenzo,
Shivonne Miller
client
California Housing Finance Agency

creative firm
GSW Worldwide
New York, (New York) USA
creatives
Ron Ballister,
Suzanne Goss
client
Y Brand

creative firm
**Perkins + Will | EvaMaddox
Branded Environments**
Chicago, (Illinois) USA
creatives
Eileen Jones,
Malgorzata Zawislak,
Emily Neville,
Anna Kania
client
Antron

creative firm
Aquea Design
Las Vegas, (Nevada) USA
creatives
Raymond Perez
client
Esprit Travel

215

creative firm
Studio Universal
Rome, Italy
creatives
Luca Marcucci
client
Universal Studios Networks Italia

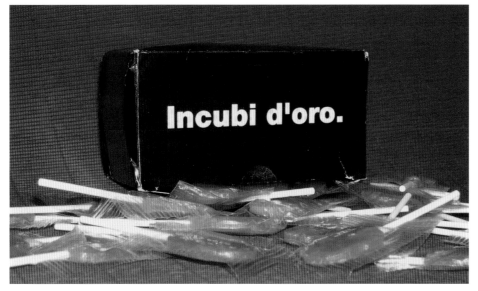

creative firm
**Ohio University
Communications & Marketing**
Athens, (Ohio) USA
creatives
Stacey Riley Stewart, Jennifer Bowie,
Mary Dillon
client
Dean of Students

creative firm
The McGraw-Hill Companies
Corporate Creative
Services Department
New York, (New York) USA
creatives
Marianne Johnston,
Paul Biedermann
client
Architectural Record

McGraw_Hill CONSTRUCTION Architectural Record

Look

August Issue
Closes July 9

Photo: © Collage Studio/CR&S B&B Italia

Feel

216

ViEW book
ohio university

2004-2006

creative firm
Ohio University
Communications & Marketing
Athens, (Ohio) USA
creatives
Mark Krumel, Mary Dillon,
Rick Fatica
client
Office of Undergraduate
Admissions

creative firm
Chris Collins Studio
New York, (New York) USA
creatives
Chris Collins,
Daniel Smith
client
Chris Collins Studio

creative firm
Bohan Advertising/Marketing
Nashville, (Tennessee) USA
creatives
Kerry Oliver, Gregg Boling
client
Northstar Destinations

Don't
Think of
it as

His Classroom

Think of it as **ID Pad Launching**

creative firm
William Berry Campaigns
*Sacramento, (California)
USA*
creatives
William Berry, Trevor Hunt
client
**Committee to Elect
Michael Merrifield**

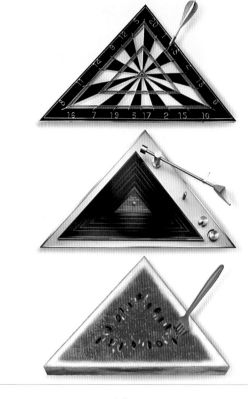

creative firm
Studio Universal
Rome, Italy
creatives
Luca Marcucci
client
**Universal Studios
Network Italy**

creative firm
Marquardht & Roche Partners
New York, (New York) USA
creatives
Gerry O'Hara, Chris Collins,
Daniel Smith
client
Fujifilm Medical Systems

217

WOMEN.
YOU WILL NEVER QUIT WATCHING THEM.

Studio
UNIVERSAL
LA TV DEL CINEMA
DA CHI FA CINEMA

creative firm
Rodgers Townsend
St. Louis, (Missouri) USA
creatives
Erik Mathre, Dawn Sorgea,
Ryan McMichael
client
SBC Communications, Inc.

creative firm
Tieken:Moret Design and Marketing
Phoenix, (Arizona) USA
creatives
Toni Cress
client
Tieken:Moret Design and Marketing

marketing strategies

Consider the dots connected.

creative firm
Ruder Finn Design
New York, (New York) USA
creatives
Lisa Gabbay, Sal Catania, Aaron Wilson
client
New York Theatre Workshop

creative firm
Walt Denson
Sausalito, (California) USA
creatives
Walt Denson
client
Walt Denson

creative firm
Empire Communications Group
Jacksonville, (Florida) USA
creatives
Chris Alcantara,
Susan Kiernan-Lewis,
Pete Helow
client
SRI/Surgical Express

A gown that talks.

218

creative firm
Design Club
Tokyo, Japan
creatives
Akihiko Tsukamoto, Masayuki Minoda,
Frank Viva, Harumi Kimura,
Kumiko Yamaguchi, Tetsuro Minorikawa,
Radical Suzuki
client
ArjoWiggins Fine Papers

creative firm
Olson/Kotowski, Inc.
Redondo Beach, (California) USA
creatives
Thad Wawro, Moira Dyer,
Paul Archer, Tony Washington,
Kevin Kotowski, Janice Olson
client
Epson America, Inc.

EPSON

EPSON
PROFESSIONAL
PRINTERS

A slightly more fleXible solution for prepress proofing

...proofers

Slips...
your...

...more fleXible,
...re cost-effective
...oofing solution

Fast, affordable ink jet proofing.

creative firm
Publicis Dialog
San Francisco, (California) USA
creatives
Lyle Lim, Alex Grossman,
Leanne Milway, Cathy Kuzia
client
HP

creative firm
Strategy One
Glen Ellyn, (Illinois) USA
creatives
Jason Thompson,
Brian Danaher,
Charles Kouri
client
**National Council of
State Boards of Nursing**

219

creative firm
Rienzi & Rienzi Communications
Montville, (New Jersey) USA
creatives
Mary Gayle Scheper, Carrie Ralston,
Kim Langley, Frank Aiello
client
Mylan Bertek Pharmaceuticals Inc.

creative firm
Fixation Marketing
Washington, (D.C.) USA
creatives
Bruce E. Morgan, Kathryn Tidyman
client
**International Association of
Amusement Parks and Attractions**

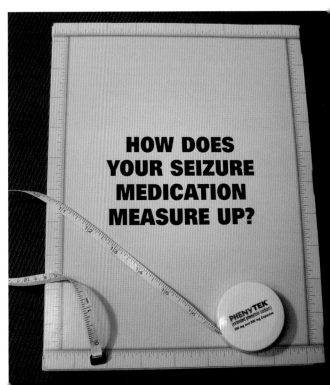

collaboration

inspiration

expression

Calling it the "finished product" wouldn't do it justice. "Ultimate detail" is much more appropriate. What began with a flash of inspiration is now a vital element of your newest project. Your vision is fulfilled. Your design is complete. And your client stands apart, with exclusive bathroom fittings that can't be found anywhere else in the world.

Whatever idea you want to express, Signature Design Studio is the one resource that can help you bring it to life — whether you have the freedom to conceive an entirely new, all-original fitting, or enough latitude to create a customized design inspired by our extensive portfolio of modifiable components.

In addition to appreciating the finer sensibilities of the design process, we also have a solid understanding of the budget and deadline realities of any project. That's because we're a division of Symmons Industries, a leader in plumbing fixtures for more than 60 years. We're recognized and respected by uncompromising designers and tough-as-nails contractors — and we're uniquely able to bring them together in peace and harmony on any project.

Learn more about how the uniquely specialized services of Signature Design Studio can help you make your next project truly your own. Contact us at 1-800-SYMMONS / (781) 848-2250, or visit www.symmons.com/signature

signature
design studio™

creative firm
Catalyst
Warwick, (Rhode Island) USA
creatives
Cindi Emery, Mike Murphy,
John Beaupre
client
Signature Design Studio

block party

Sometimes it feels like they're ganging up on you. You've got every possible creative block sitting around on your sofa with a drink, making itself at home, no sign it's going anywhere soon. Relax. Don't be afraid of creative blocks. Learn to work with them. Use them. The more you practice unblocking yourself, the easier it becomes. And by forcing you to look at things fresh, they can help you grow creatively. Remember, "no pain, no gain" applies to working your creative muscles, too.

ColorVision® Spyder2™ GEU510: $189
ColorVision Spyder2PRO™ Studio
GPU120: $299

Celebrate the best tool yet for achieving a color-managed workflow: the new ColorVision Spyder2 colorimeter and easy-to-use monitor calibration software. Enables advanced amateurs and professionals alike to create precise ICC display profiles for CRT, LCD or notebook displays.

pantone.com

Register at pantone.com for a chance to win a
ColorVision Spyder2PRO Studio.

New 2005 guides

surviving the block

PANTONE

creative firm
Pantone, Inc.
Camstadt, (New Jersey) USA
creatives
Yolanda Lamourt, Lisa Reswick
client
Pantone, Inc.

Walt DENSON photographer

creative firm
Walt Denson
Sausalito, (California) USA
creatives
Walt Denson
client
Walt Denson

220

creative firm
Ad Planet Group
Singapore
creatives
Leo Teck Chong,
Alfred Teo,
Kim Tan,
Eddie Eng,
James Tan
client
Nature Society of Singapore

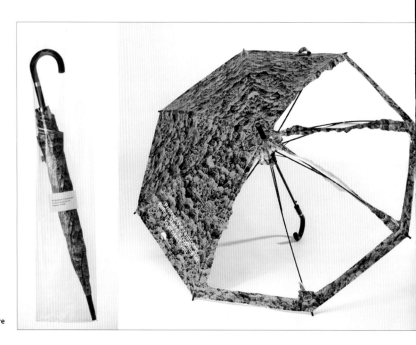

You are here

And here.

Enclosed: Your license to leave work early.

hp
invent

Inside:
Your Parent Companies
Border Crossings
Phil's Shirt Wins Again

DESTINATIONS

ISSUE 3 2004

FLIGHTS OF FA

Bahamas

Nassau International Airport (MYNN)
Governors Harbour (MYEM)

Ah, the Bahamas. Glistening pink
and white sand beaches. Emerald
green water. The serene colonial
villages. The perfect antidote to
the mid-winter blahs.

It's a refreshingly different world – a place to
bury the cell phone in the sand and relax.

But if being active is your idea of rest, there's
plenty of ways to have fun.

On Grand Bahama Island, you can take a scuba
class at the famous Underwater Explorers
Society, or swim with friendly bottlenose
dolphins at The Dolphin Experience in Lucaya.

In Nassau, you can visit the dungeon under-
neath a fort built in 1787, practice talking like
a buccaneer at the Pirate Museum or see
exotic wildlife at the Ardastra Gardens and Zoo.

You can see one of the last man-operated
lighthouses, a peppermint-striped beauty on
the beach on Great Abaco Island, or go to Bimini
to investigate the odd natural rock formations
that continue to puzzle geologists.

Speedboat tours, snorkeling among colorful s
life, casting salt flies for bonefish and drink s
with little umbrellas in them. What's not to lo
about the Bahamas?

Obsessed with cable solutions.

C&M

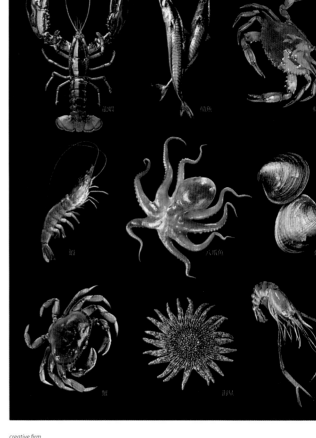

creative firm
Catalyst
Warwick, (Rhode Island) USA
creatives
Cindi Emery, John Beaupre
client
C&M Corporation

creative firm
Grafik
Alexandria, (Virginia) USA
creatives
John Vitorovich, Hal Swetnam
client
Fairmont Hotel, Washington, D.C.

creative firm
Chris Collins Studio
New York, (New York) USA
creatives
Chris Collins, Daniel Smith
client
Chris Collins Studio

222

WE'VE CREATED A HIDEAWAY
exclusively for VIPs

FAIRMONT
Gold

creative firm
Nassar Design
Brookline, (Massachusetts) USA
creatives
Nelida Nassar
client
Nassar Design

EVERY ACT OF GENEROSITY CIRCLES THE WORLD.
NASSAR DESIGN IS A REGULAR CONTRIBUTOR TO UNESCO'S LITERACY FUND.
YOUR VALUED BUSINESS HELPS SUPPORT CHILDREN IN NEED.

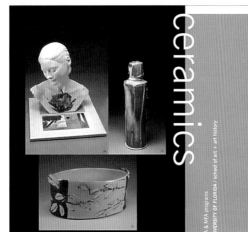

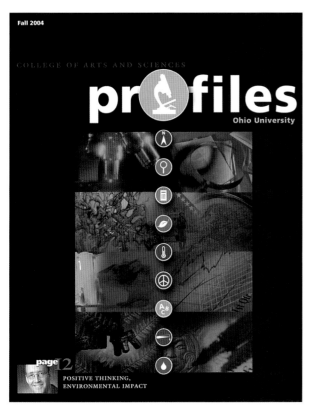

creative firm
DeBolt Photography
Chicago, Illinois

creative firm
Martin-Schaffer, Inc.
Bethesda, (Maryland) USA
creatives
Tina Martin, Steve Cohn,
Karen Falk
client
Olney Theatre Center

creative firm
BBDO Detroit
Troy, (Michigan) USA
creatives
Ryan Wald, Bill DeMink,
Susan Everhart, Fred Beal,
Oliver Hoffmann
client
Daimler Chrysler-Jeep Brand

Wonderful Then.

In the 1930s, the typewriter simplified business communication.

Free sample offer enclosed

Wonderful Now.

Today, computers help us communicate in ways we never could have imagined!

Onederfully Convenient.™

PHENYTEK, introduced in 2001, offers the benefits
of phenytoin with fewer capsules a day . . . every day*

• PHENYTEK brand extended phenytoin sodium is proven
  bioequivalent to Dilantin® Kapseals®
• The first once-daily* extended phenytoin sodium 300 mg capsule
• Provides the time-tested benefits of extended phenytoin sodium

ONCE—DAILY
PHENYTEK
(extended phenytoin sodium)
300 MG CAPSULES
Also available in 200 mg capsules

• PHENYTEK is also available as a 200 mg capsule for dosing flexibility
• There is no generic substitution for either PHENYTEK 200 mg or
  300 mg capsules

For more information or samples, please complete the attached reply card or
visit our website at www.phenytek.com

BUSINESS REPLY MAIL

MYLAN BERTEK
PHARMACEUTICALS INC
150 River Road – Bldg M
Montville NJ 07045-9803

225

Television · Silver

Television · Bronze

AT THE
MASONIC TEMPLE
SCOTTISH RITE CATHEDRAL
500 TEMPLE AVENUE, DETROIT
NOVEMBER 12
START TIME: 7:30 P.M. PROMPT

**CADDY
AWARDS**

A LUGLIO, SESSO SICURO SU STUDIO UNIVERSAL.

OGNI SERA PER TUTTO IL MESE DI LUGLIO IL MEGLIO
DELL'EROS D'AUTORE PRESENTATO DA EVA HENGER

Stand Out
It's within you

On the weekends,
I'm a rhinestone cowboy.
Peoples Jewellers

DUFFERIN MALL
SOUTH OF BLOOR ON DUFFERIN

Stand Out
It's within you

Some days I feel
like running
off to join
the circus!
Toys R Us

DUFFERIN MALL
SOUTH OF BLOOR ON DUFFERIN

creative firm
True North
Mississauga, (Ontario) Canada
creatives
Sal Iantorno, Kyle McKenna,
Tom Bargold
client
Dufferin Mall

226

creative firm
Nolin Branding & Design
Montreal, (Quebec) Canada
creatives
Louise Filion,
Caroline Blanchette,
Caroline Reumont
client
Domtar Inc.

creative firm
Campbell-Ewald
Warren, (Michigan) USA
creatives
Bill Ludwig, Joe Pas, Anne Moore,
Susan Berry, Jennifer Beaudoin,
Jim Vonseggern, Chris Scalise,
Kathy Monear, Kim Harris,
Kristen Shuart, Wescott Displays,
The EGT Group, Inc.
client
National City Corporation

227

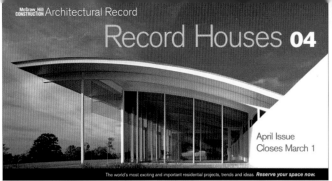

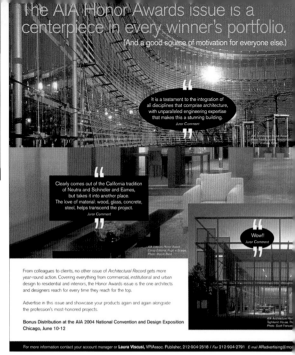

creative firm
The McGraw-Hill Companies
Corporate Creative
Services Department
New York, (New York) USA
creatives
Marianne Johnston,
Paul Biedermann
client
Architectural Record

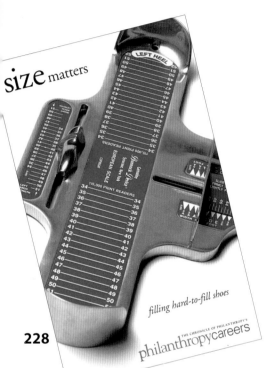

size matters

filling hard-to-fill shoes

228

THE CHRONICLE OF PHILANTHROPY'S
philanthropycareers

why settle for beans...

when you can have the whole enchilada!

creative firm
Parsons Brinckerhoff
New York, (New York) USA
creatives
Ana Tiburcio-Rivera
client
Parsons Brinckerhoff

PB PlaceMaking

add
bite to your
RECRUITING BUDGET

25% discount

THE CHRONICLE OF PHILANTHROPY
philanthropycareers
filling hard-to-fill shoes

creative firm
Greenfield/Belser Ltd.
Washington, (D.C.) USA
creatives
Burkey Belser,
Carolyn Sewell,
Alan Sciulli,
Leah Appel
client
The Chronicle
of Philanthropy

creative firm
Randi Wolf Design
Glassboro, (New Jersey) USA
creatives
Randi Wolf,
Dennis Dougherty
client
Rowan University College of
Fine & Performing Arts

creative firm
Torre Lazur McCann
Parsippany, (New Jersey) USA
creatives
Jaime Berliner, Mark Inaba,
Gargi Mukhorjee, Jessica Marvin
client
BMS/Sanofi

229

creative firm
Drew Gardner Photography
Broughton, (North Hamptonshire) England

creative firm
Studio Universal
Rome, Italy
creatives
Luca Marcucci
client
Universal Studios Networks Italy

creative firm
KPR
New York, (New York) USA
creatives
Bernard Steinman, Scott Frank,
Sal Diana, Regina Regan,
Catherine Kanner, Austin Wei
client
Janssen Pharmaceutica

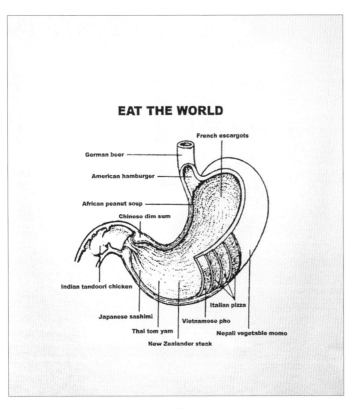

EAT THE WORLD

French escargots

German beer

American hamburger

African peanut soup

Chinese dim sum

Indian tandoori chicken

Italian pizza

Japanese sashimi

Vietnamese pho

Thai tom yam

Nepali vegetable momo

New Zealander steak

music television

stirr'n sh't up since 1981

creative firm
Move Ltd Partnership
Bangkok, Thailand
creatives
Vancelee Teng, Chatchai Boonyaprapatsara,
Subun Khow, Pornchai Sanchaichana
client
Move Ltd Partnership

creative firm
MTV Design
New York, (New York) USA
client
MTV

creative firm
Greenfield/Belser Ltd.
Washington, (D.C.) USA
creatives
Burkey Belser, Tom Cameron,
Jeff Bedrick
client
Greenfield/Belser Ltd.

creative firm
Studio Universal
Rome, Italy
creatives
Luca Marcucci
client
Universal Studios Networks Italy

GREENFIELD / BELSER / BRAND ON THE RUN

American City Busi
Greenfield/Belser and Levic

BRAND ON
TOUR D

May 29	Sea
May 30	Port
June 4	Austi
June 5	San Antonio
September 18	Charlotte
September 19	Buffalo
September 25	Washington
October 8	Sacramento
October 9	San Francisco
October 16	Atlanta
October 22	Milwaukee
October 23	Minneapolis
November 19	Kansas City
November 20	Nashville
January 15	Pittsburgh

join the unreal world
www.scifichannel.it

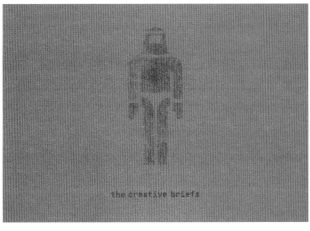

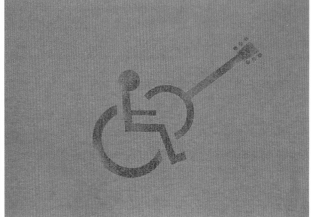

creative firm
Bohan Advertising/Marketing
Nashville, (Tennessee) USA
creatives
Kerry Oliver, Gregg Boling
client
Bohan Advertising/Marketing

creative firm
Rude Pooch
Pittsburgh, (Pennsylvania) USA
creatives
Roger Carpenter, John Carpenter,
Christina French
client
Rude Pooch

BITCHES ROCK!

creative firm
Creative Link
San Antonio, (Texas) USA
creatives
Mark Broderick
client
Ciclismo Cycling Club

231

creative firm
MTV Design
New York, (New York) USA
client
MTV

how much have you seen the world?

creative firm
Move Ltd Partnership
Bangkok, Thailand
creatives
Vancelee Teng, Chatchai Boonyaprapatsara,
Subun Khow, Pornchai Sanchaichana
client
Move Ltd Partnership

232

creative firm
Ayşe Çelem Design
Istanbul, Turkey
creatives
Ayşe Çelem, Sibel Eşen
client
Mavi Jeans

creative firm
Jack Nadel, Inc.
Los Angeles, (California) USA
creatives
Scott Brown
client
D.A.R.E. America Merchandise

creative firm
CDI Studios
Las Vegas, (Nevada) USA
creatives
Victoria Hart
client
AFAN

WANNA GET HIGH?
TAKE A
D.A.R.E.
HIKE

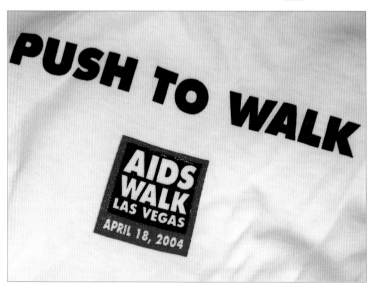

PUSH TO WALK
AIDS WALK LAS VEGAS
APRIL 18, 2004

creative firm
Dennis Y. Ichiyama
Lafayette, (Indiana) USA
creatives
Dennis Y. Ichiyama
client
Dennis Y. Ichiyama

creative firm
Jack Nadel, Inc.
Los Angeles, (California) USA
creatives
Scott Brown
client
D.A.R.E. America Merchandise

creative firm
Octavo Designs
Frederick, (Maryland) USA
creatives
Sue Hough,
Mark Burrier
client
Octavo Designs

233

creative firm
MTV Design
New York, (New York) USA
client
MTV

creative firm
Move Ltd Partnership
Bangkok, Thailand
creatives
Vancelee Teng, Chatchai Boonyaprapatsara,
Subun Khow, Pornchai Sanchaichana
client
Move Ltd Partnership

creative firm
MTV Design
New York, (New York) USA
client
MTV

creative firm
Alcone Marketing Group
Irvine, (California) USA
creatives
Luis Camano, Shivonne Miller,
Catherine Lorenzo
client
California Lottery

creative firm
Alexander Isley Inc.
Redding, (Connecticut) USA
creatives
Alexander Isley, Tara Benyei,
George Kokkinidis
client
Alexander Isley Inc.

creative firm
Portfolio Center
Atlanta, (Georgia) USA
creatives
Patricio Juarez
client
Capo Restaurant

creative firm
Catalyst
Warwick, (Rhode Island) USA
creatives
Cindi Emery, Mike Murphy,
John Beaupre
client
Signature Design Studio

creative firm
Lewis Moberly
London, England
creatives
Mary Lewis, Poppy Stedman
client
Girls Girls Girls

creative firm
Launch Creative Marketing
Chicago, (Illinois) USA
creatives
Michelle Morales
client
Sanford

236

creative firm
Greenfield/Belser Ltd.
Washington, (D.C.) USA
creatives
Burkey Belser, Carolyn Sewell
client
Greenfield/Belser Ltd.

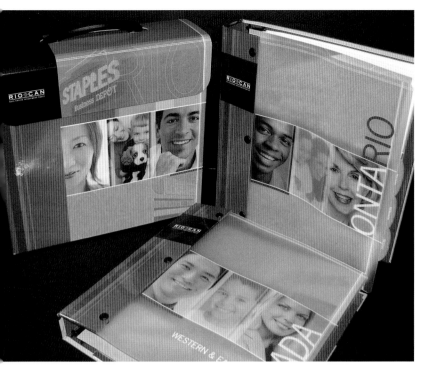

creative firm
True North
Mississauga, (Ontario) Canada
creatives
Kyle McKenna, Frank Ettore
client
Rio Can

237

creative firm
Spike TV
New York, (New York) USA
creatives
Pam Schecter, Niels Schuurmans,
Andre Razo, Milinda Zumpano, Ian Kahn
client
Spike TV

creative firm
Truefaces Creation Sdn Bhd
Subang Jaya, (Selangor Darul Ehsan) Malaysia
creatives
Truefaces Creative Team
client
Truefaces Creation

creative firm
Wallace Church, Inc.
New York, (New York) USA
creatives
Stan Church, Wendy Church,
Akira Yasuda
client
Wallace Church, Inc.

238

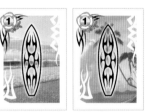

Antron®
performance fiber

creative firm
**Perkins + Will|Eva Maddox
Branded Environments**
Chicago, (Illinois) USA
creatives
Eileen Jones, Melissa Kleye,
Malgerzata Zawislak
client
Antron Performance Fiber

creative firm
Creative Link
San Antonio, (Texas) USA
creatives
Mark Broderick, Scott Iden,
Donna Santos
client
The Gambrinus Company

creative firm
**Perkins + Will|Eva Maddox
Branded Environments**
Chicago, (Illinois) USA
creatives
Eileen Jones, Brian Weatherford,
Becky Ruehl, Mary Ann Rood
client
Masland Contract

creative firm
Riordon Design
Oakville, (Ontario) Canada
creatives
Ric Riordon, Shirley Riordon
client
Riordon Design

creative firm
Tom Fowler, Inc.
Norwalk, (Connecticut) USA
creatives
Elizabeth P. Ball
client
Tom Fowler, Inc.

creative firm
Rienzi & Rienzi Communications
Montville, (New Jersey) USA
creatives
Mary Gayle Scheper, Wendy Cichy,
Mary Jo Saunders
client
Banyan School

creative firm
**Perkins + Will|Eva Maddox
Branded Environments**
Chicago, (Illinois) USA
creatives
Eileen Jones, Brian Weatherford,
Malgerzata Zawislak
client
Masland Contract

creative firm
Island Oasis
Walpole, (Massachusetts) USA
creatives
Amy Lash

240

creative firm
**Perkins + Will|Eva Maddox
Branded Environments**
Chicago, (Illinois) USA
creatives
Eva Maddox, Anna Kania,
Emily Neville
client
**The Miami Institute for Age
Management and Intervention**

creative firm
Design Nut
Kensington, (Maryland) USA
creatives
Brent M. Almond, Westland Printers,
JCG Associates
client
Nextel

creative firm
Arcanna, Inc.
Peekskill, (New York) USA
creatives
Sondra Greenspan
client
Color Tech Printers

creative firm
Ayşe Çelem Design
Istanbul, Turkey
creatives
Burcu Ayşar, Ayşe Çelem,
Arzu Şahin, Cengiz Zarlu,
Şibel Eşen
client
Ayşe Çelem Design

creative firm
Rodgers Townsend
St. Louis, (Missouri) USA
creatives
Eric Mathre,
Michelle Yesth,
Ryan McMichael,
Jim Ochu
client
SBC Communications, Inc.

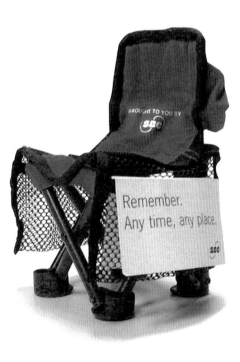

Extra care for Pleats customers comes in all forms – some you may not even think of. For starters, our reserved parking makes for a short walk. Automatic doors open as you walk in with arms full of dirty clothes. Our systems memorize your preferences so you don't have to repeat them with each visit. And our 24-hour valet service fits the hours you keep. Why not give our special care an audition today?

AUDITION CARD
TRY US. WE'LL THANK YOU WITH A $5 GIFT CARD FROM ST. LOUIS BREAD CO.

Bring in this card with your first dry cleaning order, and we'll give you a St. Louis Bread Co. gift card worth five bucks just for giving our service a try.

Offer expires 7/31/04.

IF WE CAN FOLD LIKE THIS, IMAGINE HOW WE'LL CARE FOR YOUR SHIRTS.

242

creative firm
Qualcomm
San Diego, (California) USA
creatives
Christopher Lee, Grant Kroeger
client
Qualcomm

creative firm
Rodgers Townsend
St. Louis, (Missouri) USA
creatives
Tom Hudder, Martha Koenig,
Tom Townsend, Susan Howells
client
Pleats

creative firm
Jack Nadel, Inc.
Los Angeles, (California) USA
creatives
Lauren Blaker,
Rachel Zagoren
client
Jack Nadel, Inc.

creative firm
Sayles Graphic Design
Des Moines, (Iowa) USA
creatives
John Sayles
client
Iowa State Fair

243

creative firm
Qualcomm
San Diego, (California) USA
creatives
Christopher Lee, Ken Hassen
client
Qualcomm, QLife

creative firm
Rodgers Townsend
St. Louis, (Missouri) USA
creatives
Erik Mathre,
Ron Ryan,
Susan Schultz,
Susan Session
client
SBC Communications, Inc.

creative firm
kor group
Boston, (Massachusetts) USA
creatives
James Grady,
Kjerstin Westgaard
client
**Beth Israel Deaconess
Medical Center**

244

creative firm
Lemley Design Company
Seattle, (Washington) USA
creatives
David Lemley, Bryan Pieratt,
Colleen Gray
client
Tully's Coffee

creative firm
Advantage Ltd
Hamilton, Bermuda
creatives
Sheila Semos,
Susan Tang-Petersen
client
Bermuda Festival

ANTWAAN RANDLE EL
PITTSBURGH Steelers
Steelers
DRAFTED BY UNITED WAY
United Way

creative firm
Epos, Inc.
Santa Monica, (California) USA
creatives
Gabrielle Raumberger,
Eric Martinez
client
Los Angeles Public Library

creative firm
Rottman Creative Group, LLC
La Plata, (Maryland) USA
creatives
Gary Rottman,
Robert Whetzel,
Jenna Holcombe
client
United Way/NFL

MIKE RUCKER
CAROLINA PANTHERS
NFL
United Way
UNITED WAY SPONSOR

EDWIN MULITALO
BALTIMORE
RAVENS
NFL
United Way
DRAFTED by UNITED WAY

245

creative firm
Twice Graphics
Hong Kong, China
creatives
Steve Lau
client
L'Oréal Hong Kong Ltd

creative firm
Design Guys
Minneapolis, (Minnesota) USA
creatives
Kelly Munson, Jay Theige,
Steve Sikora,
Anchalee Chambundabongse
client
Neenah Paper

246

creative firm
Gee + Chung Design
San Francisco, (California) USA
creatives
Earl Gee,
Fani Chung
client
**DCM—Doll Capital
Management**

creative firm
Ellen Bruss Design
Denver, (Colorado) USA
creatives
Jorge Lamora,
Charles Carpenter,
Ellen Bruss
client
Belmar

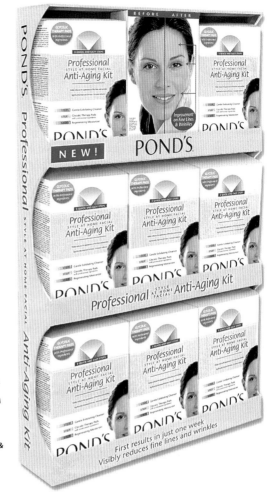

creative firm
Hornall Anderson Design Works
Seattle, (Washington) USA
creatives
Jack Anderson, Larry Anderson,
Bruce Stigler, Jay Hilburn,
Elmer dela Cruz, Bruce Branson-Meyer
client
Widmer Brothers Brewery

creative firm
Cornerstone
New York, (New York) USA
creatives
Keith Steimel
client
Swedish Match

creative firm
Tom Fowler, Inc.
*Norwalk,
(Connecticut) USA*
creatives
Elizabeth P. Ball,
Cindy Emmert
client
**Unilever Home &
Personal Care
USA**

247

creative firm
Island Oasis
Walpole, (Massachusetts) USA
creatives
Peter Buhler

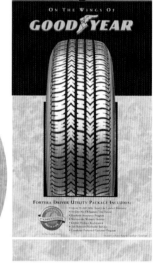

creative firm
Hornall Anderson Design Works
Seattle, (Washington) USA
creatives
Jack Anderson, Larry Anderson,
Bruce Stigler, Jay Hilburn,
Elmer dela Cruz
client
Widmer Brothers Brewery

creative firm
Launch Creative Marketing
Chicago, (Illinois) USA
creatives
Michelle Morales
client
Alberto Culver

248

creative firm
Hitchcock Fleming &
Associates, Inc.
Akron, (Ohio) USA
creatives
Bob Clancy, Chuck Repede,
Greg Pfiffner
client
Goodyear Tire & Rubber Company

creative firm
Twice Graphics
Hong Kong, China
creatives
Steve Lau
client
L'Oréal Hong Kong Ltd

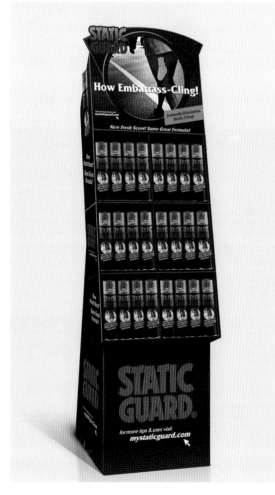

creative firm
**Launch Creative
Marketing**
Chicago, (Illinois) USA
creatives
Michelle Morales,
Jim Gelder
client
Kellogg Co.

creative firm
**Hitchcock Fleming &
Associates, Inc.**
Akron, (Ohio) USA
creatives
Bob Clancy, Mike Mickley,
Tony Fanizzi
client
Goodyear Tire & Rubber Company

249

creative firm
Cornerstone
New York, (New York) USA
creatives
Keith Steimel
client
Swedish Match

creative firm
**Empire
Communications Group**
Jacksonville, (Florida) USA
creatives
Chris Alcantara,
Susan Kiernan-Lewis,
Pete Helow
client
International Spirits

Lunch Specials
2pm

LUNCHEON-SIZED SALADS
COVENT GARDEN SALAD $5.99
SPINACH SALAD $5.99
FARMHOUSE SALAD $4.99
CAESAR SALAD $5.99
Add Blackened or Grilled Chicken $3.00
Add Grilled, Blackened or Sesame Tuna $6.00

COMBINATIONS
CUP OF SOUP and
SIDE SALAD $5.50 or
BAJA TACO Beef, Chicken or Fish $5.50 or
SHRIMP TACO Grilled or Fried $6.50

CLUB or TURKEY BACON & SWISS
HALF SANDWICH and
CUP OF SOUP $5.99 or
HALF SANDWICH & SIDE SALAD $5.99

LUNCHEON PLATTERS
FISH & CHIPS
Icelandic Cod Filet, Beer-Battered & Served with
Chips (French Fries), Tartar Sauce & Malt Vinegar.
$5.99

6 OZ. GRILLED CHICKEN BREAST
Served with Green Beans & Mashed Potatoes. $6.99

creative firm
Patrick Henry
Creative Promotions
Stafford, (Texas) USA
creatives
Summer Simmons
client
Hospitality USA

250

creative firm
Patrick Henry Creative Promotions
Stafford, (Texas) USA
creatives
Julia Austin Church
client
Z Tejas

creative firm
karacters design group
Vancouver, (British Columbia) Canada
creatives
Maria Kennedy, Marsha Larkin
client
Earls Restaurants

creative firm
**Patrick Henry
Creative Promotions**
Stafford, (Texas) USA
creatives
Rodney Allen
client
CRO-El Chico Cafe

creative firm
Island Oasis
Walpole, (Massachusetts) USA
creatives
Cindy O'Brien

creative firm
Patrick Henry Creative Promotions
Stafford, (Texas) USA
creatives
Julia Austin Church,
Smith Photography
client
Interstate Hotels & Resorts

creative firm
30sixty advertising + design
Los Angeles, (California) USA
creatives
Henry Vizcarra, David Fuscellero,
Lee Barett
client
Kings Seafood Company

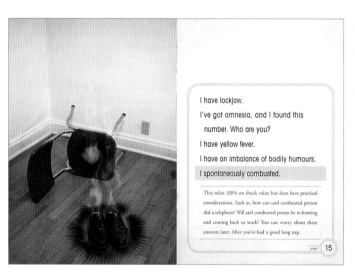

c

creative firm
Ellen Bruss Design
Denver, (Colorado) USA
creatives
Jorge Lamora,
Jim Howard,
Ellen Bruss

creative firm
Ohsan Designs
Irvine, (California) USA
creatives
Pamela Ohsan
client
Brittanie Ngo & Joe Dykhuis

creative firm
Rodgers Townsend
St. Louis, (Missouri) USA
creatives
Tom Hudder,
Luke Partridge,
Kay Cochran
client
Rodgers Townsend

creative firm
**The Design Studio of
Kean University**
Union, (New Jersey) USA
creatives
Steven Brower,
Christopher Navetta,
Ian Dorian, Janna Brower
client
**The Art Directors Club
of New Jersey**

creative firm
Twice Graphics
Hong Kong, China
creatives
Steve Lau
client
de Grisogono

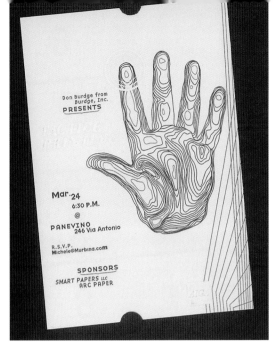

creative firm
CDI Studios
Las Vegas, (Nevada) USA
creatives
Victoria Hart
client
AIGA

15th Unisource
Annual Report
Show & Paper Fair

creative firm
Pivot Design, Inc.
Chicago, (Illinois) USA
creatives
Brock Haldeman, Don Emery,
Drew Waiss
client
Unisource

creative firm
HBO Creative Services
New York, (New York) USA
creatives
Cathy Facciola,
Mary Tchorbajian,
Venus Dennison
client
HBO

253

creative firm
Spike TV
New York, (New York) USA
creatives
Pam Schecter, Niels Schuurmans,
Andre Razo, Milinda Zumpano,
Ian Kahn
client
Spike TV

Pretty Things

Monday, July 11, 2005

7:30 P.M. Screening

The New York Public Library
For The Performing Arts
Dorothy and Lewis B.
Cullman Center

111 Amsterdam Avenue
between 64th and 65th Sts.
New York City

R.S.V.P. by July 7 to
212-512-5509

This invitation is
nontransferable.

creative firm
Bowling Green State University
Bowling Green, (Ohio) USA
creatives
Elaine Korenich,
Lori Young,
client
Elaine Korenich

Elaine Korenich
Senior BFA Exhibition
March 19–April 7, 2005
Opening March 19, 7–9:30 p.m.

Bowling Green State University
Bowling Green, OH

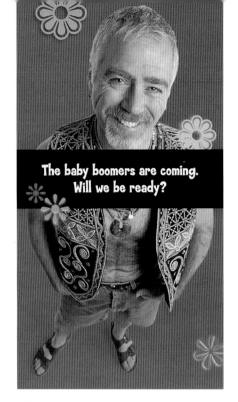

The baby boomers are coming.
Will we be ready?

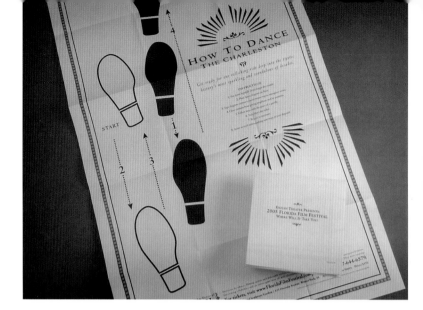

creative firm
Fry Hammond Barr
Orlando, (Florida) USA
creatives
Tim Fisher, Sean Brunson,
Lara Mann, Stephanie Ruelke
client
Enzian Theater

creative firm
Janet Hughes and Associates
Wilmington, (Delaware) USA
creatives
Felice Croul, Joyce Williams
client
**Delaware Division of Services for
Aging and Adults with Physical Disabilities**

254

creative firm
MFDI
Selinsgrove, (Pennsylvania) USA
creatives
Mark Fertig
client
Lore Degenstein Gallery

hey, let's make next year a better year
for fruitcakes everywhere

happy holidays from all of us at LOGO

creative firm
MTV Networks Creative Services
New York, (New York) USA
creatives
Cheryl Family, Scott Wadler,
Shelly Fukushima, Ken Saji,
David Lanfair
client
Logo

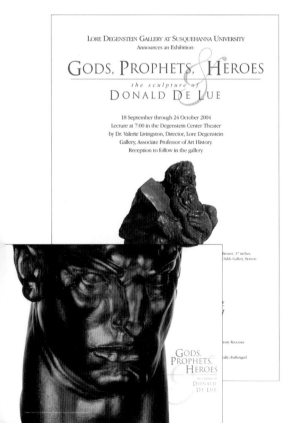

LORE DEGENSTEIN GALLERY AT SUSQUEHANNA UNIVERSITY
Announces an Exhibition:

GODS, PROPHETS, & HEROES
the sculpture of
DONALD DE LUE

18 September through 24 October 2004
Lecture at 7:00 in the Degenstein Center Theater
by Dr. Valerie Livingston, Director, Lore Degenstein
Gallery, Associate Professor of Art History.
Reception to follow in the gallery.

creative firm
Grafik
Alexandria, (Virginia) USA
creatives
Michelle Mar, Michael J. Mateos,
Lynn Umemoto, Heath Dwiggins,
Regina Esposito, Hal Swetnam
client
McKee Nelson LLP

MCKEE NELSON IS MOVING
DOWNTOWN

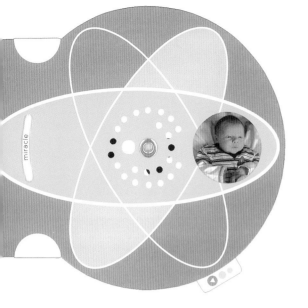

WORTH THE W8

creative firm
Salterbaxter
London, England

designer
Jeffry E. Hipp
Stone Mountain, (Georgia) USA
creatives
Jeffry E. Hipp,
Alex Robinson, Brett Tuggle,
Graphic Communications
Corporation

creative firm
Beth Singer Design, LLC
Arlington, (Virginia) USA
creatives
Chris Hoch, Sucha Snidvongs,
Beth Singer, Peter Schwartz
client
Beth Singer Design, LLC

255

creative firm
CDI Studios
Las Vegas, (Nevada) USA
creatives
Victoria Hart,
Brian Feigar
client
CDI Studios

creative firm
Nassar Design
Brookline, (Massachusetts) USA
creatives
Nelida Nassar

WE WISH YOU A YEAR 2005 THAT AT
THE IMAGE OF THE FRACTALS WILL
BRING YOU HAPPINESS AT ALL SCALES

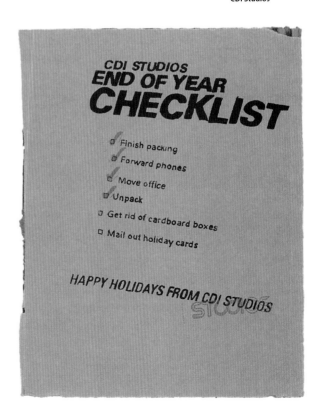

CDI STUDIOS
END OF YEAR
CHECKLIST

☑ Finish packing
☑ Forward phones
☐ Move office
☑ Unpack
☐ Get rid of cardboard boxes
☐ Mail out holiday cards

HAPPY HOLIDAYS FROM CDI STUDIOS

creative firm
Pivot Design, Inc.
Chicago, (Illinois) USA
creatives
Brock Haldeman, Liz Haldeman,
Drew Waiss, Melissa Hersam
client
Equity Office

256

creative firm
Kiku Obata + Company
St. Louis, (Missouri) USA
creatives
Amy Knopf, Kiku Obata
client
AIA/CPC St. Louis Chapter

creative firm
Premier Communications Group
Royal Oak, (Michigan) USA
creatives
Doug, Pete
client
Joe Dumars

creative firm
CMT Creative
New York, (New York) USA
creatives
James Hitchcock,
Michael Engleman,
Carla Daenninckx,
Emilie Schnick,
Nora Gaffney,
Mark Todd,
Scott McDonald
client
CMT Creative

creative firm
MTV Networks Creative Services
New York, (New York) USA
creatives
Cheryl Family, Scott Wadler,
Ken Saji, John Farrar,
Shelly Fukushima, David Lanfair
client
Spike TV

Enjoy a Friday evening where bottles are never confused as ashtrays.

BOLLA.

KORBEL
CALIFORNIA CHAMPAGNE

FETZER
VINEYARDS

creative firm
Rodgers Townsend
St. Louis, (Missouri) USA
creatives
Tom Hudder, Ron Copeland,
Ryan McMichael, Evan Willnow
client
Soulard Mardi Gras of St. Louis

NAMES OF FAMILY

I wuv Makas and Papas.
I love my Grandmas and Grandpas.

I Wauren.
My name is Lauren

Sistine, Where Unca Kiss?
Aunt Christine, can you provide the wher
of my Uncle Chris?

He Nickus Jophus.
My new baby brother's name is Nicholas J

Nicholas Joseph Mari
Born August 17, 2004
7lbs , 5oz, & 20 ½" long
Second child to Matt & Jennifer Marino.
Little brother to Lauren Marino.

THE
Lauren Marino

TWO-YEAR-OLD
TO ENGLISH

TRANSLATION
GUIDE

NEW ADDITION
2004

creative firm
Bright Rain Creative
St. Charles, (Missouri) USA
creatives
Matt Marino

257

creative firm
Ellen Bruss Design
Denver, (Colorado) USA
creatives
Steve Rura, Ellen Bruss
client
Ellen Bruss Design

creative firm
Cara Martin/Mermaid, Inc.
New York, (New York) USA
creatives
Sharon Lloyd McLaughlin,
Mike Bowman
client
205 East 59th Street

LONDON PACKAGING DINNER
FOR PACKAGING, DESIGN AND PRINT

BLACK TIE   THURSDAY 19TH MAY, 2005 7.30PM FOR 8.00PM.
THE SAVOY, THE STRAND, LONDON, WC2R 0EU
TICKET

creative firm
Turner Duckworth
London & San Francisco
London, England
creatives
David Turner, Bruce Duckworth,
Mark Waters, John Geary
client
S.A. Brain & Co. Ltd

THE ART OF LIVING
IN MANHATTAN

creative firm
Buck Consultants, an ACS Co.
St. Louis, (Missouri) USA
creatives
Jennifer Whitlow
client
Mellon HR & IS

creative firm
Lynn Cyr Design
Franklin, (Massachusetts) USA
creatives
Lynn Cyr
client
Lynn Cyr Design

creative firm
Hellbent Marketing
Redwood City, (California) USA
creatives
Deborah Shea, Mac McDougal
client
Lowell Reunion Committee

258

creative firm
Bohan Advertising/Marketing
Nashville, (Tennessee) USA
creatives
Kerry Oliver, Brooke Ludwick,
Darrell Soloman, Kristen Barlowe
client
The American Heart Association

creative firm
**D'Adda, Lorenzini,
Vigorelli, BBDO**
Rome, Italy
creatives
Giampiero Vigorelli
client
**Universal Studios
Networks Italy**

creative firm
Graphicat Limited
Hong Kong, China
creatives
Colin Tillyer
client
Noble Group Limited

creative firm
BBK Studio
*Grand Rapids,
(Michigan) USA*
creatives
Michele Chartier,
Jason Murray,
Yang Kim, SVH
client
SVH

creative firm
John Kneapler Design
New York, (New York) USA
creatives
John Kneapler, Colleen Shea
client
John Kneapler Design

Enclosed please find,
12 Drummers, 11 Pipers
10 Lords, 9 Ladies,
8 Maids, 7 Swans, 6 Geese, 5 Rings,
4 Birds, 3 Hens, 2 Doves
1 Partridge

&

Our deep wish that your
holidays bring great joy and build
fond memories.

Your 141 friends at SVH

259

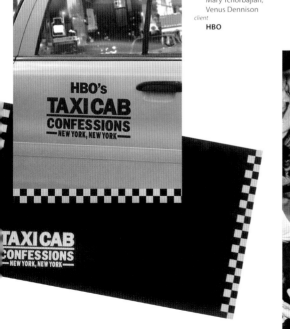

creative firm
HBO Creative Services
New York, (New York) USA
creatives
Carlos Tejeda,
Mary Tchorbajian,
Venus Dennison
client
HBO

creative firm
MTV Networks Creative Services
New York, (New York) USA
creatives
Cheryl Family, Scott Wadler, Ken Saji,
John Farrar, Kim Hemphill, Supermarket
client
MTV Networks

creative firm
Ellen Bruss Design
Denver, (Colorado) USA
creatives
Jorge Lamora, Ellen Bruss
client
The Denver Zoo

creative firm
IE Design + Communications
Hermosa Beach, (California) USA
creatives
Marcie Carson, Amy Klass
client
DaVita

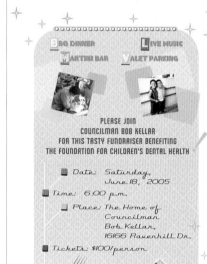

creative firm
McGregor Shott
Valencia, (California) USA
creatives
Beth Shott
client
City of Santa Clarita

260

creative firm
Zygo Communications
Wyncote, (Pennsylvania) USA
creatives
Scott Laserow
client
Josh Weinfeld

creative firm
Octavo Designs
Frederick, (Maryland) USA
creatives
Sue Hough, Mark Burrier
client
Octavo Design

creative firm
Visual Arts Press
New York, (New York) USA
creatives
Paul Sahre, Jennifer Lew, Jason Fulford
client
School of Visual Arts

creative firm
Levine & Associates
Washington, (D.C.) USA
creatives
Monica Snellings,
John Vance
client
CoreNet Global

261

creative firm
Studio Universal
Rome, Italy
creatives
Luca Marcucci
client
**Universal
Studios
Networks Italy**

creative firm
Design Nut
*Kensington,
(Maryland) USA*
creatives
Brent M. Almond,
Corbis,
Top Printing & Graphics
client
**Nicholas Pirulli &
Brent Almond**

creative firm
Solak Design
Middletown, (Connecticut) USA
creatives
Jeff Solak, Walt Solak,
Paul Horton, Robin Price
client
**Carolyn Nedderman
& Jeff Solak**

everybody has a story

the story

creative firm
Subplot Design Inc.
Vancouver,
(British Columbia) Canada
creatives
Roy White, Matthew Clark
client
Subplot Design Inc.

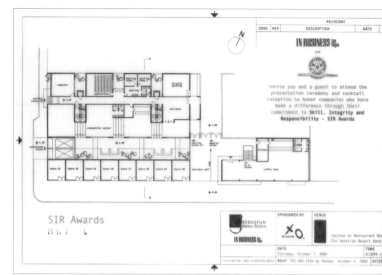

creative firm
Greenspun Media Group
Henderson, (Nevada) USA
creatives
Mami Awamura, Cintia Sasaya
client
In Business Las Vegas

262

creative firm
The College of Saint Rose
Office of Public Relations
Albany, (New York) USA
creatives
Mark Hamilton, Chris Parody,
Lisa Haley Thomson
client
The College of Saint Rose

creative firm
021 Communicaciones
Mexico City, Mexico
creatives
Gabriel Flores, Dahian Rau
client
General Motors Mexico

creative firm
LekasMiller Design
Walnut Creek, (California) USA
creatives
Lana Ip, Tina Lekas Miller
client
Cork Supply USA, Inc. and Newpak USA, Inc.

Happy Holidays

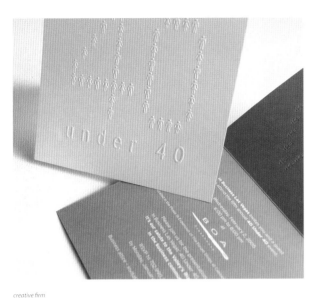

creative firm
Island Oasis
Walpole, (Massachusetts) USA
creatives
Jenny Keech

creative firm
Greenspun Media Group
Henderson, (Nevada) USA
creatives
Mami Awamura
client
In Business Las Vegas

creative firm
Lemley Design Company
Seattle, (Washington) USA
creatives
David Lemley
client
Leatherback

263

creative firm
Desbrow
Pittsburgh, (Pennsylvania) USA
creatives
Kimberly Miller, Jason Korey
client
Read! 365

creative firm
Semmer Group
Minneapolis, (Minnesota) USA
creatives
Emily Oberg, Matt McKee,
Joan Semmer
client
RAINN

creative firm
Rainy Day Designs
Carbondale, (Colorado) USA
creatives
Erin Rigney, Craig Wheeless, Stanley Bell
client
Town of Carbondale

creative firm
LF Banks & Associates
Philadelphia, (Pennsylvania) USA
creatives
Lori Banks, Travis Schnupp
client
John Templeton Foundation

creative firm
yellobee studio
Atlanta, (Georgia) USA
creatives
Alison Scheel, Gregory Krumm
client
Via Elisa

264

creative firm
Liska + Associates, Inc.
Chicago, (Illinois) USA
creatives
Sabine Krauss, Deborah Schneider,
Steve Liska
client
Tricoci University of Beauty Culture

creative firm
stressdesign
Syracuse, (New York) USA
creatives
Marc Stress
client
LeaseADE

creative firm
Designwrite Advertising
Deephaven, (Minnesota) USA
creatives
John C. Jensen
client
Kent Hrbek Outdoors Television Show

creative firm
John Wingard Design
Honolulu, (Hawaii) USA
creatives
John Wingard
client
Rock Solid Surf Technologies

creative firm
Hornall Anderson Design Works
Seattle, (Washington) USA
creatives
Kathy Saito, Sonja Max
client
Screamer Hats

265

creative firm
KARAKTER
London, England
creatives
Clive Rohald, Kam Devsi,
Mei Wing Chan, Martin Watkins
client
Jamaica National Building Society

creative firm
Octavo Designs
Frederick, (Maryland) USA
creatives
Sue Hough, Mark Burrier
client
BlueNoise

creative firm
Design Nut
Kensington, (Maryland) USA
creatives
Brent M. Almond
client
Ser Humanos

creative firm
Mark Oliver, Inc.
Solvang, (California) USA
creatives
Mark Oliver, Sudi McCollum
client
Bellwether Farms

creative firm
John Wingard Design
Honolulu, (Hawaii) USA
creatives
John Wingard
client
Four Points LLC

creative firm
Liska + Associates, Inc.
Chicago, (Illinois) USA
creatives
Kristen Merry, Steve Liska
client
Bitch Music

creative firm
KARAKTER
London, England
creatives
Clive Rohald, Kam Devsi,
Mei Wing Chan, Martin Watkins
client
Jamaica National Building Society

creative firm
Sherman Advertising/Mermaid, Inc.
New York, (New York) USA
creatives
Sharon Lloyd McLaughlin, Andrew OcKeen,
Stephen Morse
client
Sutton 57

creative firm
WestGroup Creative
New York, (New York) USA
creatives
Chip Tolaney, Marvin Berk
client
International Studio of Music

creative firm
Pat Taylor Graphic Designer
Washington, (D.C.) USA
creatives
Pat Taylor
client
Handcrafted Project

creative firm
Buitenkant Advertising
New York, (New York) USA
creatives
Vava Buitenkant
client
The Humpty Dumpty Institute

267

creative firm
Hornall Anderson Design Works
Seattle, (Washington) USA
creatives
Daymon Bruck, Yuri Shvets
client
Virtutech

creative firm
Gill Fishman Associates
Cambridge, (Massachusetts) USA
creatives
Alicia Ozyjowski
client
Schneider Associates

creative firm
Mind's Eye Creative
New Albany, (Indiana) USA
creatives
Stephen Brown
client
Mind's Eye Creative

creative firm
stressdesign
Syracuse, (New York) USA
creatives
Christine Walker
client
Clayscapes Pottery Inc.

creative firm
Kiku Obata & Company
St. Louis, (Missouri) USA
creatives
Troy Guzman
client
Bike St. Louis

GOOSE
ISLAND
BOATYARD

creative firm
Liska + Associates, Inc.
Chicago, (Illinois) USA
creatives
Kristen Merry, Steve Liska
client
Goose Island Boatyard

luminet
SYSTEMS GROUP

creative firm
John Wingard Design
Honolulu, (Hawaii) USA
creatives
John Wingard
client
Luminet Systems Group

creative firm
Willius Marketing Communications
Minneapolis, (Minnesota) USA
creatives
Jeffrey Willius
client
Volcan Wall Companies

268

Vineyard Lane

creative firm
Daigle Design
Bainbridge Island, (Washington) USA
creatives
Candace Daigle, Jessi Carpenter
client
Vineyard Lane

zero gravity design group

creative firm
Zero Gravity Design Group
Smithtown, (New York) USA
creatives
Zero Gravity Design Group
client
Zero Gravity Design Group

THE NIGHTCLUB

creative firm
CDI Studios
Las Vegas, (Nevada) USA
creatives
Eddie Roberts
client
5150 Night Club

THE OUTLETS AT
VERO BEACH℠
FASHION, STYLE & MORE

creative firm
Kiku Obata & Company
St. Louis, (Missouri) USA
creatives
Amy Knopf
client
Stoltz

FESTIVE
FAVORITES

creative firm
Brand Engine
Sausalito, (California) USA
creatives
Eric Read, Coralie Russo
client
Nancy's Specialty Foods

creative firm
WestGroup Creative
New York, (New York) USA
creatives
Chip Tolaney, Marvin Berk
client
Arbore Design

creative firm
BBK Studio
Grand Rapids, (Michigan) USA
creatives
Brian Hauch, Sharon Oleniczak
client
Cuisine Art

creative firm
Acme Communications, Inc.
New York, (New York) USA
creatives
Kiki Boucher
client
Robin Drake Design

creative firm
John Wingard Design
Honolulu, (Hawaii) USA
creatives
John Wingard
client
Ocean Club

creative firm
Gill Fishman Associates
Cambridge, (Massachusetts) USA
creatives
Fred Golinko
client
The Meadows

creative firm
Mad Dog Graphx
Anchorage, (Alaska) USA
creatives
Brett Rawalt
client
Out North Contemporary Art House

creative firm
Ruder Finn Design
New York, (New York) USA
creatives
Lisa Gabbay, Kaven Lam
client
Affymetrix

creative firm
Steven Lee Design
San Francisco, (California) USA
creatives
Steven Lee
client
Hot Steel

creative firm
Addison Whitney
Charlotte, (North Carolina) USA
creatives
Kimberlee Davis, Kelly Brewster, Trey Walsh
client
Ocean Embassy

creative firm
Brand Engine
Sausalito, (California) USA
creatives
Eric Read, Rebecca Escalera
client
Propello

creative firm
Design Objectives Pte Ltd
Singapore
creatives
Ronnie S C Tan, Lawrence Tong
client
Sheraton Hotel Taipei

creative firm
Mind's Eye Creative
New Albany, (Indiana) USA
creatives
Stephen Brown
client
Noewire

creative firm
Mark Oliver, Inc.
Solvang, (California) USA
creatives
Mark Oliver, Sudi McCollum
client
Bellwether Farms

creative firm
Creative Link
San Antonio, (Texas) USA
creatives
Mark Broderick, Ricardo Barrera
client
Catholic Television of San Antonio

creative firm
Hornall Anderson Design Works
Seattle, (Washington) USA
creatives
Jack Anderson, Kathy Saito, Henry Yiu,
Elmer dela Cruz, Sonja Max, Hayden Schoen
client
CitationShares

creative firm
Ventress Design Group
Franklin, (Tennessee) USA
creatives
Tom Ventress
client
DigiScript

Israel.
An American
Value

creative firm
Beth Singer Design, LLC
Arlington, (Virginia) USA
creatives
Chris Hoch
client
American Israel Public Affairs Committee

creative firm
Ruder Finn Design
New York, (New York) USA
creatives
Lisa Gabbay, Kaven Lam
client
Affymetrix

ORCHIN
ORTHODONTICS

creative firm
Greenfield/Belser Ltd.
Washington, (D.C.) USA
creatives
Burkey Belser, Maureen Meyer, Paul Clements
client
Orchin Orthodontics

creative firm
Impact Advertising
Williamsport, (Pennsylvania) USA
creatives
Christopher Johnson
client
Barone's Bakery

creative firm
Gill Fishman Associates
Cambridge, (Massachusetts) USA
creatives
Alicia Ozyjowski, Michael Persons
client
CommonAngels

UNIVERSITY
MALL

271

creative firm
Kiku Obata & Company
St. Louis, (Missouri) USA
creatives
Joe Floresca
client
Stoltz

creative firm
Ruder Finn Design
New York, (New York) USA
creatives
Lisa Gabbay, Kaven Lam
client
Affymetrix

creative firm
Pat Taylor Graphic Designer
Washington, (D.C.) USA
creatives
Gretchen Maxwell, Pat Taylor
client
GLM Design

creative firm
Qualcomm
San Diego, (California) USA
creatives
Christopher Lee
client
La Jolla Playhouse

creative firm
Landor Associates
San Francisco, (California) USA
creatives
Jon Weden, Jeanne Reimer
client
Frito Lay

creative firm
Perkins + Will | EvaMaddox Branded Environments
Chicago, (Illinois) USA
creatives
Eva Maddox, Anna Kania, Emily Neville, Kevin Carlin
client
The Miami Institute for Age Management & Intervention

creative firm
Qualcomm
San Diego, (California) USA
creatives
Christopher Lee
client
La Jolla Playhouse

272

creative firm
Mind's Eye Creative
New Albany, (Indiana) USA
creatives
Stephen Brown
client
Loop Island Wetlands

creative firm
Zero Gravity Design Group
Smithtown, (New York) USA
creatives
Zero Gravity Design Group
client
Pharmalogical, Inc.

creative firm
Octavo Designs
Frederick, (Maryland) USA
creatives
Sue Hough, Mark Burrier
client
Healing Connections

creative firm
Lewis Moberly
London, England
creatives
Mary Lewis, Poppy Stedman
client
Girls Girls Girls

creative firm
Elias/Savion Productionstudios
Pittsburgh, (Pennsylvania) USA
creatives
Jim Kashak
client
ESP Studios

creative firm
Kiku Obata & Company
St. Louis, (Missouri) USA
creatives
Jennifer McBath,
Patrick Davis Communications
client
Boot Loot

creative firm
Gill Fishman Associates
Cambridge, (Massachusetts) USA
creatives
Michael Persons
client
The Lenny Fund

creative firm
Ventress Design Group
Franklin, (Tennessee) USA
creatives
Tom Ventress
client
University of Virginia Press

creative firm
kor group
Boston, (Massachusetts) USA
creatives
Karen Dendy Smith, Tony Bartolucci
client
kor group

creative firm
Gill Fishman Associates
Cambridge, (Massachusetts) USA
creatives
Michael Persons
client
The Prospero Group

creative firm
Brand Engine
Sausalito, (California) USA
creatives
Yusuke Asaka, Eric Read, Rebecca Escalera,
Meghan Zodrow, Casey Coyle
client
Vista Center for the Blind & Visually Impaired

creative firm
Design Systemat, Inc.
Makati City, Philippines
creatives
Belandre M. Nepumoceno
client
Christine Int'l. Phil., Inc.

creative firm
Suka Design
New York, (New York) USA
creatives
Brian Wong
client
Northstar Realty Finance Corp

creative firm
Gill Fishman Associates
Cambridge, (Massachusetts) USA
creatives
Michael Persons
client
Gamen Group

creative firm
Murphy Design
Philadelphia, (Pennsylvania) USA
creatives
Rosemary Murphy
client
Sit (a Pet Boutique)

creative firm
Fixation Marketing
Washington, (D.C.) USA
creatives
Bruce E. Morgan, Randy Guseman
client
Christian Booksellers Association

274

GORDIE

one night

creative firm
Jowaisas Design
Winter Park, (Florida) USA
creatives
Elizabeth Jowaisas, Margaret Youngblood,
Leslie Lanahan
client
The Gordie Foundation

creative firm
Pat Taylor Graphic Designer
Washington, (D.C.) USA
creatives
Pat Taylor
client
Equalogy Play Rights

CH1CAGO
VISIONS

creative firm
BreedWorks
Oneonta, (New York) USA
creatives
Susan Muther
client
Morgan's Fortunato Farm

creative firm
Liska + Associates, Inc.
Chicago, (Illinois) USA
creatives
Steve Liska
client
The Art Institute of Chicago

creative firm
Tieken:Moret Design and Marketing
Phoenix, (Arizona) USA
creatives
Toni Cress
client
Monarch Dunes

creative firm
Creative Link
San Antonio, (Texas) USA
creatives
Mark Broderick, Ricardo Barrera
client
Siouxland Sampler Quilt Guild

creative firm
Landor Associates
San Francisco, (California) USA
creatives
Jon Weden, Rolando Diep
client
Frito Lay

creative firm
Design Objectives Pte Ltd
Singapore
creatives
Ronnie S C Tan, Andy Koh
client
Meritus Hotel Bangkok, Thailand

creative firm
Empire Communications Group
Jacksonville, (Florida) USA
creatives
Chris Alcantara
client
Inmotion Pictures

creative firm
Gill Fishman Associates
Cambridge, (Massachusetts) USA
creatives
Michael Persons, Alicia Ozyjowski
client
TriSixty Security

creative firm
Mortensen Design, Inc.
Mountain View, (California) USA
creatives
Gordon Mortensen, Heleno Seo
client
Newground Resources

creative firm
Kiku Obata & Company
St. Louis, (Missouri) USA
creatives
Rich Nelson
client
Southeast Missourian

creative firm
Stephen Longo Design Assoc.
West Orange, (New Jersey) USA
creatives
Stephen Longo
client
Ekko Fusion Restaurant

creative firm
Iridium
Ottawa, (Ontario) Canada
creatives
David Daigle, Jean-Luc Denat
client
Promomedia Group

creative firm
Greenfield/Belser Ltd.
Washington, (D.C.) USA
creatives
Burkey Belser, Tom Cameron, Steve McCracken
client
Arent Fox

creative firm
The Humane Society of the United States
Washington, (D.C.) USA
creatives
Paula Jaworski
client
The Humane Society of the United States

276

creative firm
Liquefire Design
Emeryville, (California) USA
creatives
Anthony Luk
client
TableZest, Inc.

creative firm
Tom Fowler, Inc.
Norwalk, (Connecticut) USA
creatives
Thomas G. Fowler, Elizabeth P. Ball
client
Unilever Home & Personal Care
Creative Package Design Department

creative firm
Very Memorable Design
New York, (New York) USA
creatives
Michael James Pinto
client
Excira Technologies, Inc.

creative firm
Focus Design and
Marketing Solutions
Pasadena, (California) USA
creatives
Aram Youssefian
client
Boutique Hotel Network

creative firm
Mortensen Design, Inc.
Mountain View, (California) USA
creatives
Gordon Mortensen, Patricia Margaret
client
Epic Bancorp

creative firm
VSA Partners
Chicago, (Illinois) USA
creatives
Curt Scheiber, Ashley Lippard, Wendy Belt
client
IBM

creative firm
Kellum McClain Inc.
New York, (New York) USA
creatives
Ron Kellum
client
Jane Rose Reporting

creative firm
Ruder Finn Design
New York, (New York) USA
creatives
Lisa Gabbay, Kaven Lam
client
Affymetrix

creative firm
WindChaser Design Team
Marina del Rey, (California) USA
creatives
Nathan A.S. Adams, Joey Garcia Jr.
client
WindChaser Products, Inc.

277

creative firm
MetaDesign
San Francisco, (California) USA
creatives
Brett Wickens, Peter Saville,
Hui-Ling Chen, Corey Holms
client
Current TV

creative firm
Foth & Van Dyke
Green Bay, (Wisconsin) USA
creatives
Daniel Green
client
South Central Iowa Solid Waste Agency

creative firm
Skidmore, Inc.
Royal Oak, (Michigan) USA
creatives
Andre Foster, Barrett Streu
client
Big Love Detroit

creative firm
Jowaisas Design
Winter Park, (Florida) USA
creatives
Elizabeth Jowaisas
client
**Orlando Area Chapter of the
Florida Public Relations Association**

creative firm
CDI Studios
Las Vegas, (Nevada) USA
creatives
Victoria Hart, Brian Felgar
client
Industrial Power

creative firm
Hitchcock Fleming & Associates, Inc.
Akron, (Ohio) USA
creatives
Nick Betro, Todd Moser, Kim Bruns
client
American Cancer Society

creative firm
Signi
Mexico City, Mexico
creatives
Daniel Castelao
client
Tarme

creative firm
AdVantage Ltd
Hamilton, Bermuda
creatives
Susan Tang-Petersen, Karen Martin
client
Greenman Landscaping

creative firm
Curio
Hoboken, (New Jersey) USA
creatives
Carrie Brunk
client
Liz Oliver, Oliver Productions

278

creative firm
Hitchcock Fleming & Associates, Inc.
Akron, (Ohio) USA
creatives
Nick Betro, Mark Collins, Scott Kristoff
client
Geauga Lake Park & Wildwater Kingdom

creative firm
Grizzell & Co
St. Louis, (Missouri) USA
creatives
John H. Grizzell
client
Thompson Civil Trademark

creative firm
Design Nut
Kensington, (Maryland) USA
creatives
Brent M. Almond
client
**National Association for
College Admission Counseling**

creative firm
Vince Rini Design
Huntington Beach, (California) USA
creatives
Vince Rini
client
Children's Hospital Los Angeles

creative firm
T+T
Chicago, (Illinois) USA
creatives
Theodore C. Alexander, Jr., Therese Alexander
client
Road America

creative firm
Phoenix Creative Group
Potomac Falls, (Virginia) USA
creatives
Jeremiah Austin, Nick Lutkins
client
Alpha Natural Resources

David & Garcia PR
Public Relations

creative firm
Goldforest
Miami, (Florida) USA
creatives
Ana Teresa Mellet, Bibiana Pulido, Michael Gold
client
David & Garcia PR

creative firm
Iridium
Ottawa, (Ontario) Canada
creatives
David Daigle, Jean-Luc Denat
client
Funkdawgs

creative firm
Creative Link
San Antonio, (Texas) USA
creatives
Mark Broderick, Donna Santos
client
Spectrum Health Clubs

279

creative firm
Bertz Design Group
Middletown, (Connecticut) USA
creatives
John Gibson
client
Pratt & Whitney

creative firm
Spring Design Partners
New York, (New York) USA
creatives
Ron Wong, May Wong
client
Coca Cola (Frederic Kahn)

creative firm
CDI Studios
Las Vegas, (Nevada) USA
creatives
Victoria Hart
client
Shufflemaster Inc.

creative firm
X Design Company
Denver, (Colorado) USA
creatives
Alex Valderrama
client
Danielle Racing

creative firm
Mortensen Design, Inc.
Mountain View, (California) USA
creatives
Gordon Mortensen, Chris Rossi, Patricia Margaret
client
Department B

creative firm
Shea, Inc.
Minneapolis, (Minnesota) USA
creatives
Susan Donahue
client
Fortuneland, Dalian, China

creative firm
Hellbent Marketing
Redwood City, (California) USA
creatives
Deborah Shea, Mac McDougal
client
Savvy Cellar

creative firm
Sunspots Creative
Hoboken, (New Jersey) USA
creatives
Rick Bonelli, Dave Vioreanu, Deena Hartley
client
New Jersey Seeds

creative firm
Design Objectives Pte Ltd
Singapore
creatives
Ronnie S C Tan, Luke Tan Shixin
client
SP Chemicals Ltd

280

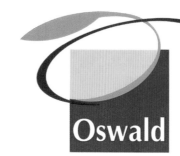

creative firm
Scott Adams Design Associates
Columbus, (Ohio) USA
creatives
Scott Adams
client
Nationwide Realty Investors

creative firm
House of Design
Graz, Austria
creatives
André Stangl
client
Oswald Obst und Wacdfrüchte

creative firm
Mendes Publicidade
Belém, (Pará) Brazil
creatives
Oswaldo Mendes, Marcelo Amorim
client
Sebrae/PA.

creative firm
Stream Companies
Malvern, (Pennsylvania) USA
creatives
Kate Heskett, Christian O'Neil
client
Couture Laser & Skin

creative firm
FullSteam Marketing & Design
Salines, (California) USA
creatives
Craig Kauffman, Karen Nardozza
client
Monterey Bay Botanical Gardens

creative firm
A3 Design
Charlotte,(North Carolina) USA
creatives
Alan Altman, Amanda Altman
client
DR Horton

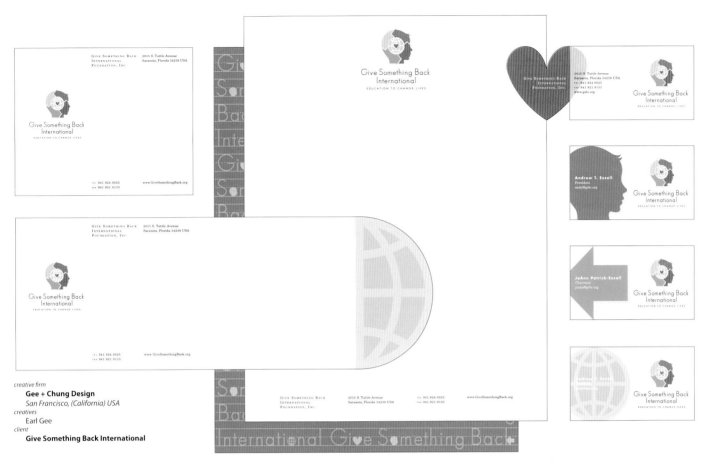

creative firm
Gee + Chung Design
San Francisco, (California) USA
creatives
Earl Gee
client
Give Something Back International

281

creative firm
Coates and Coates
Naperville, (Illinois) USA
creatives
Jim Brophy
client
Wierenga Consulting

creative firm
Sheriff Design
Elkins Park, (Pennsylvania) USA
creatives
Lori Bilodeau
client
Towers and Turrets

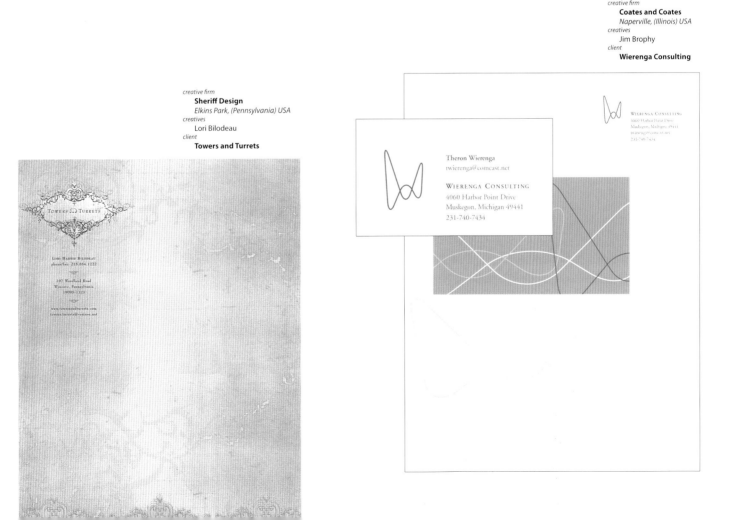

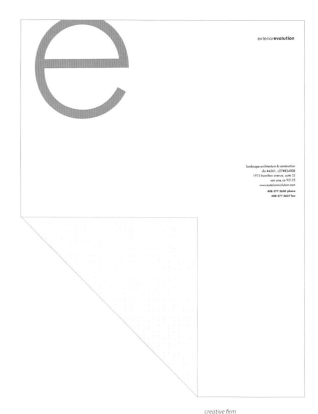

creative firm
MFDI
Selinsgrove, (Pennsylvania) USA
creatives
Mark Fertig
client
Haight Street Garage

creative firm
Melissa Passehl Design
San Jose, (California) USA
creatives
Melissa Passehl,
Nextpress
client
Exterior Evolution

282

creative firm
Mermaid, Inc.
New York, (New York) USA
creatives
Sharon Lloyd McLaughlin
client
Mermaid, Inc.

creative firm
Hornall Anderson Design Works
Seattle, (Washington) USA
creatives
Jack Anderson, Larry Anderson,
Henry Yiu
client
SOVArchitecture

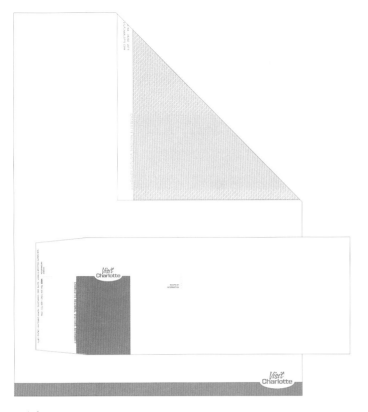

creative firm
A3 Design
Charlotte, (North Carolina) USA
creatives
Alan Altman, Amanda Altman
client
Visit Charlotte

creative firm
CDI Studios
Las Vegas, (Nevada) USA
creatives
Victoria Hart, Michelle Georgilas
client
CDI Studios

283

creative firm
Design Nut
Kensington, (Connecticut) USA
creatives
Brent M. Almond,
Westland Printers
client
Design Nut

creative firm
X Design Company
Denver, (Colorado) USA
creatives
Alex Valderrama
client
Danielle Racing

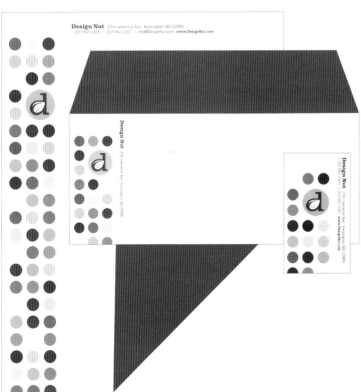

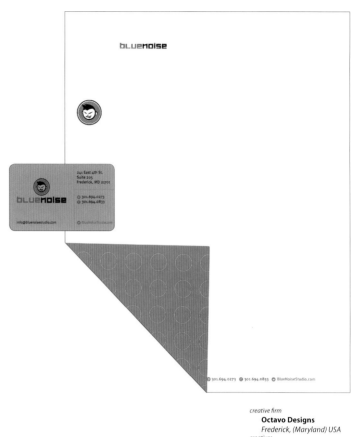

creative firm
Mortensen Design, Inc.
Mountain View, (California) USA
creatives
Gordon Mortensen, Patricia Margaret
client
Department B

creative firm
Octavo Designs
Frederick, (Maryland) USA
creatives
Sue Hough, Mark Burrier
client
Blue Noise

284

creative firm
PHP Communications
Birmingham, (Alabama) USA
creatives
Joan Perry, Lynn Smith
client
PHP Communications

creative firm
Daniel Stanford
Savannah, (Georgia) USA
creatives
Daniel Stanford
client
Third Degree I.D.

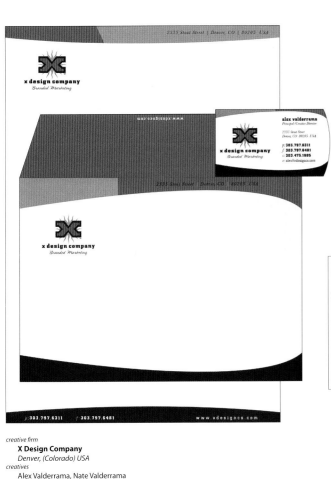

creative firm
X Design Company
Denver, (Colorado) USA
creatives
Alex Valderrama, Nate Valderrama
client
X Design Company

creative firm
Original Impressions
Miami, (Florida) USA
creatives
Frank Irias
client
Conrad Miami

creative firm
Sayles Graphic Design
Des Moines, (Iowa) USA
creatives
John Sayles
client
Sloan Brothers Painting

creative firm
Interrobang Design Collaborative
Richmond, (Vermont) USA
creatives
Mark D. Sylvester
client
Viewfinder Productions

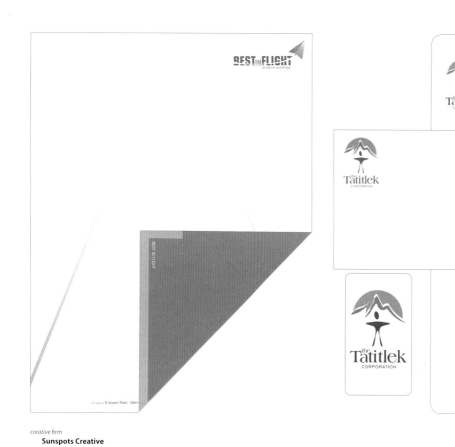

creative firm
Sunspots Creative
Hoboken, (New Jersey) USA
creatives
Rick Bonelli, Dave Vioreanu,
Deena Hartley
client
Best in Flight Academy

creative firm
Mad Dog Graphx
Anchorage, (Alaska) USA
creatives
Kris Ryan-Clarke
client
The Tatitlek Corporation

creative firm
Simple Design
Evergreen, (Colorado) USA
creatives
Robert Mitchell
client
RMC Inc.

creative firm
Scott Adams Design Associates
Columbus, (Ohio) USA
creatives
Scott Adams
client
Matt White Consulting

creative firm
Octavo Designs
Frederick, (Maryland) USA
creatives
Sue Hough, Mark Burrier
client
RAM Digital

creative firm
Design Guys
Minneapolis, (Minnesota) USA
creatives
Steven Sikora, Jay Theige
client
Design Guys

creative firm
Erwin Zinger Graphic Design
Groningen, The Netherlands
creatives
Erwin Zinger
client
ISD Noordenkwartier

creative firm
ESP Studios
Pittsburgh, (Pennsylvania) USA
creatives
Monica Watt, Jim Kashak
client
ESP Studios

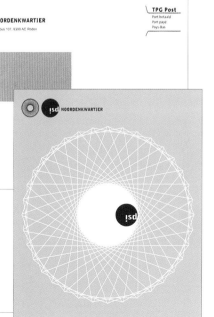

creative firm
Elevator
Sput, Croatia
creatives
Lana Vitas, Tony Adamic
client
Ulola Cosmetics

288

creative firm
Squarehand
New York, (New York) USA
creatives
Mónica Torrejón Kelly
client
**Stunning Models on
Display Records**

creative firm
**Focus Design and
Marketing Solutions**
Pasadena, (California) USA
creatives
Aram Youssefian
client
Studio 4 Networks

creative firm
Five Visual Communication & Design
West Chester, (Ohio) USA
creatives
Rondi Tschopp, Tonya Henry
client
West Chester Chamber Alliance

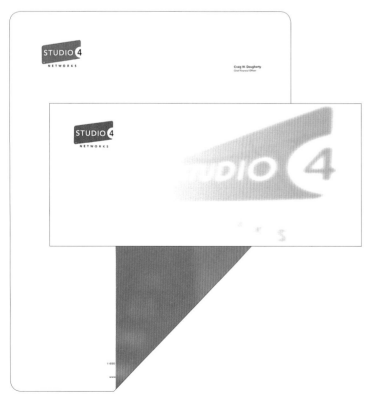

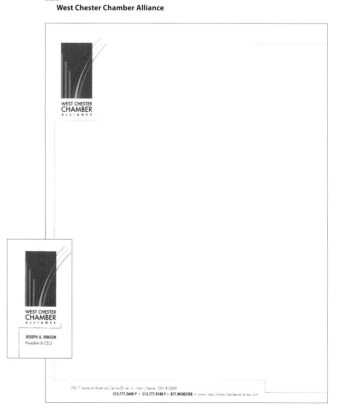

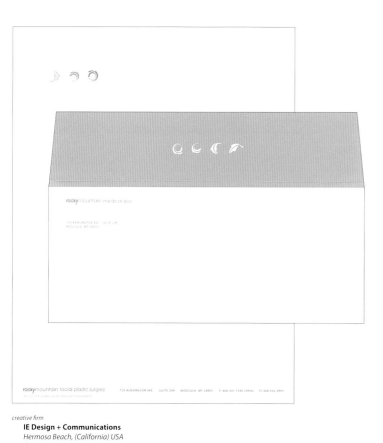

creative firm
IE Design + Communications
Hermosa Beach, (California) USA
creatives
Cya Nelson, Marie Carson
client
Rocky Mountain

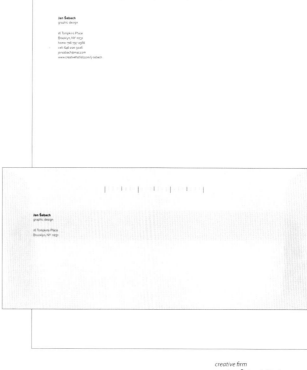

creative firm
Jan Šabach Design
Brooklyn, (New York) USA
creatives
Jan Šabach
client
Jan Šabach

creative firm
KROG
Ljubljana, Slovenia
creatives
Edi Berk
client
Hotel Mons, Ljubljana

creative firm
KFR Communications, LLC
New Egypt, (New Jersey) USA
creatives
Glenn Foster
client
KFR Communications, LLC

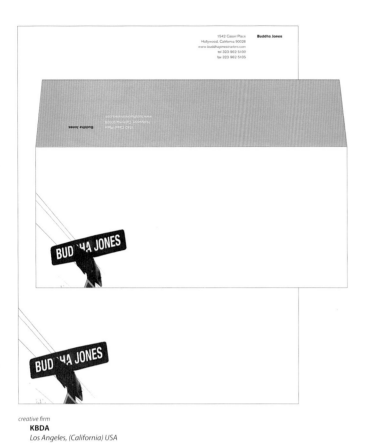

creative firm
KBDA
Los Angeles, (California) USA
creatives
Kim Baer, Keith Knueven
client
Buddha Jones

290

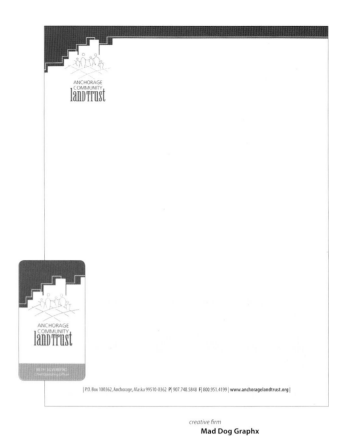

creative firm
Mad Dog Graphx
Anchorage, (Alaska) USA
creatives
Kris Ryan-Clarke
client
Anchorage Community Land Trust

creative firm
Michael Patrick Partners
Palo Alto, (California) USA
creatives
Eko Tjoek, Duane Maidens
client
Michael Patrick Partners, Inc.

creative firm
ESP Studios
Pittsburgh, (Pennsylvania) USA
creatives
Monica Watt, Jim Kashak
client
ESP Studios

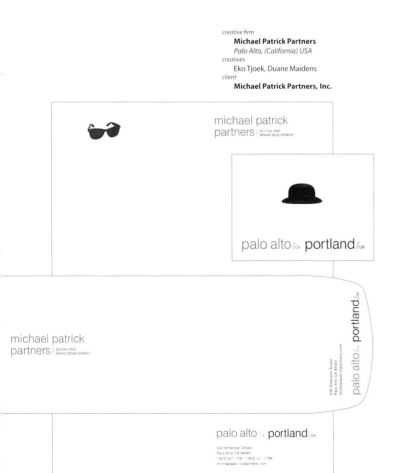

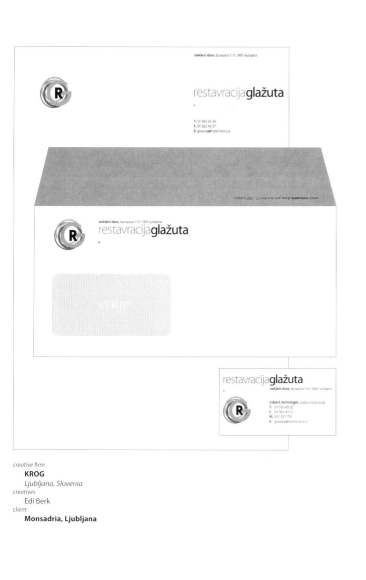

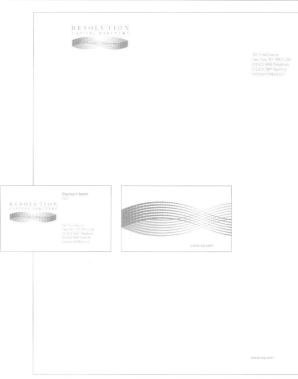

creative firm
KROG
Ljubljana, Slovenia
creatives
Edi Berk
client
Monsadria, Ljubljana

291

creative firm
Colemanbrandworx
New York, (New York) USA
creatives
Jim Williams
client
Resolution Capital Partners

creative firm
Daigle Design
Bainbridge Island, (Washington) USA
creatives
Callie Butler-Goodrich,
Candace Daigle,
Paul Dunning,
Jessi Carpenter
client
Calico Cat

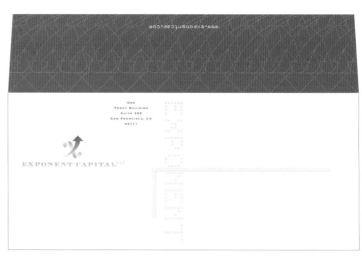

292

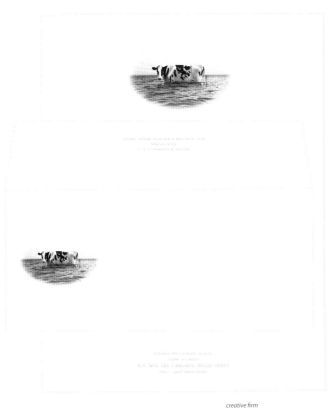

creative firm
Colemanbrandworx
New York, (New York) USA
creatives
Jim Williams
client
Udder Holdings, LLC

creative firm
Octavo Designs
Frederick, (Maryland) USA
creatives
Sue Hough
client
Top 2 Bottom Professional Cleaning

creative firm
Perkins + Will | EvaMaddox
Branded Environments
Chicago, (Illinois) USA
creatives
Eva Maddox, Anna Kania,
Emily Neville
client
The Miami Institute for Age
Management and Intervention

creative firm
Interrobang Design Collaborative
Richmond, (Vermont) USA
creatives
Mark D. Sylvester,
Lisa Taft Sylvester
client
Interrobang Design Collaborative

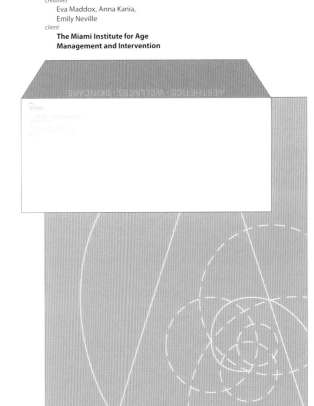

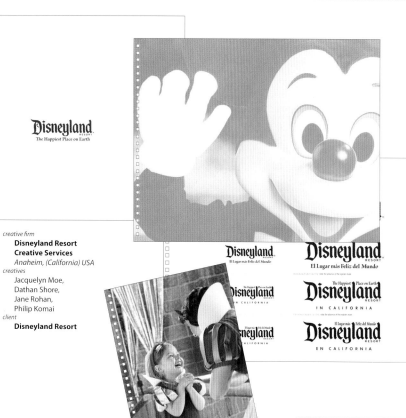

creative firm
Disneyland Resort
Creative Services
Anaheim, (California) USA
creatives
Jacquelyn Moe,
Dathan Shore,
Jane Rohan,
Philip Komai
client
Disneyland Resort

creative firm
Nickelodeon Creative Resources
New York, (New York) USA
creatives
Tim Blankley, Andrew Faw,
Oona Stern, Jessica Gladstone,
Phil Falco, Piero Piluso, Joe Bianco,
Annie Tao
client
Nickelodeon/Viacom
Consumer Products

creative firm
Phoenix Creative Group
Potomac Falls, (Virginia) USA
creatives
Jeremiah Austin, Nick Lutkins
client
ALPHA Natural Resources

Identity Standards

creative firm
Cisco Brand Strategy
San Jose, (California) USA
creatives
Art Kilinski, Gary McCavitt,
Bob Jones, Jeff Brand
client
Cisco Systems

295

creative firm
Cisco Brand Strategy
San Jose, (California) USA
creatives
Art Kilinski,
Gary McCavitt
client
Cisco Systems

creative firm
Brand Engine
Sausalito, (California) USA
creatives
Will Burke, Yusuke Asaka,
Monica Schlaug
client
Pekoe Siphouse

creative firm
Brand Engine
Sausalito, (California) USA
creatives
Will Burke, Yusuke Asaka,
Casey Coyle, Kinkel Rowan,
David Eichhorn
client
Pixie Maté

296

creative firm
Nickelodeon Creative Resources
New York, (New York) USA
creatives
Tim Blankley, Russ Spina,
Jordana Furcht, Peggy Doody,
Piero Pinso, Joe Bianco,
Erik Chichester, Erin Hicks, Annie Tao
client
**Nickelodeon/Viacom
Consumer Products**

creative firm
Shimokochi-Reeves
Los Angeles, (California) USA
creatives
Mamoku Shimokochi, Anne Reeves
client
Angstrom Lighting, Inc.

297

creative firm
Turner Duckworth
London & San Francisco
Chiswick, England
creatives
David Turner, Bruce Duckworth,
Mark Waters, John Geary
client
S.A. Brain & Co Ltd

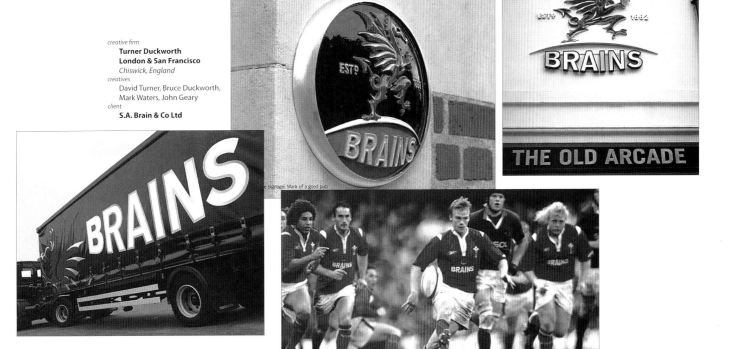

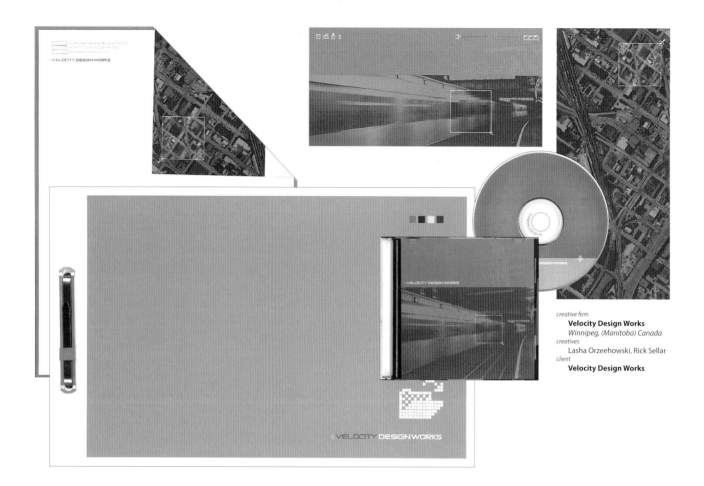

creative firm
Velocity Design Works
Winnipeg, (Manitoba) Canada
creatives
Lasha Orzeehowski, Rick Sellar
client
Velocity Design Works

298

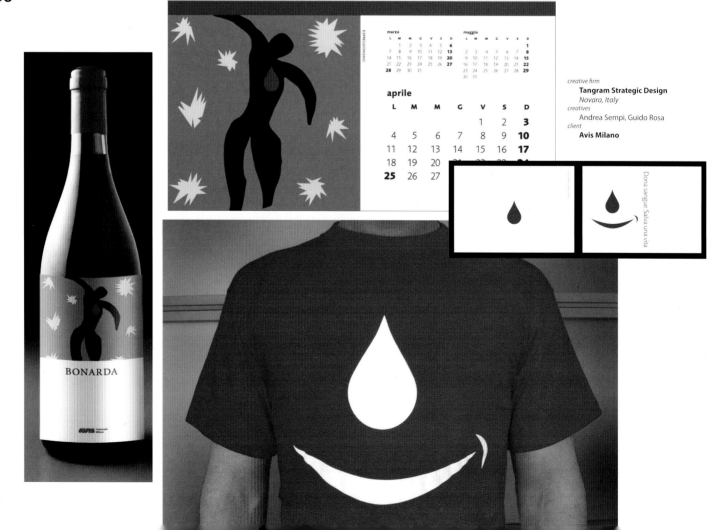

creative firm
Tangram Strategic Design
Novara, Italy
creatives
Andrea Sempi, Guido Rosa
client
Avis Milano

creative firm
Stephen Longo Design Assoc.
West Orange, (New Jersey) USA
creatives
Stephen Longo, Harvey Hirsch
client
Matsuya Japanese Steak House

N.J.'s Largest
Selection of
Fresh Sushi

creative firm
karacters design group
Vancouver (British Columbia) Canada
creatives
James Bateman, Kara Bohl,
Monica Martinez
client
Vancity

creative firm
Qualcomm
San Diego, (California) USA
creatives
Christopher Lee
client
Rush Press

300

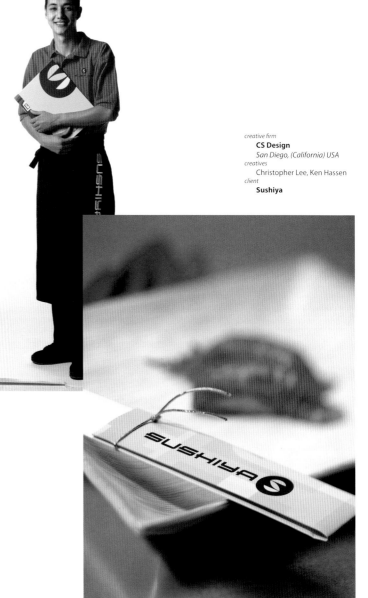

creative firm
CS Design
San Diego, (California) USA
creatives
Christopher Lee, Ken Hassen
client
Sushiya

creative firm
Kiku Obata & Company
St. Louis, (Missouri) USA
creatives
Kiku Obata, Kevin Flynn, AIA, David Leavey, AIA,
Amy Knopf, Eleanor Safe, Jeff Ebers,
Lisa Bollman, Jon Miller
client
Mirasol

301

C

creative firm
Wallach Glass Studio
Santa Rosa, (California) USA
creatives
Tenaya Wallach, Christina Wallach
client
University of California, Berkeley

creative firm
Brand Engine
Sausalito, (California) USA
creatives
Will Burke, Monica Schlaug
client
Pekoe Siphouse

creative firm
Kolano Design
Pittsburgh, (Pennsylvania) USA
creatives
Joshua Welsh
client
Boy Scouts of America

creative firm
Design Objectives Pte Ltd
Singapore
creatives
Ronnie S C Tan
client
Sheraton Hotel Taipei

creative firm
Kiku Obata & Company
St. Louis, (Missouri) USA
creatives
Kiku Obata, Denise Fuehne, Russell Buchanan, Jr.,
Laura McCanna, Carole Jerome, Albert Vecerka/Esto
client
Wild Pair/Bakers Footwear

302

creative firm
Les Cheneaux Design
Bowling Green, (Ohio) USA
creatives
Luc Hughart, Lori Young
client
Snook's Dream Cars

creative firm
Suka Design
New York, (New York) USA
creatives
Adrian Levin, Brian Wong,
John Moon
client
United Federation of Teachers

creative firm
Edge Advertising
Washington, (D.C.) USA
creatives
Karin Edgett, David Tull,
Monika Górnikiewics, Peter Corcoran
client
Level Green Landscaping

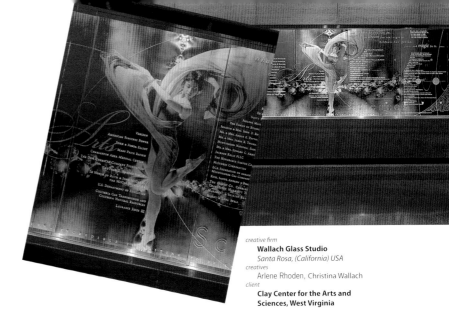

creative firm
Wallach Glass Studio
Santa Rosa, (California) USA
creatives
Arlene Rhoden, Christina Wallach
client
**Clay Center for the Arts and
Sciences, West Virginia**

creative firm
Design Objectives Pte Ltd
Singapore
creatives
Ronnie S C Tan
client
Sheraton Hotel Taipei

creative firm
Simple Design
Evergreen, (Colorado) USA
creatives
Robert Mitchell,
Doug Oldham
client
RMC Inc.

303

creative firm
Cornerstone
New York, (New York) USA
creatives
Keith Steimel
client
Coca-Cola Co.

creative firm
Design Systemat, Inc.
Makati City, Philippines
creatives
Stefano Paolo G. Bunag
client
Delifrance

creative firm
Perkins + Will | EvaMaddox
Branded Environments
Chicago, (Illinois) USA
creatives
Eva Maddox,
Burke Greenwood,
Becky Ruehl,
Ron Steumarski,
Maron Demissie
client
Art Institute of Chicago

creative firm
Brand Lounge GmbH
Dusseldorf, Germany
creatives
Janine Peters
client
Wehmeyer GmbH

creative firm
Island Oasis
Walpole, (Massachusetts)
USA
creatives
Jennifer Howard

creative firm
Kolano Design
Pittsburgh, (Pennsylvania) USA
creatives
Joshua Welsh
client
Friends of the Riverfront

creative firm
Perkins + Will | EvaMaddox
Branded Environments
Chicago, (Illinois) USA
creatives
Eileen Jones, Anna Kania, Melissa Kleve,
Brian Weatherford, Patrick Grzybek
client
Antron

creative firm
Kiku Obata & Company
St. Louis, (Missouri) USA
creatives
Kiku Obata, Kevin Flynn, AIA,
Dennis Hyland, AIA, Troy Guzman,
Jon Miller, Todd Owyoung
client
Big Shark Bicycle Company

creative firm
Stephen Longo Design Assoc.
West Orange, (New Jersey) USA
creatives
Stephen Longo
client
Ekko Fusion Restaurant

305

creative firm
**Perkins + Will | EvaMaddox
Branded Environments**
Chicago, (Illinois) USA
creatives
Christina Wallach, Eva Maddox, Eileen Jones,
Rod Vickroy, Frank Pettinati, Ron Stelmarksi,
Jason Hall, Anna Kania, Malgorzata Zawislak,
Lindsey Steinacher, Patrick Grzybek,
Bryce de Reynier, Maron Demissie, Becky Ruehl,
Emily Neville, Daniel VonderBrink, Kevin Carlin,
Lisa Estep, David Powell, Austin Zike,
Nicolette Daly, Gary Wheeler
client
Haworth, Inc.

creative firm
Wallach Glass Studio
Santa Rosa, (California) USA
creatives
Christina Wallach
client
**Columbus Children's
Research Institute**

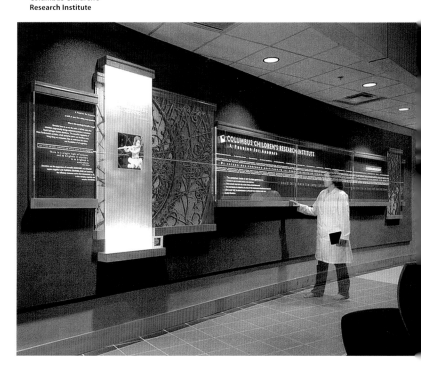

Editorial Design, single page

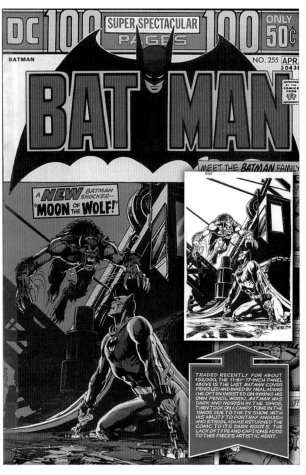

creative firm
Playboy Enterprises International, Inc.
Chicago, (Illinois) USA
creatives
Tom Staebler, Scott Anderson
client
PLAYBOY Magazine

creative firm
Selling Power
Fredericksburg, (Virginia) USA
creatives
Colleen Quinnell, Peter Hoey
client
Selling Power Magazine

creative firm
Akron Beacon Journal
Akron, (Ohio) USA
creatives
Dennis Balogh,
Edna Jakubowski
client
Akron Beacon Journal

creative firm
Playboy Enterprises International, Inc.
Chicago, (Illinois) USA
creatives
James Imbrogno, Tom Staebler,
Len Willis
client
PLAYBOY Magazine

creative firm
Playboy Enterprises International, Inc.
Chicago, (Illinois) USA
creatives
Tom Staebler,
Scott Anderson
client
PLAYBOY Magazine

Land of extremes
Open skies and dramatic, sweeping vistas are typical of the region of India that is Ladakh

creative firm
Emphasis Media Limited
Hong Kong, China
creatives
Davide Butson, Locky Lai
client
China Airlines

307

Your 2004 Main LIBRARY

After $57 million and countless hours of preparation and hard labor, Akron-Summit County's main library at 60 S. High St. in downtown Akron is reopening at nearly twice its original size. Space for patron use has tripled and includes a state-of-the-art auditorium, a children's room, a teen area, a cafe and an exterior park and amphitheater.

The main library over the years

1874
Jan. 26: Akron City Council establishes first free public library in Ohio.

March 1: Akron Public Library opens on second floor of Masonic Temple at Mill and Howard streets (above), using books from Akron Library Association, and funding, from Akron City Council. Patrons can't take books from shelves, and children under 12 can't check out books themselves.

1898
June 8: Library triples in size when it dedicates space on second floor of Everett building at Main and Market streets. Main library consists of a room about 104 by 70 feet, with some smaller rooms adjoining. It is described as "second to none for beauty, light, convenience, and necessary furnishings."

1904
April 23: Library moves into a new Renaissance-style building of Ohio sandstone at High and Market streets, built with $82,000 donated by Andrew Carnegie. The site, Bierce Park, was deeded to city by Gen. Lucius V. Bierce, whose house was used years earlier to harbor slaves escaping to Canada.

1942
Nov. 15: Library dedicates former Akron Beacon Journal building at East Market and Summit streets, tripling its floor space. Building is purchased for $300,000, with renovation costing about $100,500.

1968
March 24: Library moves to $5.36 million building at 55 S. Main St., downtown. In first year, 67,742 more books are borrowed than in previous year.

White ash veneer
The wood paneling covering many surfaces in the entire building comes from a tough hardwood known as American ash, Biltmore ash and cane ash. It has been called the All-American leisure wood because it often is used in baseball bats, canoe paddles, tool handles and boat building, as well as veneer.

Old library building
135,000 square feet of the old building was renovated and includes an elevated glass block walkway to a 600-space parking deck. Free parking for up to one hour will be offered.

Auditorium
The auditorium has seating for 430 and will feature digital projection capabilities and a 16-by-26-foot screen. It also has an 850-square-foot stage and a Steinway baby grand piano for live performances.

Zinc tile
Zinc tiles cover the exterior of the auditorium in an interlocking diamond pattern. They were made in Germany and are 99 percent zinc, with small amounts of titanium and copper.

Marmoleum floor
Marmoleum, a type of linoleum used in the children's section, is made from linseed oil, woodflour, pine rosin, jute and limestone. The colorful flooring is hygienic, anti-static and biodegradable. It provides no place for dust mites to hide, and it's easy to clean and hardwearing — perfect for kids.

Terrazo floor
Much of the uncarpeted floor areas of the library are made of terrazo. Terrazo consists of marble chips and an epoxy binder that is poured into forms like concrete and when dry, it is then polished. This type of flooring is not only durable and visually pleasing, but also bacteria resistant.

Library Park
The park features a handicapped-accessible serpentine sidewalk, with combination retaining/seating walls along its length. Plants including hydrangea, ornamental grasses and Black-eyed Susans were chosen for the garden because of their interesting textures, colors, forms and seasonal characters. Junipers were chosen to provide year-round color, and large planting areas have been set aside for masses of colorful annuals.

A floor-by-floor look at the main library

First level
(accessed from Main Street)

The Cleveland Cavaliers in cooperation with Project: LEARN will be sponsoring an adult literacy program in a classroom in the library's lower level.

Highlights
The first floor has two computer training rooms, where two full-time trainers will conduct hands-on classes beginning in November.

Second level
(accessed from High Street entrance, Library park pathway and midlevel amphitheater)

Highlights
The 430-seat auditorium has specially designed acoustics and theatrical lighting, and the gently sloping floor makes just about every seat a good one.

Third level
(accessed from elevator tower and stairs)

Highlights
Windows, windows and more windows on the third floor make for some spectacular views and wonderful natural lighting.

creative firm
Akron Beacon Journal
Akron, (Ohio) USA
creatives
Rick Steinhauser
client
Akron Beacon Journal

creative firm
Playboy Enterprises International, Inc.
Chicago, (Illinois) USA
creatives
Tom Staebler, Scott Anderson
client
PLAYBOY Magazine

creative firm
CCM
West Orange, (New Jersey) USA
creatives
Stephen Longo, German Salazar,
Jorawer Singh, Trebor Ricadela,
Elizabeth Bacon
client
County College of Morris

308

Get OVER It!

Post-9/11 everything changed — except the need to see prospects.

BY GEOFFREY JAMES • ILLUSTRATION BY DAV BORDELEAU

creative firm
Selling Power
Fredericksburg, (Virginia) USA
creatives
Colleen Quinnell,
Dav Bordeleau
client
Selling Power Magazine

A FATAL LEGACY

THE RISE AND FALL OF CAVIARTERIA

1
DREAMLAND

BY SIMON COOPER

creative firm
**Playboy Enterprises
International, Inc.**
Chicago, (Illinois) USA
creatives
Jim Imbrogo, Tom Staebler,
Scott Anderson
client
PLAYBOY Magazine

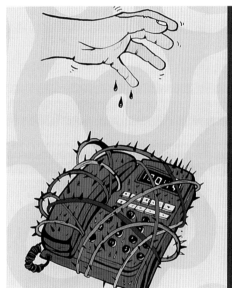

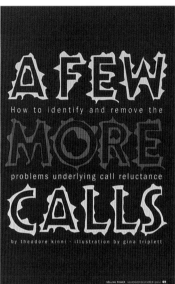

309

THE MICRO**MANAGER**

ILLUSTRATION BY GERARD DUBOIS

BY GEOFFREY JAMES

How to get the most from your team – without micromanaging them into the ground

Nearly every sales rep has experienced it. Times get tough, sales tank and suddenly your sales manager becomes an obsessive micromanager. A manager who demands detailed sales reports, requires reams of customer documentation, requests forecast after forecast, and checks up on every move the sales reps make is simply trying to save the situation. In reality, such managers make a bad time worse. No crisis ever resolved itself because of detail mania. And no team hates being micromanaged more than a sales team. When the manager begins to micromanage, the sales reps start finding ingenious ways around the incessant demands, or worse, downshift their sales activities to accommodate the paranoia, with the end result that sales drop even further.

It doesn't have to be this way, though. While the desire to micromanage can sprout up in even the most talented manager, there are ways to keep the beast at bay. In short, it is definitely possible to manage a sales force to get the best work and the most sales – without driving them crazy.

JULY/AUGUST 2004 SELLING POWER

IS THIS MAN THE FUTURE OF POKER?

MEET DAVID WILLIAMS. HE'S A NERD WHO PLAYED MAGIC. HE'S STILL IN COLLEGE. AND HE JUST WON $3.5 MILLION PLAYING TEXAS HOLD 'EM

BY PAT JORDAN

brand name

How to differentiate your company and your product from **the rest of the herd**

By Theodore B. Kinni
Illustration by Dav Bordeleau

MARCH 2005 SELLING POWER

310

TRADITIONAL ART

DECORATIVE Dolls

人形

THE WORD FOR "DOLL" IN JAPANESE IS WRITTEN with the characters for "person" and "shape," together meaning "something in the shape of a person."

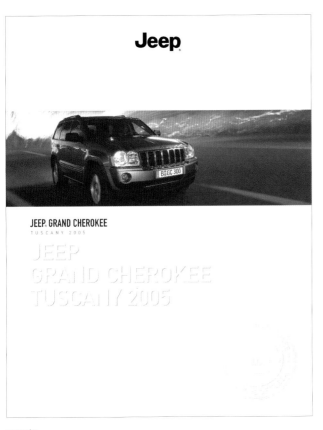

Jeep

JEEP® GRAND CHEROKEE
TUSCANY 2005

JEEP
GRAND CHEROKEE
TUSCANY 2005

creative firm
Design Hoch Drei
Stuttgart, Germany
creatives
Ingo Bitges
client
Daimler Chrysler

Sales
Calls
From
HELL

Nine proven recovery techniques for when your sales calls turn downright disastrous

When your demo products don't work, you mangle your prospect's name or blood splatters over a surgeon who could make or break your entry into a new market, it may seem as if the game is over. Perhaps you should call it a day and head for the nearest boxing ring, where you could take a real beating. Hold on now. Yes, it's tough on the road. And yes, sometimes a sales call can turn into a total disaster. But there's always the hope that you can still pull off the sale. After all, nobody's perfect. Even customers make mistakes. You're allowed to fail – miserably. The key is not in what happened that turned the sale south, but what you did next. Here are nine sales calls from hell. After reading these true stories of real disasters, you'll discover how top salespeople salvage deals from situations that have gone impossibly, horribly wrong.

creative firm
Selling Power
Fredericksburg, (Virginia) USA
creatives
Michael Aubrecht,
Rick Sealock
client
Selling Power Magazine

311

creative firm
Business Travel News
New York, (New York) USA
creatives
Colin Anderson
client
Business Travel News

creative firm
KF Design
Takasaki, Japan
creatives
Kevin Foley, Hiroshi Ohashi,
Hisashi Kondo
client
Jiji Gaho Sha, Inc./APP:Japan+

AL ART

White porcelain, a delicate ceramic of shining purity. Throughout the history of ceramics, surely no other type has been as sought-after and treasured as porcelain. The creation of vessels of white porcelain is an exacting task, demanding pure white clay and highly transparent glazes.

White porcelain is always described as a white ceramic, but the white actually varies according to where and when the porcelain was produced, the people that produced it—even the character of the individual potter. There is also, of course, great variety in the shapes produced; even when vessels are produced in the same

E DELICATE WHITE OF
P O R C E L A I N

Business Travel News
THE NEWSPAPER FOR THE CORPORATE TRAVEL BUYER
November 29, 2004 $15

Redefining Business Travel

creative firm
Dever Designs
Laurel, (Maryland) USA
creatives
Jeffrey Dever, Kristin Devel Duffy,
Jack Gallagher
client
APICS

creative firm
Peterson & Company
Dallas, (Texas) USA
creatives
Miler Hung
client
**Dallas Society of
Visual Communication**

312

creative firm
Heye&Partner GmbH
Unterhaching, (Bavaria) Germany
creatives
Thomas Feicht, Norbert Herold,
Jöerg Stöeckigt, Marc Herold,
Peter Hirrlinger, Andreas Forberger,
Thilo v Büren, Gunnar Immisch,
Dietmar Henneka, Ono Mothwurf,
Florian Ege, Martin Kiebling,
Lothar Hackethal, Jan Okusluk,
Thomas Winkbauer, Otward Buchner
client
INSTANT Corporate Culture

creative firm
Dever Designs
Laurel, (Maryland) USA
creatives
Jeffrey Dever, Sara Tyson
client
Liberty Magazine

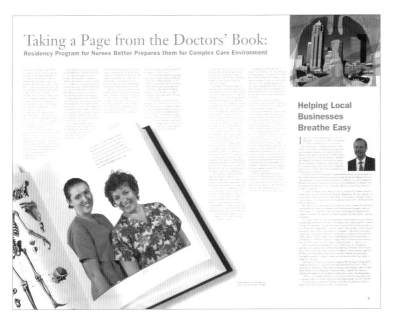

Taking a Page from the Doctors' Book:
Residency Program for Nurses Better Prepares them for Complex Care Environment

Helping Local Businesses Breathe Easy

creative firm
Bertz Design Group
Middletown, (Connecticut) USA
creatives
Richard Uccello,
John Giammatteo
client
Middlesex Hospital

MAXIMUM MEANING MINIMUM MEANS
by Jeff Barfoot

Hello, My Name Is Abram Games
(1914 - 1996)

men who mean business read
THE FINANCIAL TIMES
every day

creative firm
Peterson & Company
Dallas, (Texas) USA
creatives
Dorit Suffness
client
Dallas Society of Visual Communication

creative firm
Portfolio Center
Atlanta, (Georgia) USA
creatives
Curtis Jenkins
client
Interval Magazine

creative firm
Greenspun Media Group
Henderson, (Nevada) USA
creatives
Mami Awamura, Alex Cao
client
The Forum Shops at Caesars

FORUM MOMENTUM

FASHION FORWARD
Experience the newest looks
of The Forum Shops

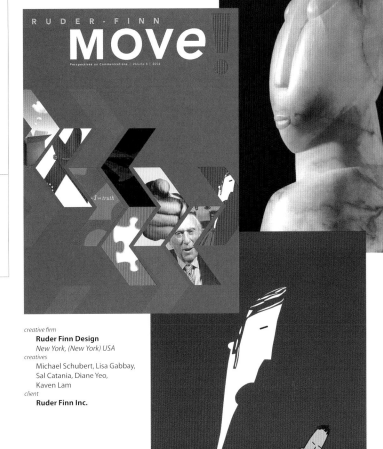

creative firm
Advanstar Medical Economics
Montvale, (New Jersey) USA
creatives
Cheryl Gloss
client
Medical Economics Magazine

creative firm
Ruder Finn Design
New York, (New York) USA
creatives
Michael Schubert, Lisa Gabbay,
Sal Catania, Diane Yeo,
Kaven Lam
client
Ruder Finn Inc.

creative firm
Firefly Studio Pte Ltd
Singapore
creatives
Muhammad Yazid M,
Irene Wong,
Ng Kok Choon
client
The China Club

315

creative firm
Bertz Design Group
Middletown, (Connecticut) USA
creatives
Mark Terranova, Jeff Solak, Richard Uccello,
Dawn Droskoski, John Gibson
client
ING

creative firm
Erwin Zinger Graphic Design
Groningen, The Netherlands
creatives
Erwin Zinger, Marcel Bosma,
Bart Vliegen
client
Aventura Entertainment

Privacy protection is good business

By Michael Mastron

The development of a comprehensive policy on the treatment and use of personal information has involved all of PEO. The engineering regulator is acting voluntarily to show its commitment not only to new government expectations, but also to better protect an easily overlooked but increasingly important commodity.

creative firm
Professional Engineers Ontario
Toronto, (Ontario) Canada
creatives
Luciano Filauro
client
Professional Engineers Ontario

Finding a Job

In this new series, we'll advise you on how to get your career up and running—or get an unsatisfying career back on track somewhere else.

creative firm
Advanstar Medical Economics
Montvale, (New Jersey) USA
creatives
Roger Dowd,
George Baquero,
Gail Garfinkel Weiss
client
Medical Economics

creative firm
Portfolio Center
Atlanta, (Georgia) USA
creatives
Lorenzo Gonzales

creative firm
Dever Designs
Laurel, (Maryland) USA
creatives
Jeffrey Dever, Jim Frazier
client
Psychotherapy Networker

EMPATHY IS THE CONNECTIVE TISSUE of good therapy. It's what enables us to establish bonds of trust with clients, and to meet them with our hearts as well as our minds. Empathy enhances our insights, sharpens our hunches, and, at times, seems to allow us to "read" a client's mind. Yet, vital as it is to our work, empathy has remained a rather fuzzy concept in psychotherapy. To many of us, it seems to arise from a kind of potluck stew of emotional resonance and insight, seasoned with lots of attuned presence and a generous dollop of luck. ■ Far from the therapy office, in the precisely measured environment of the research lab, brain scientists are discovering that a particular cluster of our neurons is specifically designed and primed to mirror another's bodily responses and emotions. We're

EMOTION IN
THE CONSULTING
ROOM IS MORE
CONTAGIOUS THAN
WE THOUGHT

by BABETTE ROTHSCHILD

Mirror

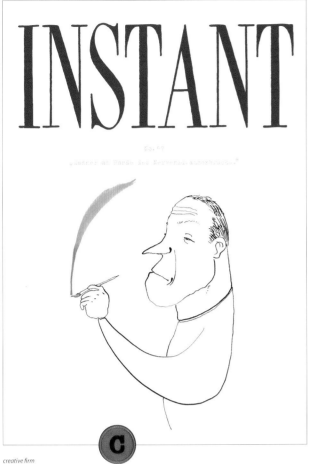

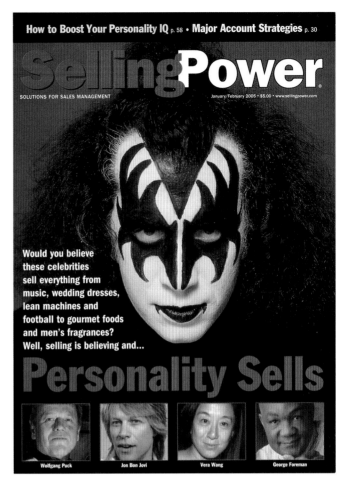

creative firm
Heye&Partner GmbH
Unterhaching, (Bavaria) Germany
creatives
Thomas Feicht, Norbert Herold,
Jöerg Stöeckigt, Marc Herold
client
INSTANT Corporate Culture

creative firm
Greenspun Media Group
Henderson, (Nevada) USA
creatives
Mami Awamura, Alex Cao
client
The Forum Shops at Caesars

creative firm
Creative Link
San Antonio, (Texas) USA
creatives
Mark Broderick, Donna Santos,
Ricardo Barrera, Scott Iden,
Jordan Merson
client
Spurs Sports & Entertainment

creative firm
Selling Power
Fredericksburg, (Virginia) USA
creatives
Colleen Quinnell
client
Selling Power Magazine

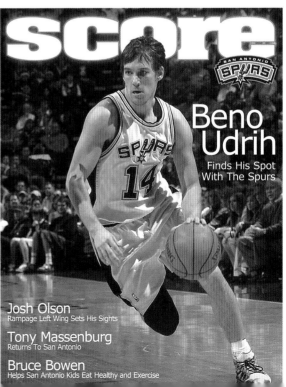

creative firm
Stan Gellman Graphic Design Inc.
St. Louis, (Missouri) USA
creatives
Meg Zelenovich, Bryan Wakeland,
Megan Miller, Barry Tilson
client
St. Louis Commerce Magazine

creative firm
Above Media
Mexico City, Mexico
creatives
Juan Carlos Rivera,
Natalia Velazquez
client
American Express

creative firm
Emphasis Media Limited
Hong Kong, China
creatives
Davide Butson, Julie Man
client
Pernod Ricard Asia

318

creative firm
AMVETS Design Department
Lanham, (Maryland) USA
creatives
Sara Walters,
Ann-Marie Sedor

creative firm
Emphasis Media Limited
Hong Kong, China
creatives
Davide Butson, Alison Lam
client
Dragonair

A SPECIAL SUPPLEMENT TO

DRUGTOPICS
Women's Health

BUSINESSTYLE
El placer de hacer negocios

Javier Sordo Madaleno
La Arquitectura
como emoción

Gilberto Aceves I El negocio del futbol I Scottsdale I Aseguradoras I IAP: viaje 2x1

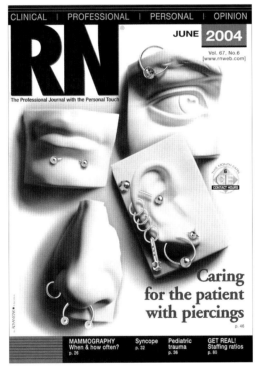

CLINICAL I PROFESSIONAL I PERSONAL I OPINION

RN
JUNE **2004**
Vol. 67, No.6
[www.rnweb.com]

The Professional Journal with the Personal Touch

Caring for the patient with piercings
p. 46

| MAMMOGRAPHY When & how often? p. 26 | Syncope p. 32 | Pediatric trauma p. 36 | GET REAL! Staffing ratios p. 80 |

319

05 SPRING EDITION

HANG SENG BANK

RESTIGE
超越 A Life Full of Achievements

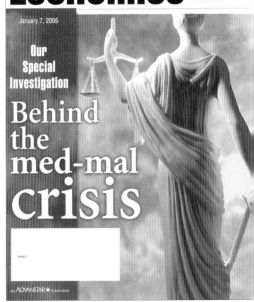

Smarter Business Better Patient Care

Medical Economics
www.memag.com

Answers to your tax questions
p. 44

January 7, 2005

Our Special Investigation

Behind the med-mal crisis

AN ADVANSTAR PUBLICATION

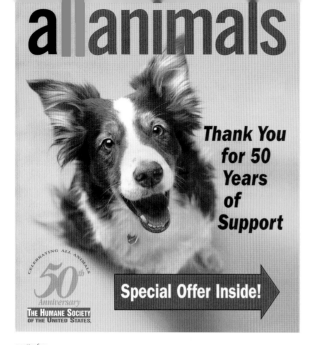

Thank You for 50 Years of Support

CELEBRATING ALL ANIMALS
50th Anniversary
THE HUMANE SOCIETY OF THE UNITED STATES.

Special Offer Inside!

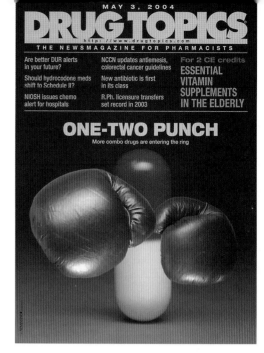

DRUG TOPICS
http://www.drugtopics.com
THE NEWSMAGAZINE FOR PHARMACISTS

Are better DUR alerts in your future?

Should hydrocodone meds shift to Schedule II?

NIOSH issues chemo alert for hospitals

NCCN updates antiemesis, colorectal cancer guidelines

New antibiotic is first in its class

R.Ph. licensure transfers set record in 2003

For 2 CE credits
ESSENTIAL VITAMIN SUPPLEMENTS IN THE ELDERLY

ONE-TWO PUNCH
More combo drugs are entering the ring

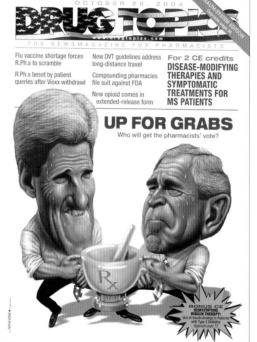

HEALTH-SYSTEM EDITION

DRUG TOPICS
www.drugtopics.com
THE NEWSMAGAZINE FOR PHARMACISTS

Flu vaccine shortage forces R.Ph.s to scramble

R.Ph.s beset by patient queries after Vioxx withdrawl

New DVT guidelines address long-distance travel

Compounding pharmacies file suit against FDA

New opioid comes in extended-release form

For 2 CE credits
DISEASE-MODIFYING THERAPIES AND SYMPTOMATIC TREATMENTS FOR MS PATIENTS

UP FOR GRABS
Who will get the pharmacists' vote?

Rx
2004

BONUS CE
DEMYSTIFYING INSULIN THERAPY:
Use of Insulin Analogs in Patients with Type 2 Diabetes

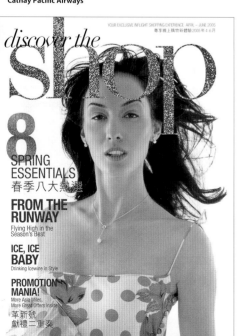

discover the
Shop

YOUR EXCLUSIVE INFLIGHT SHOPPING EXPERIENCE APRIL – JUNE 2005
春季網上購物新體驗 2005年 4-6月

8 SPRING ESSENTIALS
春季八大熱選

FROM THE RUNWAY
Flying High in the Season's Best

ICE, ICE BABY
Drinking Icewine In Style

PROMOTION MANIA!
More Asia Miles, More Great Offers Inside!
革新號
獻禮二重奏

SCORE
SPURS

Edna Campbell
New Silver Stars Guard Has A Story Worth Hearing

Sean Elliott
Retired But Calling The Shots

The Legends Continue
George Gervin
Johnny Moore
David Robinson
James Silas

Dan Hughes
Silver Stars Coach Turning Talent Into Winners

WNBA

Lone Star:
Edna Campbell has a unique perspective as a WNBA player/breast cancer survivor.

3731 1138333
JOHN Q. MEMBER
210.258.1234
sacu.com

Official Credit Union of the San Antonio Spurs

creative firm
Emphasis Media Limited
Hong Kong, China
creatives
Davide Butson, Percy Chung
client
Cathay Pacific Airways

creative firm
Selling Power
Fredericksburg, (Virginia) USA
creatives
Colleen Quinnell
client
Selling Power Magazine

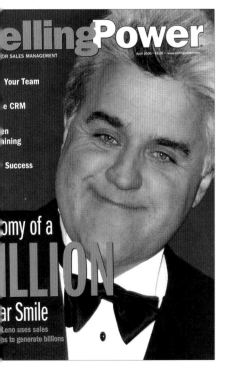

creative firm
Above Media
Mexico City, Mexico
creatives
Juan Carlos Rivera,
Natalia Velazquez
client
American Express

creative firm
Peterson & Company
Dallas, (Texas) USA
creatives
Scott Ray
client
**Dallas Society of
Visual Communication**

321

creative firm
Nesnadny + Schwartz
Cleveland, (Ohio) USA
creatives
Mark Schwartz, Joyce Nesnadny,
Michelle Moehler, Nicholas Watts
client
The Hearst Corporation

creative firm
Wendell Minor Design
Washington,
(Connecticut) USA
creatives
Wendell Minor, Al Cetta
client
Harper Collins

creative firm
Phil Jordan and Associates, Inc.
Arlington, (Virginia) USA
creatives
Michael Deas
client
U.S. Postal Service

creative firm
Advanstar Medical Economics
Montvale, (New Jersey) USA
creatives
Thomas Darnsteadt, Dale Stephanos
client
Drug Topics Magazine

creative firm
Playboy Enterprises
International, Inc.
Chicago, (Illinois) USA
creatives
Mike Benny, Tom Staebler,
Rob Wilson
client
PLAYBOY Magazine

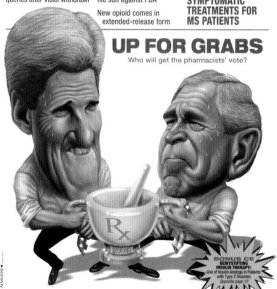

creative firm
Q
Wiesbaden, Germany
creatives
Thilo von Debschitz, von Zubinski Labor
client
Arjo Wiggins

creative firm
Heye&Partner GmbH
Unterhaching, (Bavaria)
Germany
creatives
Thomas Feicht, Norbert Herold,
Jöerg Stöeckigt, Marc Herold
client
INSTANT Corporate Culture

creative firm
Rodgers Townsend
St. Louis, (Missouri) USA
creatives
Tom Hudder,
Luke Partridge,
Kris Wright,
Mike McCormick
client
Ameren UE

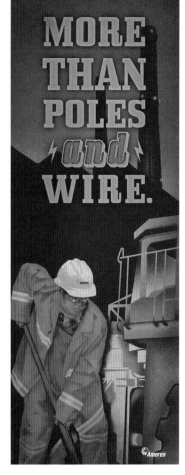

323

creative firm
Rick Sealock
Kitchener, (Ontario) Canada
creatives
Rick Sealock
client
Rick Sealock

creative firm
Hitchcock Fleming & Associates, Inc.
Akron, (Ohio) USA
creatives
Nick Betro, Bob Clancy, Max Ulichney
client
Dunlop

creative firm
Wendell Minor Design
*Washington,
(Connecticut) USA*
creatives
Wendell Minor, Al Cetta
client
Harper Collins

324

creative firm
**Playboy Enterprises
International, Inc.**
Chicago, (Illinois) USA
creatives
Dade Orgeron, Tom Staebler,
Scott Anderson
client
PLAYBOY Magazine

creative firm
Rick Sealock
Kitchener, (Ontario) Canada
creatives
Rick Sealock
client
Rick Sealock

HOLY WAR

IT'S EASY
TO RECOGNIZE
RELIGIOUS
EXTREMISM ABROAD.
BUT CAN WE
RECOGNIZE IT
AT HOME?

creative firm
Playboy Enterprises International, Inc.
Chicago, (Illinois) USA
creatives
John Thompson, Tom Staebler,
Rob Wilson
client
PLAYBOY Magazine

Paper and
plastic jewels
Making necklace,
bracelet, ring sure to keep
babe sitter happy, too.
E2

PETS
Vet-assisted farewells poignant and humane

Good bad black cat stole piece of her heart

HOME SECURITY

Know the neighbors.
Landscaping, lights,
even a dog dish
may deter
intruders. And
close garage door

Story by **MARY BETH BRECKENRIDGE** / Illustration by **JEMAL R. BRINSON**

HOMEBODY

Apartment dweller has green thumb

Gardens, bird feeders benefit fellow tenants

Keep mower in tiptop shape

325

creative firm
Sagon-Phior
Los Angeles, (California) USA
creatives
Sagon-Phior
McCormick Distilling Co.

creative firm
Akron Beacon Journal
Akron, (Ohio) USA
creatives
Jemal R. Brinson
client
Akron Beacon Journal

creative firm
Playboy Enterprises International, Inc.
Chicago, (Illinois) USA
creatives
Ralph Steadman, Tom Staebler,
Scott Anderson
client
PLAYBOY Magazine

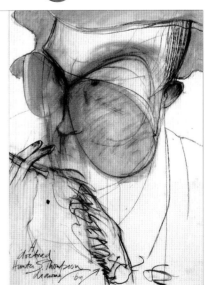

creative firm
Akron Beacon Journal
Akron, (Ohio) USA
creatives
Kathy Hagedorn
client
Akron Beacon Journal

creative firm
**Playboy Enterprises
International, Inc.**
Chicago, (Illinois) USA
creatives
Dave McKean, Tom Staebler
client
PLAYBOY Magazine

327

creative firm
Kessler Design Group
Arlington, (Virginia) USA
creatives
John Dawson
client
U.S. Postal Service

creative firm
**Playboy Enterprises
International, Inc.**
Chicago, (Illinois) USA
creatives
Nick Dewar, Tom Staebler
client
PLAYBOY Magazine

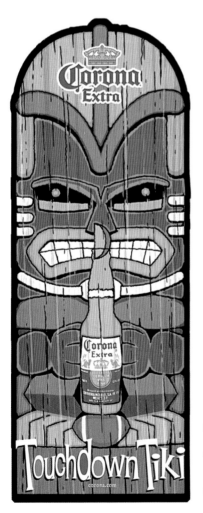

creative firm
Creative Link
San Antonio, (Texas) USA
creatives
Mark Broderick,
Scott Iden,
Ricardo Barrera
client
The Gambrinus Company

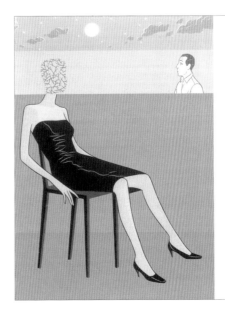

328

creative firm
Rodgers Townsend
St. Louis, (Missouri) USA
creatives
Tom Hudder, Luke Partridge,
Kris Wright, Mike McCormick
client
Ameren UE

creative firm
Derry Noyes Graphics
Arlington, (Virginia) USA
creatives
Derry Noyes
client
U.S. Postal Service

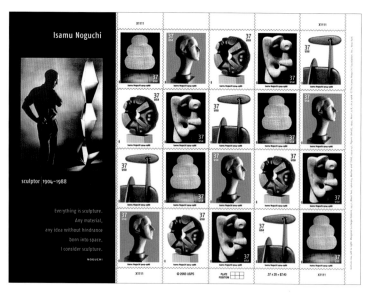

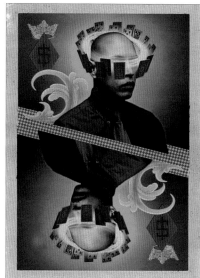
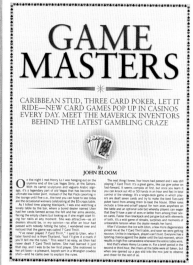

creative firm
Playboy Enterprises International, Inc.
Chicago, (Illinois) USA
creatives
Amy Guip, Tom Staebler,
Rob Wilson
client
PLAYBOY Magazine

creative firm
**Playboy Enterprises
International, Inc.**
Chicago, (Illinois) USA
creatives
Phil Hale, Tom Staebler
client
PLAYBOY Magazine

ART OF THE AMERICAN INDIAN

mbres bowl USA37 Kutenai parfleche USA37 Tlingit sculptures USA37 Ho-Chunk bag USA37 Seminole doll USA37

ississippian effigy USA37 Acoma pot USA37 Navajo weaving USA37 Seneca carving USA37 Luiseño basket USA37

creative firm
Rodgers Townsend
St. Louis, (Missouri) USA
creatives
Tom Hudder,
Luke Partridge,
Kris Wright,
Mike McCormick
client
Ameren UE

SLEEP EASY. *we* NEVER REST.

creative firm
R. Dana Sheaff & Company
Arlington, (Virginia) USA
creatives
Richard Sheaff
client
U.S. Postal Service

329

Lawyers Gone Wild

Was Ness Motley the legal world's Animal House?

By Heather Smith
Illustration by Craig LaRotonda

creative firm
The American Lawyer
New York, (New York) USA
creatives
Darlene Simidian,
Craig LaRotonda
client
The American Lawyer

overheard

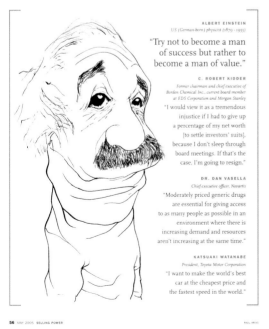

ALBERT EINSTEIN
US (German-born) physicist (1879 - 1955)
"Try not to become a man
of success but rather to
become a man of value."

C. ROBERT KIDDER
*Former chairman and chief executive of
Borden Chemical Inc.; current board member
at EDS Corporation and Morgan Stanley*
"I would view it as a tremendous
injustice if I had to give up
a percentage of my net worth
[to settle investors' suits],
because I don't sleep through
board meetings. If that's the
case, I'm going to resign."

DR. DAN VASELLA
Chief executive officer, Novartis
"Moderately priced generic drugs
are essential for giving access
to as many people as possible in an
environment where there is
increasing demand and resources
aren't increasing at the same time."

KATSUAKI WATANABE
President, Toyota Motor Corporation
"I want to make the world's best
car at the cheapest price and
the fastest speed in the world."

56 MAY 2005 SELLING POWER

creative firm
Selling Power
Fredericksburg, (Virginia) USA
creatives
Colleen Quinnell,
Raul Arias
client
Selling Power Magazine

creative firm
Rick Sealock
*Kitchener, (Ontario)
Canada*
creatives
Rick Sealock
client
Rick Sealock

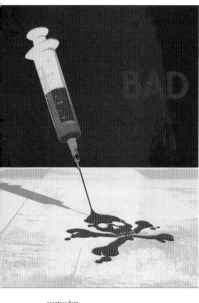

BLOOD

In the 1980s, thousands of hemophiliacs around the world became infected with HIV after using tainted blood products. Could their illnesses and deaths have been prevented?

By Elizabeth Amon

BLOOD, SWEAT & TRADE SECRETS
In which our reporter-spy conducts a personal investigation into Mexican border factories known as maquiladoras

by William T. Vollmann

creative firm
The American Lawyer
New York, (New York) USA
creatives
Joan Ferrell, John Ritter
client
The American Lawyer

creative firm
**Playboy Enterprises
International, Inc.**
Chicago, (Illinois) USA
creatives
James Jean, Tom Staebler,
Rob Wilson
client
PLAYBOY Magazine

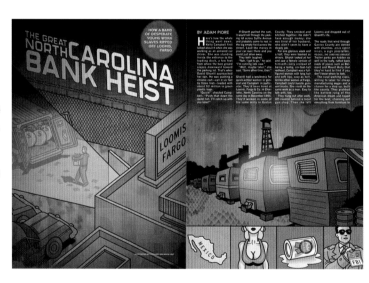

THE GREAT NORTH CAROLINA BANK HEIST

HOW A BAND OF DESPERATE YOUNG WORK SLAVES RIPPED OFF LOOMIS FARGO

BY ADAM PIORE

330

creative firm
**Playboy Enterprises
International, Inc.**
Chicago, (Illinois) USA
creatives
Tom Staebler,
Rob Wilson
client
PLAYBOY Magazine

creative firm
**Playboy Enterprises
International, Inc.**
Chicago, (Illinois) USA
creatives
Martin Hoffman, Tom Staebler,
Scott Anderson
client
PLAYBOY Magazine

creative firm
Ice House Graphics
Arlington, (Virginia) USA
creatives
Howard Paine
client
U.S. Postal Service

CLOUDSCAPES

Cirrus radiatus	Cirrostratus fibratus	Cirrocumulus undulatus	Cumulonimbus mammatus	Cumulonimbus incus
Altocumulus stratiformis	Altostratus translucidus	Altocumulus undulatus	Altocumulus castellanus	Altocumulus lenticularis
Stratocumulus undulatus	Stratus opacus	Cumulus humilis	Cumulus congestus	Cumulonimbus with tornado

© 2003 USPS

37 x 15 $5.55

X1111   PLATE POSITION   X1111

THE HANDYMAN

BY RICH COHEN

AFTER COLLEGE AND BEFORE SHAME SET IN, LUKE MADE A CAREER OUT OF BEING USEFUL TO THE MARRIED WOMEN OF HIS TOWN

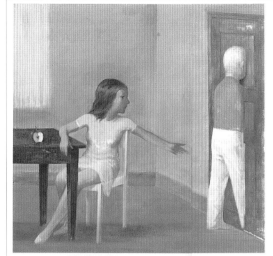

EVEN WHEN HE WAS SURROUNDED
BY WOMEN, DAD KEPT FADING
INTO THE FUTURE

THE
AFTER
LIFE

FICTION BY AMY HEMPEL

creative firm
Rick Sealock
Kitchener, (Ontario) Canada
creatives
Robert Parsons, Rick Sealock
client
Boston Magazine

creative firm
**Playboy Enterprises
International, Inc.**
Chicago, (Illinois) USA
creatives
Gerard Dubois, Tom Staebler
client
PLAYBOY Magazine

Business,
INTERRUPTED

By Carlyn Kolker

COMMERCIAL LITIGATION

331

creative firm
The American Lawyer
New York, (New York) USA
creatives
Joan Ferrell,
Poul Hans Lange
client
The American Lawyer

creative firm
**Playboy Enterprises
International, Inc.**
Chicago, (Illinois) USA
creatives
Phil Hale, Tom Staebler
client
PLAYBOY Magazine

creative firm
**Playboy Enterprises
International, Inc.**
Chicago, (Illinois) USA
creatives
Geoffrey Grahn, Tom Staebler
client
PLAYBOY Magazine

THE REVENGE OF THE
GODFATHER

A STARTLING PREVIEW
OF THE NEW SEQUEL
TO MARIO PUZO'S
THE GODFATHER

FICTION BY MARK WINEGARDNER

PUNCHDRUNK
WHEN ALL ELSE FAILS, VIOLENCE IS THE ONLY WAY TO GIVE PEACE A CHANCE

FICTION BY CHUCK PALAHNIUK

creative firm
Rienzi & Rienzi Communications
Montville, (New Jersey) USA
creatives
Mary Gayle Scheper, Edward Horvath,
Frank Aiello, Kim Langley
client
Mylan Pharmaceuticals Inc.

creative firm
Emerson, Wajdowicz Studios
New York, (New York) USA
creatives
Jurek Wajdowicz, Lisa LaRochelle, Yoko Yoshida
Members of Magnum Photos
client
Smart Papers

creative firm
Emerson, Wajdowicz Studios
New York, (New York) USA
creatives
Jurek Wajdowicz, Lisa LaRochelle,
Jonas Bendiksen, Yoko Yoshida
client
The Rockefeller Foundation

creative firm
People Magazine Specials
New York, (New York) USA
creatives
Jessica Bryan, Joe Schmelzer
client
People Magazine

Off the Charts

Usher, Johnny, Colin, Brad . . . the sexiness of these superstars can't be measured

USHER

He's smooth as silk and hard as rock, able to sing a steamy slow jam and get clubs pounding to the lola oh! oh! C'mon willing Oh Confessions. When did former teen phenom Usher Ray mond IV, now 26, grow up? And where did he get the kind of wisdom that separates the men from the boys? To wit:

> **"THE BEST PRESENT A MAN CAN GIVE A WOMAN IS HIS UNDIVIDED ATTENTION."**

Photographs by MATTHIAS CLAMER

82

creative firm
People Magazine Specials
New York, (New York) USA
creatives
Maddy Miller, Matthias Clamer
client
People Magazine

Beauty CLOSE-UP

MARTHA STEWART

Making the best of a bad thing, Stewart is back and looking better than ever. She speaks candidly about surviving Alderson, her post-prison routine and the joys of fitting into her favorite jeans

106

333

creative firm
Nesnadny + Schwartz
Cleveland, (Ohio) USA
creatives
Mark Schwartz, Stacie Ross, Lois Conner
client
Vassar College

White Oak (Quercus alba), 1930 Class Tree, near the Shakespeare Garden

creative firm
People Magazine Specials
New York, (New York) USA
creatives
Maddy Miller, John Huba
client
People Magazine

creative firm
People Magazine Specials
New York, (New York) USA
creatives
Maddy Miller
client
People Magazine

creative firm
People Magazine Specials
New York, (New York) USA
creatives
Jessica Bryan, Anthony Mandler
client
People Magazine

ANN-MARGRET & LINDSAY LOHAN

film star and the 18-year-old ingenue have often been compared. We get them together for the first time

> There's a certain fire with red-heads. Spunk"
> —LINDSAY LOHAN

JAKE GYLLENHAAL

Five reasons we love Jake Gyllenhaal

Do You Think I'm Sexy?

These women of *The Apprentice* don't agree on much, but they all say Donald Trump is one hot mogul

"Donald is definitely one of the sexiest men on earth. Being sexy is not always looking like a Tom Cruise—it's the whole package. Plus, he's got these pouty little lips I just love."
—Heidi Bressler

"When Trump walks into the room he commands it. Most men are not capable of this type of aura. The way he looks at you is sexy. You know he's a man and not a boy."
—Stacie J.

"The man exudes immediate appeal by exerting an unparalleled sense of self. This is an attribute that excites many a woman in today's society. Confidence is sexy."
—Katrina Campins

"I've always been attracted to strong and powerful men. Smart, rich and funny equals sexy in my book. His mega sense of humor really does match his big personality."
—Omarosa Manigault-Stallworth

"He's the kind of guy who is comfortable in his shoes. When a man just walks in the room and moves in his body so comfortably—that's a sexy trait."
—Elizabeth Jarosz

"He's quite a man. After getting fired it's pretty hard to call him sexy, but there is a softer side that people don't get to see. He has a little gleaming sparkle of sexiness, and when you're in his presence, you can't help but be attracted to that."
—Jennifer Crisafulli

Clockwise from bottom left: Heidi Bressler, Stacie J., Katrina Campins, Omarosa Manigault-Stallworth, Elizabeth Jarosz and Jennifer Crisafulli.

134

DONALD TRUMP
"THESE ARE SPECIAL WOMEN, SO IF THEY THINK I'M SEXY, THAT'S OKAY WITH ME. I DON'T RATE MY SEXY, I LET OTHER PEOPLE DO IT"

Photograph by TROY WORD

creative firm
People Magazine Specials
New York, (New York) USA
creatives
Maddy Miller, Troy Word
client
People Magazine

04 LIBERIA 03 **Independence in action**
As Liberia's Civil War Escalates, MSF Responds with Medical Care for Thousands

creative firm
Emerson, Wajdowicz Studios
New York, (New York) USA
creatives
Jurek Wajdowicz, Lisa LaRochelle, Francisco Zizola, Jodi Biber, Teun Voeten, Jean-Marc Giboux, Kris Torgeson, Yoko Yoshida
client
Médecins Sans Frontiéres USA

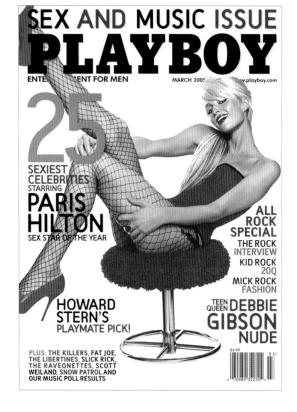

SEX AND MUSIC ISSUE
PLAYBOY
ENTERTAINMENT FOR MEN   MARCH 2005   www.playboy.com

25 SEXIEST CELEBRITIES STARRING
PARIS HILTON
SEX STAR OF THE YEAR

ALL ROCK SPECIAL
THE ROCK INTERVIEW
KID ROCK 20Q
MICK ROCK FASHION

TEEN QUEEN DEBBIE GIBSON NUDE

HOWARD STERN'S PLAYMATE PICK!

PLUS: THE KILLERS, FAT JOE, THE LIBERTINES, SLICK RICK, THE RAVEONETTES, SCOTT WEILAND, SNOW PATROL AND OUR MUSIC POLL RESULTS

$4.99   03>

creative firm
Playboy Enterprises International, Inc.
Chicago, (Illinois) USA
creatives
Odette Sugerman, Tom Staebler
client
PLAYBOY Magazine

334

creative firm
People Magazine Specials
New York, (New York) USA
creatives
Rina Migliaccio, Maddy Miller, Kenneth Willardt
client
People Magazine

creative firm
Playboy Enterprises International, Inc.
Chicago, (Illinois) USA
creatives
Ken Nahoum, Tom Staebler, Scott Anderson
client
PLAYBOY Magazine

Drew Barrymore

She started exercising and eating better

AGE 30 ACTRESS

Why? "It wasn't about my figure. I felt heavy and lethargic, so I started exercising to feel more fit and have more energy. Then it snowballed into, 'Oh, I feel good, and I want to keep it going.'"

How much did you lose? "20 lbs."

And now? "I eat anything I want. Sometimes my portions are smaller. Or I eat more protein than carbs. But here's a radical statement: I refuse to give up the foods I love—macaroni and cheese, anything fried, potatoes any style, iceberg lettuce and avocados."

Were you really called Fatso as a kid? "Yeah, my hair and I were getting made fun of."

What would you say to that person now? "Thank you for being so mean to me. You only made me stronger."

MY LOOK

TRANSFORMATIONS

These stars come clean about their beauty evolutions

Photographed by KENNETH WILLARDT

PLAY
Terrell Owens
20

The media doesn't like the opinionated Eagle attitude, but he still lets loose—on and off the f

Interview by Dovey Mama

They're Back
...and better than ever!

Where have you been, hunky stars of '90s shows?
And thanks for returning in such fine form!

MATTHEW FOX

AGE: 38 **NOW:** Dr. Jack Shephard on ABC's hit drama *Lost*. **YOU REMEMBER HIM AS:** Charlie Salinger (left), the oldest orphan on *Party of Five*. **WHERE HE'S BEEN:** Spending time with his family (wife Margherita and their two children). "I needed to find more of a balance with my work and being a father and husband," he says. **STAYED HOT BY:** Running, surfing and road biking. But, Fox confesses, "I've almost made an effort to booze and smoke just to give myself a little more character." **HE STILL HAS IT:** "He's matured beautifully," says his *Lost* costar Evangeline Lilly. "Before, he was just a boy." Says Fox: "I'm not no baby-faced. I feel like more of a man." **WHY HE'S HAVING THE TIME OF HIS LIFE:** All the pistons are firing both professionally and personally. "I'm in a really great place now," he says. "I've been doing this for 15 years, and I feel like I'm better at it than I've ever been."

138 November 29, 2004 PEOPLE

Photograph by ALISON DYER

creative firm
People Magazine Specials
New York, (New York) USA
creatives
Ann Tortorelli, Alison Dyer
client
People Magazine

FARNSWORTH BENTLEY

REAL NAME: DEREK WATKINS
AGE: 30 **HEIGHT:** 6'1¾"
PROFESSION: RENAISSANCE MAN
RESIDENCE: WEST HOLLYWOOD, CALIF.

Here's what he can do for you:
Sing. "I'm doing dissertation over instrumental, which other people call rapping." See him do it in a Tommy Jeans ad campaign next month and an upcoming Kanye West video.
Shop. He recalls a date at the mall when he was in his early 20s. "I got her some $22 earrings. They were fabulous."
Hold your umbrella. (Remember? He shot to fame as P. Diddy's umbrella holder.)
Cover your phone. "I usually have different phone covers on my phone. Right now I have a dalmatian. And I just got a pug."
Give hugs. "You need seven hugs a day to be adequate," he says. "I truly believe that."

Photograph by LARSEN & TALBERT

95

creative firm
People Magazine Specials
New York, (New York) USA
creatives
Brian Belovitch, Larsen & Talbert
client
People Magazine

creative firm
People Magazine Specials
New York, (New York) USA
creatives
Maddy Miller, Tamara Reynolds
client
People Magazine

creative firm
CSC-P2 Communications Services
Falls Church, (Virginia) USA
creatives
Aaron Robilis
client
CSC

335

STEVEN LOPEZ

AGE: 25 **HEIGHT:** 6'2"
SPORT: TAE KWON DO
RESIDENCE: SUGARLAND, TEXAS

Laurels: First Olympic gold medalist and two-time world champion in tae kwon do.
How training cramps his love life: "My routine is home, train, home, train, eat, sleep, train," he says. "In high school I didn't date at all."
What he means when he says he's a mama's boy. "I was brought up in a Latin-Hispanic family, where my mother did most everything. The woman in my life is going to have to treat she as well as my mother has."
Why a woman might not mind: "He has the biggest heart of any human I've ever met in my life," says older brother Jean. "He's supportive and compassionate and intelligent and is going to make a lady very lucky."

88

Photograph by TAMARA REYNOLDS

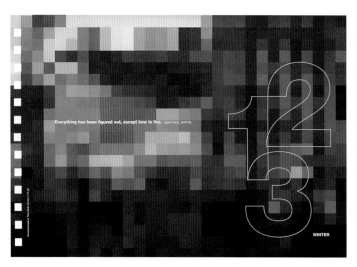

creative firm
Emerson, Wajdowicz Studios
New York, (New York) USA
creatives
Jurek Wajdowicz, Lisa LaRochelle, Yoko Yoshida
Members of Magnum Photos,
client
Smart Papers

creative firm
Bowling Green State University
Bowling Green, (Ohio) USA
creatives
Elaine Korenich, Lori Young
client
Elaine Korenich

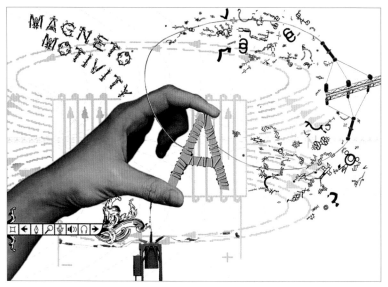

creative firm
Les Cheneaux Design
Bowling Green, (Ohio) USA
creatives
Lori Young
client
Les Cheneaux Design

creative firm
Grafik
Alexandria, (Virginia) USA
creatives
Michael J. Mateos,
John Vitorovich
client
Grafik

creative firm
Stream Companies
Malvern, (Pennsylvania) USA
creatives
Jason Brennan, Michael Robinson
client
Stream Companies

creative firm
30sixty advertising+design
Los Angeles, (California) USA
creatives
Henry Vizcarra, David Fuscellero,
Lee Barett
client
30sixty advertising+design

creative firm
Axion Design Inc.
San Anselmo, (California) USA
client
Axion Design Inc.

creative firm
ds & f
Washington, (D.C.) USA
creatives
Don Schaaf & Staff
client
Don Schaaf & Friends, Inc.

338

creative firm
Hornall Anderson Design Works
Seattle, (Washington) USA
creatives
Sonja Max, Henry Yiu,
Andrew Wicklund, Leo Raymundo
client
Hornall Anderson Design Works

creative firm
Dezainwerkz
Singapore
creatives
Xavier Sanjiman, Shawn Yeo
client
Dezainwerkz

creative firm
CMT Creative
New York, (New York) USA
creatives
James Hitchcock, Michael Engleman,
Carla Daeninclex, Emilie Schnick,
Nora Gaffney, David Bennett
client
CMT Creative

creative firm
Torre Lazur McCann
Parsippany, (New Jersey) USA
creatives
Gail Benlese, Maureen O'Rourke

creative firm
Levine & Associates
Washington, (D.C.) USA
creatives
Jennie Jariel, Lena Markley,
Monica Snellings, Megan Riordan,
Kari Laerden, Maureen Myer
client
Levine & Associates

creative firm
Design Nut
Kensington, (Maryland) USA
creatives
Brent M. Almond, CopyCraft
client
Design Nut

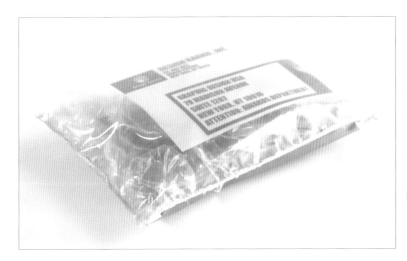

creative firm
DesignKarma Inc.
New York, (New York) USA
creatives
Vitaliy Yasch,
Timofei Yuriev,
Sherri Valenti
client
DesignKarma Inc.

339

creative firm
Turner Duckworth
 London & San Francisco
Chiswick, (London) England
creatives
David Turner, Bruce Duckworth,
Shawn Rosenberger, Wendi Nordeck
client
Turner Duckworth
London & San Francisco

creative firm
Riordon Design
Oakville, (Ontario) Canada
creatives
Ric Riordon, Alan Krpan,
Dawn Charney
client
Riordon Design

What I did on my summer vacation...   *I went out on a boat,*   *and went out to eat,*   *played on my computer,*   *and got a sun tan*

ASTRA PHARMACEUTICALS,
NEW YORK CONVENTION INVITATION

ZOE RESTAURANT LOGO,
SOHO, NEW YORK CITY

SHERLOCK, WINDOWS SOFTWARE
PACKAGING & ADVERTISING

NATIONAL SUN PROTECTION
ADVISORY COUNSEL LOGO

creative firm
John Kneapler Design
New York, (New York) USA
creatives
John Kneapler, Chris Dietrich
client
John Kneapler

340

creative firm
Zunda Design Group
South Norwalk, (Connecticut) USA
creatives
Charles Zunda, Dan Price
client
Zunda Design Group

creative firm
Fixation Marketing
Washington, (D.C.) USA
creatives
Bruce E. Morgan, John Frantz,
Elizabeth Ellen, Randy Guseman,
Kathryn Tidyman
client
Fixation Marketing

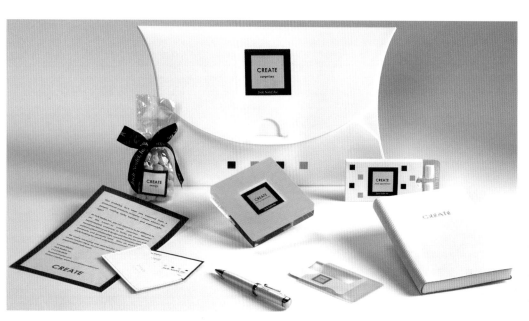

creative firm
Jack Nadel, Inc.
Los Angeles, (California) USA
creatives
Lauren Blaker,
Rachel Zagoren
client
Jack Nadel, Inc.

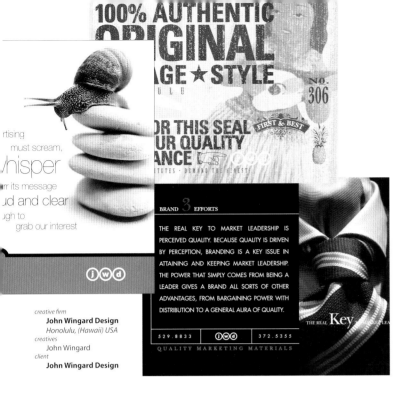

BRAND **3** EFFORTS

THE REAL KEY TO MARKET LEADERSHIP IS PERCEIVED QUALITY. BECAUSE QUALITY IS DRIVEN BY PERCEPTION, BRANDING IS A KEY ISSUE IN ATTAINING AND KEEPING MARKET LEADERSHIP. THE POWER THAT SIMPLY COMES FROM BEING A LEADER GIVES A BRAND ALL SORTS OF OTHER ADVANTAGES, FROM BARGAINING POWER WITH DISTRIBUTION TO A GENERAL AURA OF QUALITY.

529.8833   372.5355

QUALITY MARKETING MATERIALS

THE REAL Key

creative firm
John Wingard Design
Honolulu, (Hawaii) USA
creatives
John Wingard
client
John Wingard Design

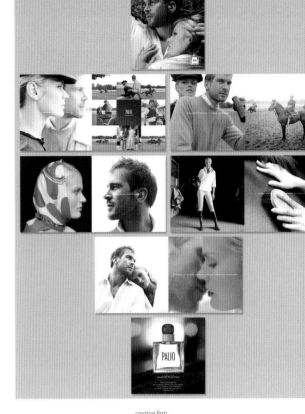

creative firm
Palio Communications
Saratoga Springs, (New York) USA
creatives
Guy Mastrion, Todd LaRoche,
Jack Hyndman, Michael Costello,
Alan Steele, Chip Quayle,
John Elford, Marcia Lyon
client
Palio Communications

341

creative firm
X Design Company
Denver, (Colorado) USA
creatives
Alex Valderrama,
Nate Valderrama
client
X Design Company

creative firm
Coates and Coates
Naperville, (Illinois) USA
creatives
Carolin Coates
client
Coates and Coates

creative firm
LTD Creative
Frederick, (Maryland) USA
creatives
Timothy Finnen,
Louanne Welgoss,
Kimberly Dow
client
LTD Creative

creative firm
KBDA
Los Angeles, (California) USA
creatives
Kim Baer, Keith Knueven,
Jill Vacarra
client
KBDA

creative firm
Jack Nadel, Inc.
Los Angeles, (California) USA
creatives
Debbie Abergel
client
Jack Nadel, Inc.

creative firm
DesignKarma Inc.
New York, (New York) USA
creatives
Vitaliy Yasch,
Timofei Yuriev,
Sherri Valenti
client
DesignKarma Inc.

342

creative firm
LTD Creative
Frederick, (Maryland) USA
creatives
Timothy Finnen, Louanne Welgoss,
Kimberly Dow
client
LTD Creative

creative firm
30sixty advertising+design
Los Angeles, (California) USA
creatives
Henry Vizcarra, Pär Larsson
client
30sixty advertising+design

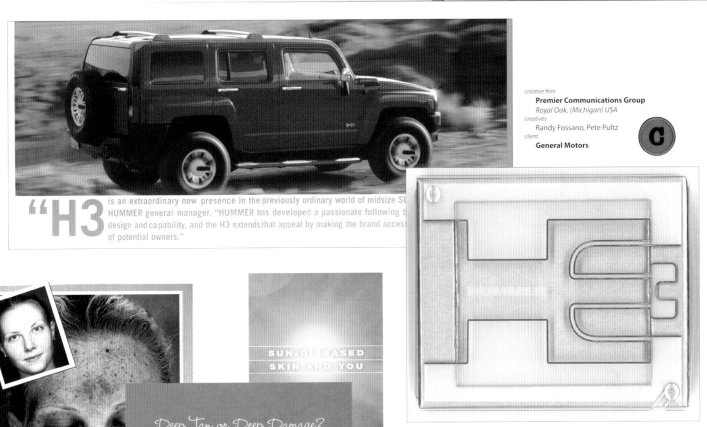

"**H3** is an extraordinary new presence in the previously ordinary world of midsize SU[...] HUMMER general manager. "HUMMER has developed a passionate following b[...] design and capability, and the H3 extends that appeal by making the brand access[...] of potential owners."

creative firm
Premier Communications Group
Royal Oak, (Michigan) USA
creatives
Randy Fossano, Pete Pultz
client
General Motors

SUN-DISEASED
SKIN AND YOU

Deep Tan or Deep Damage?

Take a Look Inside.

Skin Remembers...

[...] long recognized the harmful effects of the sun and ultravio[...]
[...] by this UV detect photo depicting sun-damage lurking be[...]
[...] trigger your skin to burn, age prematurely and can lead to[...]
[...] is not a diagnostic tool and should not be used to detect sk[...]
[...] ks of UV rays and discuss any potential sun-damage you m[...]
[...] k-up with a dermatologist.

creative firm
KPR
New York, (New York) USA
creatives
Bernard Steinman, Letty Albarran,
Mitch Siegel, Ianine Chianese,
Annie Yoo
client
3M Pharmaceuticals

creative firm
Premier Communications Group
Royal Oak, (Michigan) USA
creatives
Randy Fossano, Patrick Hatfield
client
General Motors

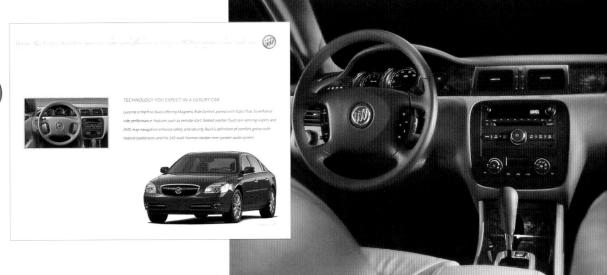

TECHNOLOGY YOU EXPECT IN A LUXURY CAR

Lucerne is the first Buick offering Magnetic Ride Control, paired with StabiliTrak, to enhance
ride performance. Features such as remote start, heated washer fluid, rain-sensing wipers and
DVD map navigation enhance safety and security. Buick's definition of comfort grows with
heated/cooled seats and the 245-watt Harman Kardon nine-speaker audio system.

press release

helped complete the Solstice's design efficiently and economically. For example, the rear corner lamps are from the GMC Envoy, while door handles, fog lamps, seats, engine and transmission are shared with other GM vehicles.

However, some parts are all Solstice. The taillamps, for instance, were designed with special reflectors to eliminate the need for a separate side marker light. This not only contributes to the car's sleek design, but also eliminates the cost of a separate marker lens and bulb.

Interior design is equally purposeful and clever, with details like pedals placed for easy heel-and-toe driving and a cockpit-style instrument panel that sweeps around the driver. Designers also worked with chassis engineers to optimize the placement of the shifter. Manual shifter throws between gear changes were studied and shortened.

05

PERFORMANCE

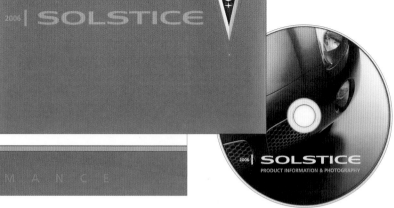

"When you interior des between ge tune the be

A turning p The produc already incl

"Solstice is "Everyone statement a

Its fast-track process that

"The GTO a performanc dimension t

creative firm
Premier Communications Group
Royal Oak, (Michigan) USA
creatives
Randy Fossano, Patrick Hatfield
client
General Motors

344 creative firm
Dever Designs
Laurel, (Maryland) USA
creatives
Jeffrey Dever, Caroline Cruz
client
**IAAPA-International Association
of Amusement Parks and Attractions**

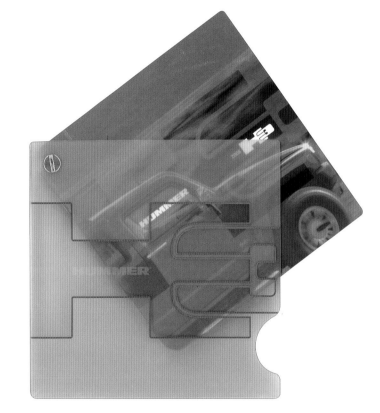

creative firm
Premier Communications Group
Royal Oak, (Michigan) USA
creatives
Randy Fossano, Pete Pultz
client
General Motors

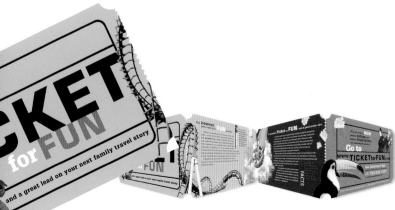

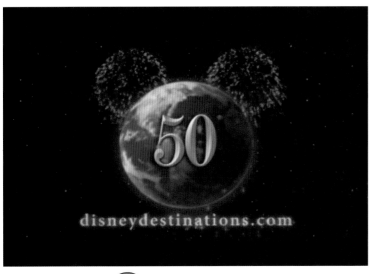

creative firm
Leo Burnett/Chicago
Chicago, (Illinois) USA
creatives
Ned Crowley, Jon Moore,
Joe Pytka
client
Disneyland Resort

creative firm
McCann Erickson Korea
Seoul, Korea
creatives
KY An, JH Cho, Moonsun Choi
client
Hanaro Telecom

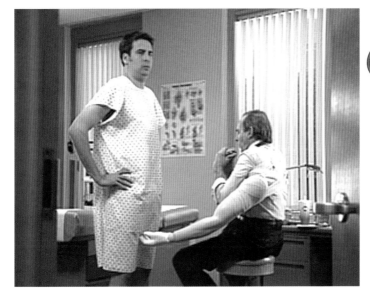

creative firm
Grey Worldwide NY
New York, (New York) USA
creatives
Tim Mellors,
Jonathan Rodgers,
Ari Halper,
Steve Krauss,
Diana Gay
client
Dairy Queen

345

creative firm
Bruketa & Zinic
Zagreb, Croatia
creatives
Tonka Lujanac
client
Jamnica d.d.

creative firm
Dieste Harmel & Partners
Dallas, (Texas) USA
creatives
Dieste Harmel & Partners
Creative Team
client
Anheuser-Busch, Bud Light

creative firm
EyeballNYC
New York, (New York) USA
creatives
Limore Shur, Andrea Dionisio,
Adam Gault, Stuart Simms,
Carl Mok, Danny Kamhaji,
Allison Kocar, John Brennick
client
Outdoor Life Network

creative firm
Grey Worldwide NY
New York, (New York) USA
creatives
Tim Mellors, Mark Catalina,
Mike Ryniec, Lori Bullock
client
NY Jets

346

creative firm
MARC USA
Pittsburgh, (Pennsylvania) USA
creatives
Tony Jaffe, Ron Sullivan,
Laurie Habeeb, Marianne Shaffer
client
Mohawk Flooring

creative firm
Fry Hammond Barr
Orlando, (Florida) USA
creatives
Tim Fisher, Sean Brunson,
Lara Mann, Melissa Cooney
client
McDonalds Central Fl Co-op

creative firm
Bohan Advertising/Marketing
Nashville, (Tennessee) USA
creatives
Kerry Oliver, Gregg Boling, Darrell Soloman,
Brooke Ludwick, Tom Gibney, Kristin Barlowe
client
Centennial Medical Center

creative firm
EyeballNYC
New York, (New York) USA
creatives
Limore Shur, Julian Bevan, Brian Sensebe, Carl Mok,
Neil Stuber, Danny Kamhaji, Federico Saenz, Stuart Simms,
John Brennick, Ghazia Jalal, Carlo Vega, Allison Kocar,
Johan Wiberg, John Lake Harvey
client
VH-1

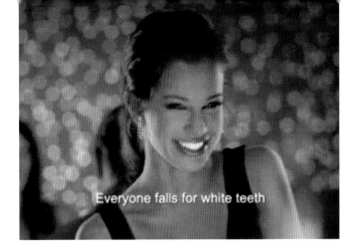

creative firm
Bruketa & Zinic
Zagreb, Croatia
creatives
Maro Pitarevic, Tomislav Jurica Kacunic,
Vlatko Pejic
client
Neva d.o.o.

creative firm
McCann Erickson Korea
Seoul, Korea
creatives
YC Kim, RH Lee
client
UNICEF Korea

creative firm
Revolución
New York, (New York) USA
creatives
Alberto Rodriguez, Roberto Pedroso,
Abby Lee
client
Palm Bay Imports

347

creative firm
Grey Worldwide NY
New York, (New York) USA
creatives
Tim Mellors, Rob Baiocco, Graham Button,
Aaron Royer, Andy Murillo, Stephanie Gottlieb
client
Parrot Bay

creative firm
Hoffman/Lewis
San Francisco, (California) USA
creatives
Sharon Krinsky, Patti Bott, James Cabral
client
Northern California Toyota Dealers

creative firm
Grey Worldwide NY
New York, (New York) USA
creatives
Tim Mellors, Rob Baiocco,
Shawn Couzens, Gary Ennis,
Lori Bullock
client
Frontier Airlines

creative firm
Rodgers Townsend
St. Louis, (Missouri) USA
creatives
Tom Hudder, Luke Partridge,
Mike McCormick
client
Ameren

creative firm
Grey Worldwide NY
New York, (New York) USA
creatives
Tim Mellors, Jonathan Rodgers,
Ari Halper, Steve Krauss, Diana Gay
client
Dairy Queen

creative firm
Liska + Associates, Inc.
Chicago, (Illinois) USA
creatives
Steve Liska, Gloria Almada
client
Hubbard Street Dance Chicago

348

creative firm
Brand Lounge GmbH
Duesseldorf, Germany
creatives
Christian Labonté, Ralph Bayer
client
Ferrero OHGmbH

creative firm
Rodgers Townsend
St. Louis, (Missouri) USA
creatives
Tom Hudder, Tom Townsend
client
SBC Communications Inc.

passion for Doritos chips.

creative firm
Dieste Harmel & Partners
Dallas, (Texas) USA
creatives
Dieste Harmel & Partners
Creative Team
client
Frito Lay

creative firm
Campbell-Ewald Adv.
Warren, (Michigan) USA
creatives
Bill Ludwig, Mark Simon,
Eric Olis, Dan Ames, Jim Gilmore
client
Navy

creative firm
Design Guys
Minneapolis, (Minnesota) USA
creatives
Steve Sikora
client
Target

349

creative firm
Grey Worldwide NY
New York, (New York) USA
creatives
Tim Mellors, Mark Catalina,
Mike Ryniec, Aaron Royer
client
NY Jets

creative firm
Rodgers Townsend
St. Louis, (Missouri) USA
creatives
Tom Hudder, Luke Partridge,
Mike McCormick
client
Ameren

creative firm
BMR (Brooks Marketing Resources)
Sault Ste. Marie, (Ontario) Canada
creatives
Mark Falkins, Rob Doda
client
Tourism Sault Ste. Marie

creative firm
Campbell-Ewald Adv.
Warren, (Michigan) USA
creatives
Mark Simone, Marcia Levenson,
Tim Kenum, Michael Stelmaszek
client
United States Post Office

creative firm
Grey Worldwide NY
New York, (New York) USA
creatives
Tim Mellors, Rob Baiocco,
Graham Button, Aaron Royer,
Andy Murillo, Stephanie Gottlieb
client
Parrot Bay

creative firm
Grey Worldwide NY
New York, (New York) USA
creatives
Tim Mellors, Mike Ryniec, Jess Vendley,
Mark Catalina, Denise O'Bleness,
Aaron Royer, Chad Hopenwasser
client
Panasonic

350

creative firm
Rodgers Townsend
St. Louis, (Missouri) USA
creatives
Tom Hudder, Tim Varner,
Mike Dillon
client
Circus Flora

creative firm
Heye&Partner GmbH
Unterhaching, Germany
creatives
Jan Okusluk, Oliver Diehr, Janet Fox,
Pieter Lony, Sebastian Strasser
client
GMX

creative firm
Nick @ Nite
New York, (New York) USA

creative firm
Grey Worldwide NY
New York, (New York) USA
creatives
Tim Mellors, Jonathan Rodgers,
Peter Foster, Paul Safsel,
Bart Culberson, Adam Seely
client
Progressive Insurance

creative firm
Campbell-Ewald Adv.
Warren, (Michigan) USA
creatives
Bill Ludwig, Brent Bouchez,
Robin Todd, Patrick O'Leary,
Joe Puhy, Mary Ellen Krawczyk
client
Chevrolet

creative firm
Rodgers Townsend
St. Louis, (Missouri) USA
creatives
Tom Hudder, Scott Lawson,
Mike Dillon
client
SBC Communications, Inc.

351

creative firm
Grey Worldwide NY
New York, (New York) USA
creatives
Tim Mellors, Jonathan Rodgers,
Ari Halper, Steve Krauss,
Diana Gay
client
Dairy Queen

creative firm
Hoffman/Lewis
San Francisco, (California) USA
creatives
Sharon Krinsky, Patti Bott, James Cabral
client
Northern California Toyota Dealers

creative firm
Rodgers Townsend
St. Louis, (Missouri) USA
creatives
Tom Hudder, Tom Townsend
client
SBC Communications, Inc.

creative firm
Grey Worldwide NY
New York, (New York) USA
creatives
Tim Mellors, Mike Ryniec,
Jess Vendley, Mark Catalina,
Denise O'Bleness, Aaron Royer,
Chad Hopenwasser
client
Panasonic

creative firm
Grey Worldwide NY
New York, (New York) USA
creatives
Tim Mellors, Rob Baiocco,
Brian Lefkowitz, Angela Denise,
Sean Burns, Elizabeth Salkoff,
Aaron Royer, Chad Hopenwasser
client
Starburst

creative firm
BMR (Brooks Marketing Resources)
Sault Ste. Marie, (Ontario) Canada
creatives
Mark Falkins, Derong Chen,
Art Taylor, Becky St. John
client
Atlas Auto Parts

352

creative firm
Grey Worldwide NY
New York, (New York) USA
creatives
Tim Mellors, Rob Baiocco,
Shawn Couzens, Gary Ennis, Lori Bullock
client
Frontier Airlines

creative firm
Brand Lounge GmbH
Duesseldorf, Germany
creatives
Christian Labonté, Jan Skolik
client
Coca-Cola GmbH

354

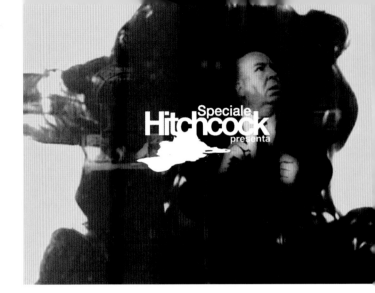

creative firm
Grey Worldwide NY
New York, (New York) USA
creatives
Tim Mellors, Rob Baiocco,
Graham Button, Aaron Royer,
Andy Murillo, Stephanie Gottlieb
client
Parrot Bay

creative firm
Universal Studios Network Italy
Rome, Italy
creatives
Theresia Braun, Ernesto Spinelli,
Monica Clarli
client
Universal Studios Network Italy

creative firm
Bohan Advertising/Marketing
Nashville, (Tennessee) USA
creatives
Kerry Oliver, Gregg Boling,
Darrell Soloman, Brooke Ludwick,
Tom Gibney, Kristen Barlowe
client
Centennial Medical Center

355

creative firm
Servicio-ejecutivo
New York, (New York) USA
creatives
Tatiana Arocha, Jeff Nichols,
Karen Parmelee
client
CMT

creative firm
Keller Crescent Advertising
Evansville, (Indiana) USA
creatives
Randall L. Rohn, Lee Bryant,
Carson Catlin, John Chaddock
client
Ubiquitel-Sprint

creative firm
Grey Worldwide NY
New York, (New York) USA
creatives
Tim Mellors, Jonathan Rodgers,
Peter Foster, Paul Safsel,
Bart Culberson, Adam Seely
client
Progressive Insurance

creative firm
Hitchcock Fleming & Associates, Inc.
Akron, (Ohio) USA
creatives
Nick Betro, Bob Clancy,
Scott Kristoff
client
**Geauga Lake Park &
Wildwater Kingdom**

creative firm
MTV On-Air Promos
New York, (New York) USA
creatives
Kevin Mackall, David Horowitz,
Betsy Blakemore, Jim Fealy,
Nathan Byrne/Post Millennium (NYC)
Paul Goldman/Eargoo (NYC)
client
MTV

creative firm
Spike TV
New York, (New York) USA
creatives
Alan Roll, Jennifer Brogle,
Michael Foronda
client
Spike TV

356

ONE PLACE YOU
NEVER NEED TO PUT
THE SEAT DOWN.

creative firm
Grey Worldwide NY
New York, (New York) USA
creatives
Tim Mellors, Rob Baiocco,
Graham Button, Aaron Royer,
Andy Murillo, Stephanie Gottlieb
client
Parrot Bay

creative firm
Dieste Harmel & Partners
Dallas, (Texas) USA
creatives
Dieste Harmel & Partners Creative Team
client
Clorox, Glad

creative firm
Campbell-Ewald Adv.
Warren, (Michigan) USA
creatives
Bill Ludwig, Brent Bouchez,
Whitney Jenkins, Nathan O'Brien,
Mary Ellen Krawczyk
client
Chevrolet

creative firm
Grey Worldwide NY
New York, (New York) USA
creatives
Tim Mellors, Jonathan Rodgers,
Ari Halper, Steve Krauss,
Diana Gay
client
Dairy Queen

creative firm
Scheer Advertising Group
Woodmere, (New York) USA
creatives
H. Robert Greenbaum,
Don Jacobs
client
Burlington Coat Factory

357

creative firm
Grey Worldwide NY
New York, (New York) USA
creatives
Tim Mellors, Rob Baiocco,
Shawn Couzens, Gary Ennis,
Lori Bullock
client
Frontier Airlines

creative firm
Grey Worldwide NY
New York, (New York) USA
creatives
Tim Mellors, Mark Catalina,
Mike Ryniec, Aaron Royer
client
NY Jets

creative firm
Spike TV
New York, (New York) USA
creatives
Alan Rolls, Jennifer Brogle,
Chris Cushing, Michael Foronda
client
Spike TV

creative firm
Grey Worldwide NY
New York, (New York) USA
creatives
Tim Mellors, Rob Baiocco,
Graham Button, Aaron Royer,
Andy Murillo, Stephanie Gottlieb
client
Parrot Bay

creative firm
Rodgers Townsend
St. Louis, (Missouri) USA
creatives
Tom Hudder, Luke Partridge,
Mike McCormick
client
Ameren

creative firm
Keller Crescent Advertising
Evansville, (Indiana) USA
creatives
Randall L. Rohn, Lee Bryant,
John Chaddock
client
St. Mary's

creative firm
Grey Worldwide NY
New York, (New York) USA
creatives
Tim Mellors, Jonathan Rodgers,
Peter Foster, Paul Safsel,
Bart Culberson, Adam Seely
client
Progressive Insurance

creative firm
Fry Hammond Barr
Orlando, (Florida) USA
creatives
Tim Fisher, Sean Brunson,
Lara Mann, Shannon Hallare
client
YMCA

creative firm
Hoffman/Lewis
San Francisco, (California) USA
creatives
Sharon Krinsky, Patti Bott, James Cabral
client
Northern California Toyota Dealers

creative firm
Grey Worldwide NY
New York, (New York) USA
creatives
Tim Mellors, Mike Ryniec,
Jesse Vendley, Mark Catalina,
Denise O'Bleness, Aaron Royer,
Chad Hopenwasser
client
Panasonic

creative firm
McCann Erickson Korea
Seoul, Korea
creatives
Ky An, JH Cho, Moonsun Choi
client
Coca-Cola Korea

359

creative firm
Grey Worldwide NY
New York, (New York) USA
creatives
Tim Mellors, Jonathan Rodgers,
Steve Krauss, Diana Gay
client
Showhound Naturals

creative firm
Universal Studios Network Italy
Rome, Italy
creatives
M.T. Braun
client
Universal Studios Network Italy

You can't make a dog happier.

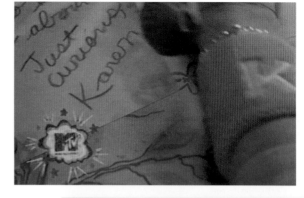

creative firm
McCann Erickson Korea
Seoul, Korea
creatives
KY An,
JH Cho,
Moonsun Choi
client
Hanaro Telecom

creative firm
MTV On-Air Promos
New York, (New York) USA
creatives
Kevin Mackall, Brent Stoller,
Tom Coleman, Trooper,
Marcelo Gondola/Burst,
Crandall Miller/The Whitehouse
client
MTV

360

creative firm
VH1
New York, (New York) USA
creatives
Nigel Cox-Hagen, Phil Delbourgo,
Amanda Havey, Bex Schwartz,
Scott Galinsky, Scott Pittinsky,
Tina Mintus
client
VH1

creative firm
RT&E Integrated Communications
Wilmington, (Delaware) USA
creatives
Randall Jones
client
Delaware Lottery

creative firm
MTV On-Air Promos
New York, (New York) USA
creatives
Kevin Mackall, Sophia Cranshaw,
Terence King, Paul Goldman/Eargoo
client
MTV

361

creative firm
Grey Worldwide NY
New York, (New York) USA
creatives
Tim Mellors, Mike Ryniec,
Jesse Vendley, Mark Catalina,
Denise O'Bleness, Aaron Royer,
Chad Hopenwasser
client
Panasonic

creative firm
Grey Worldwide NY
New York, (New York) USA
creatives
Tim Mellors, Jonathan Rodgers,
Ari Halper, Steve Krauss,
Diana Gay
client
Dairy Queen

creative firm
Eyeball NYC
New York, (New York) USA
creatives
James Hitchcock, Michael Engleman,
Jeff Nichols, Carla Daeninckx, Santos Lopez
client
CMT

creative firm
Campbell-Ewald Adv.
Warren, (Michigan) USA
creatives
Bill Ludwig, Debbie Karnowsky,
Mark Simon, Neville Anderson,
Tim Kenum, Mike Conboy,
Michael Stelmaszek, Laura McGowan
client
Kaiser Permenante

creative firm
Grey Worldwide NY
New York, (New York) USA
creatives
Tim Mellors, Jonathan Rodgers,
Peter Foster, Paul Safsel,
Bart Culberson, Adam Seely
client
Progressive Insurance

creative firm
Fry Hammond Barr
Orlando, (Florida) USA
creatives
Tim Fisher, Sean Brunson,
Lara Man, Jessica Hill
client
The Enzian Theater

creative firm
Universal Studios Network Italy
Rome, Italy
creatives
Theresia Braun, Alessandra Vincenti,
Monica Ciarli, Giovanni Stacione
client
Universal Studios Network Italy

creative firm
Grey Worldwide NY
New York, (New York) USA
creatives
Tim Mellors, Rob Baiocco,
Graham Button, Aaron Royer,
Andy Murillo, Stephanie Gottlieb
client
Parrot Bay

creative firm
TV Land
New York, (New York) USA

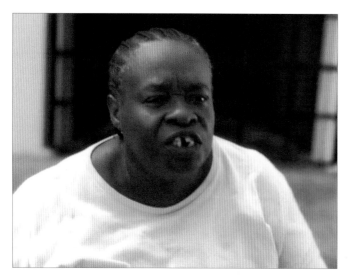

creative firm
Grey Worldwide NY
New York, (New York) USA
creatives
Tim Mellors, Rob Baiocco,
Graham Button, Aaron Royer,
Andy Murillo, Stephanie Gottlieb
client
Parrot Bay

creative firm
Gunter Advertising
Madison, (Wisconsin) USA
creatives
Randy Gunter, Bill Patton, Trevlin Utz,
Brandon Moore, Paul Bartlett, Billy
Branch,
Eric Sardinas
client
The Joseph Huber Brewing Co.

creative firm
Grey Worldwide NY
New York, (New York) USA
creatives
Tim Mellors, Mark Catalina,
Mike Ryniec, Aaron Royer
client
NY Jets

creative firm
Grey Worldwide NY
New York, (New York) USA
creatives
Tim Mellors, Rob Baiocco,
Shawn Couzens, Gary Ennis, Lori Bullock
client
Frontier Airlines

365

creative firm
Grey Worldwide NY
New York, (New York) USA
creatives
Tim Mellors, Jonathan Rodgers,
Ari Halper, Steve Krauss,
Diana Gay
client
Dairy Queen

creative firm
Fry Hammond Barr
Orlando, (Florida) USA
creatives
Tim Fisher, Sean Brunson,
Lara Mann, Shannon Hallare
client
YMCA

creative firm
Noggin/The N Brand.comm
New York, (New York) USA
creatives
Joe Pappalardo, Mike Tricario,
Matthew Duntemann, Riss Design
client
The N

366

creative firm
Noggin/The N Brand.comm
New York, (New York) USA
creatives
Emily Campion, Matthew Duntemann,
Jennifer Juliano
client
The N

creative firm
EyeballNYC
New York, (New York) USA
creatives
Limore Shur, Adam Gault, Stefanie Augustine,
Jason Conradt, John Lake Harvey, Ali Kocar
client
Country Music Television

creative firm
Noggin/The N Brand.comm
New York, (New York) USA
creatives
Clark Stubbs, Matthew Duntemann,
Melinda Beck, Shel Silverstein
client
Noggin

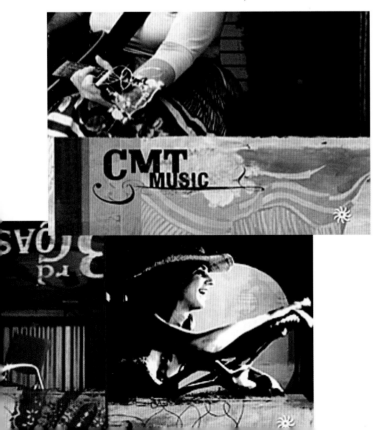

creative firm
Y&R Germany
Frankfurt, Germany
creatives
Christian Daul,
Uwe Marquardt
client
Y&R Germany

Corporate TVc, campaign

creative firm
Universal Studios Network Italy
Rome, Italy
creatives
Theresia Braun, Paolo Costa,
Francesca Schiavone
client
Universal Studios Network Italy

367

Banner Ads

creative firm
First Marketing
Pompano Beach, (Florida) USA
creatives
Keith Johnson, Jack Behar,
Larry Poccia
client
Nextel Partners

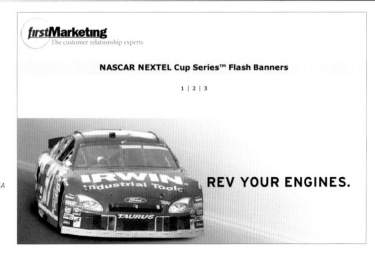

creative firm
Rodgers Townsend
St. Louis, (Missouri) USA
creatives
Tom Hudder, Scott Lawson,
Kay Cochran
client
Arts & Education Council

creative firm
Keller Crescent Advertising
Evansville, (Indiana) USA
creatives
Randall L. Rohn, Carson Catlin,
Nancy Kirkpatrick, Keith Rios,
Bill Shuman
client
Evansville, IN

creative firm
The Foundation for a Better Life
Denver, (Colorado) USA
creatives
Grant Baird, Brandt Lambermont
client
The Foundation for a Better Life

creative firm
MTV On-Air Promos
New York, (New York) USA
creatives
Kevin Mackall, Ted Pauly, Eric Eckelman,
Matt Giulvezan, Bryan Newman, Paul Ewen,
David Skinner, Jenn Leong, Ted Marcus
client
MTV

369

creative firm
Nickelodeon Creative Resources
New York, (New York) USA
creatives
Frank Czuchan, Samantha Berger,
Sohini Das, Holly Gregory,
Tracey Allred, Anna Yoon

creative firm
MTV Design
New York, (New York) USA
client
MTV

creative firm
MTV Design
New York, (New York) USA
client
MTV

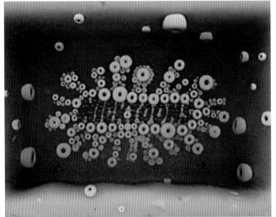

creative firm
1st Ave Machine
New York, (New York) USA
client
Nicktoons

creative firm
EyeballNYC
New York, (New York) USA
creatives
Nigel Cox-Hagan, Phil Delbourgo,
Amanda Havey, Shannon Horan,
Expansion Team
client
VH1

creative firm
Nicktoons
New York, (New York) USA
creatives
Jeremy Fernsler,
Euralis Weekes
client
Nicktoons

creative firm
bangbang studios
New York, (New York) USA
creatives
Rick Morris, James Hitchcock,
Michael Engleman, Carla Daeninckx,
Emilie Schnick, David Bennett
client
CMT Creative

creative firm
EyeballNYC
New York, (New York) USA
creatives
Limore Shure,
James Hitchcock,
Michael Engleman
client
CMT

creative firm
Spike TV
New York, (New York) USA
creatives
Alan Roll, Jennifer Brogle,
Obi Onyejekwe, Zach Shukan
client
Spike TV

creative firm
**Universal Studios
Network Italy**
Rome, Italy
creatives
Theresia Braun,
Monica Ciarli,
Giovanni Staccone
client
**Universal Studios
Network Italy**

creative firm
**Nickelodeon
Creative Resources**
New York, (New York) USA
creatives
Frank Czuchan,
Lisa Versaci,
Samantha Berger,
Aaron McDannell,
Manny Galan,
Tom Lynch,
Erik Chichester

creative firm
Hitchcock Fleming & Associates, Inc.
Akron, (Ohio) USA
creatives
Nick Betro, Bob Clancy, Scott Kristoff
client
Geauga Lake Park & Wildwater Kingdom

371

creative firm
Nick @ Nite
*New York, (New York)
USA*

creative firm
Spike TV
New York, (New York) USA
creatives
Alan Roll, Jennifer Brogle,
Obi Onyejekwe
client
Spike TV

creative firm
Conor O'boyle
New York, (New York) USA
creatives
Conor O'boyle
client
Nicktoons

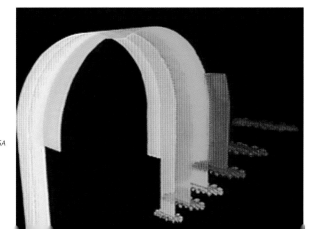

creative firm
CMT Creative
New York, (New York) USA
creatives
James Hitchcock, Michael Engleman,
Carla Daeninckx, Emilie Schnick,
Traylor Woodall, John Lane
client
CMT Creative

creative firm
Nick @ Nite
New York, (New York) USA

creative firm
Conor O'boyle
New York, (New York) USA
creatives
Conor O'boyle
client
Nicktoons

372 creative firm
MTV Design
New York, (New York) USA

creative firm
INTERspectacular
New York, (New York) USA
creatives
Kendrick Reid, Michael Uman,
Luis Blanco
client
Comedy Central

creative firm
NTERspectacular
New York, (New York) USA
creatives
Kendrick Reid, Michael Uman,
Luis Blanco
client
Comedy Central

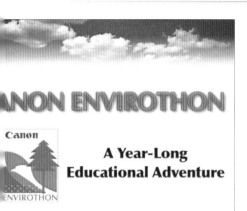

creative firm
Marketing Department of America Ltd
New York, (New York) USA
creatives
Dr. John Tantillo, Tomoniko Sueaya, Rolf Graeber, Michael Jump, Christin Paglen, Keith Paglen
client
Canon Envirothon

creative firm
MTV Networks Creative Services
New York, (New York) USA
creatives
Cheryl Family, Scott Wadler, Ken Saji, Matt Herron, Edwin Rogers, Marty Buccafusco, Tom Arnold, Elizabeth Smith
client
MTV Networks International

373

creative firm
RT&E Integrated Communications
Wilmington, (Delaware) USA
creatives
Rick Clemons, Mike Strunk
client
INVISTA

creative firm
Keller Crescent Advertising
Evansville, (Indiana) USA
creatives
Randall L. Rohn, Carson Catlin
client
HPNOTIQ

Corporate Films/Videos

creative firm
Brian J. Ganton & Assoc.
Cedar Grove, (New Jersey) USA
creatives
Brian Ganton, Jr.,
Brian Ganton, Sr.
client
Oldcastle Glass

374

creative firm
3Inc Creative
Kew Gardens, (New York) USA
creatives
Vito Incorvaia, Patrick Incorvaia
client
NPA Wildposting

Sales Films/Videos

creative firm
RT&E Integrated Communications
Wilmington, (Delaware) USA
creatives
Randall Jones, Kevin Watts
client
DuPont Sorona

creative firm
Revolución
New York, (New York) USA
creatives
Alberto Rodriguez, Roberto Pedrosa,
Abby Lee
client
Citi Bank

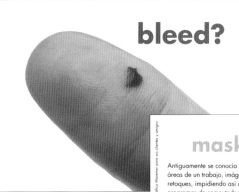

bleed?

creative firm
Maremar Graphic Design
Bayamon, Puerto Rico
creatives
Marina Rivón
client
Maremar Graphic Design

mask = mascarilla

Antiguamente se conocía como mascarilla al material utilizado para proteger ciertas áreas de un trabajo, imágenes o partes de una página, a la hora de imprimir o hacer retoques, impidiendo así que salieran en la copia impresa. En la actualidad hay programas de computadoras que permiten realizar este trabajo de manera electrónica, con la ventaja adicional de que las mascarillas preparadas pueden ser guardadas para ser utilizadas en futuros trabajos de ser necesario.

Tenemos una amplia experiencia utilizando ésta y otras técnicas para hacer que su producto resalte y se venda.

Resolver su problema de comunicación es nuestra meta. Permítanos ayudarle con su próximo proyecto; llámenos al 787.731.8795

Identidades Corporativas • Publicaciones • "Brochures" • Invitaciones • Piezas de Promoción • Empaques

www.maremar.com

T 787.731.8795   M 787.647.5993   F 787.287.9867   E-m info@maremar.com

En este proyecto, ganador de un premio Excel, utilizamos mascarillas para retocar ciertas áreas de las fotografías y así poder realzar la belleza del producto.

creative firm
BCN Communications
Chicago, (Illinois) USA
creatives
Michael Neu, Harri Boller

375

1) We are problem solvers, and we are strategic thinkers.
We define solid solutions to convey the right creative message.

5) We have a long history of success.
We've worked closely with our clients for over fifteen years to identify and drive their message.

scope

y, the e-movie.

creative firm
BCN Communications
Chicago, (Illinois) USA
creatives
Michael Neu, Harri Boller

creative firm
BrandSpeak Communications
Chaska, (Minnesoata) USA
client
Entegris, Inc.

creative firm
Launch Creative Marketing
Chicago, (Illinois) USA
creatives
Michelle Morales, Jim Gelder
client
Kellogg Co.

376

creative firm
Datagraf
Auning, Denmark
creatives
Dennis Vestergaard
client
Danisco

creative firm
Premier Communications Group
Royal Oak, (Michigan) USA
creatives
Randy Fossano, Patrick Hatfield
client
General Motors

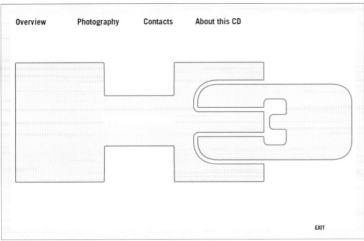

creative firm
Premier Communications Group
Royal Oak, (Michigan) USA
creatives
Randy Fossano, Pete Pultz
client
General Motors

creative firm
Mind & Media
Alexandria, (Virginia) USA
creatives
Sophia Lambroe, Berry Blanton,
Jill Tullo
client
Army National Gaurd

377

creative firm
Kutoka Interactive
Montreal, (Quebec) Canada

creative firm
Launch Creative Marketing
Chicago, (Illinois) USA
creatives
Michelle Morales, Erin Cronin
client
Kellogg Co.

creative firm
RT&E Integrated Communications
Wilmington, (Delaware) USA
creatives
Rick Clemons, Mike Strunk
client
Delaware Lottery

creative firm
Publicis Dialog
San Francisco, (California) USA
creatives
Jonathan Butts, Joe Lin, Alan Riddle,
Christopher St. John, David Giles
client
Google

creative firm
Curio
Hoboken, (New Jersey) USA
creatives
Carrie Brunk, Dominic Poon
client
Kevin Schochat
www.kevinschochat.com

creative firm
Fry Hammond Barr
Orlando, (Florida) USA
creatives
Tim Fisher, Sean Brunson,
Lara Mann
client
The Enzian Theater

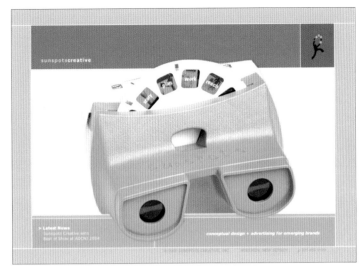

creative firm
Sunspots Creative
Hoboken, (New Jersey) USA
creatives
Rick Bonelli, Deena Hartley,
Dave Vioreanu
client
Sunspots Creative
www.sunspotscreative.com

creative firm
Skidmore, Inc.
Royal Oak, (Michigan) USA
creatives
Barrett Streu, Mae Skidmore,
Tim Smith
client
Skidmore, Inc.
www.skidmorestudio.com

creative firm
GOLD & Associates
Ponte Vedra Beach, (Florida) USA
creatives
Noone Savage,
Brian Gold
client
Golf 20/20
www.golf2020.com

creative firm
Big Spaceship
Brooklyn, (New York) USA
creatives
Michael Lebowitz, Jens Karlsson,
Karen Dahlstrom, Drew Horton,
Ron Thompson, Kimba Granlund,
Tai U, Jamie Kosoy,
Jesse Greenberg, Chris Wei
client
Warner Bros.
www.batmanbegins.com

creative firm
Velocity Design Works
Winnepeg, (Manitoba) Canada
creatives
Velocity Design Works
Creative Team
client
The Community Endowment Fund
www.thecef.com

creative firm
aijalon
Lincoln, (Nebraska) USA
creatives
Lance Ford, Quiller Caudill, Ben Swift,
Melissa Kirchner, Jason Petersen
client
GroovePuppet
www.groovepuppet.com

380

creative firm
BBK Studio
Grand Rapids, (Michigan) USA
creatives
Kevin Budelmann, Alison Popp,
John Winkelman,
Marie-Claire Camp, Clark Malcolm
client
Herman Miller
www2.hermanmiller.com/discoveringdesign/

creative firm
Big Spaceship
Brooklyn, (New York) USA
creatives
Michael Lebowitz, D. Garrett Nantz,
Edward Looram, Dexter Cruz,
Michael Dillingham, David Chau,
Michael Trezza, Tai U, Christian Stadler,
Karen Dahlstrom, Andrew Payne
client
Warner Bros.
www.catwomanmovie.com

creative firm
Rodgers Townsend
St. Louis, (Missouri) USA
creatives
Erik Mathre, Michelle Vesth,
Matt Clement, Sean Young
client
SBC Communications, Inc.
http://projects.rodgerstownsend.com/
uploaded/customer/sbc_holiday_ecard.htm

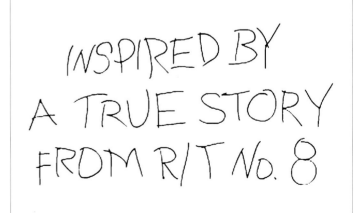

creative firm
Big Spaceship
Brooklyn, (New York) USA
creatives
Michael Lebowitz, Ron Thompson,
Joshua Hirsch, Karen Dahlstrom,
Michael Dillingham, Frank Campanella,
Tai U, George Murray, Christine Yu,
Chris Wei, Krissy Weisman
client
Warner Bros.
http://pdl.warnerbros.com/wbmovies/charlie/
flashsite/index.html

creative firm
kor group
Boston, (Massachusetts) USA
creatives
Jim Gibson, Tyler Hawes
client
Saint Joseph's Abbey
www.spencerabbey.org

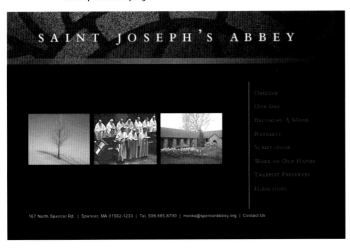

creative firm
The Mixx
New York, (New York) USA
creatives
Courtney Darling
client
REMI Companies.com
www.remicompanies.com

creative firm
aijalon
Lincoln, (Nebraska) USA
creatives
Lance Ford, Quiller Caudill,
Jason Petersen
client
Youth with a Mission-Taoyuan
www.ywamtaoyuan.com

creative firm
BreedWorks
Oneonta, (New York) USA
creatives
Susan Muther, Hazen Reed,
Heath Stein
client
a Suri Farm
www.asurifarm.com

creative firm
Very Memorable Design
New York, (New York) USA
creatives
Michael James Pinto,
Joshua Mack
client
Definitive Ink
www.definitiveink.com

382

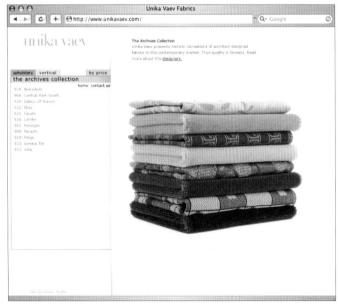

creative firm
Jones Studio Limited
Staten Island, (New York) USA
creatives
Eric Jones
client
Unika Vaev
www.unikavaev.com

creative firm
Big Spaceship
Brooklyn, (New York) USA
creatives
Michael Lebowitz, James Widegren,
Joshua Hirsch, Karen Monahan,
Frank Campanella, David Chau,
Tai U, Karen Dahlstrom,
D. Garrett Nantz, Ian Bellomy
client
20th Century Fox
www.elektramovie.com

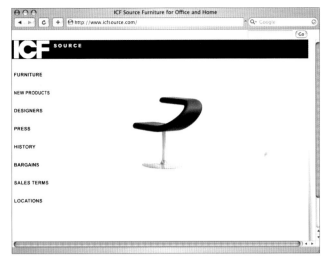

creative firm
Jones Studio Limited
Staten Island, (New York) USA
creatives
Eric Jones
client
ICF
www.icfsource.com

creative firm
JPL Productions
Harrisburg, (Pennsylvania) USA
creatives
Brandon Craig, Chris Buccholz,
Chelsie Markel
client
KC Distance Learning, Inc.
www.iqacademies.com

creative firm
MTV Networks Creative Services
New York, (New York) USA
creatives
Cheryl Family, Scott Wadler,
Alan Perler, Ken Saji,
Patrick O'Sullivan, Mark Malabrigo,
Scott Galbraith, Sara Swartz,
Jared Stanley, Brian Bason,
Russ Ferguson, Cynara Webb,
Tori Turner, Chris McKenzie,
Mugor Marculescu, Diana Davis
client
Viacom

383

creative firm
Big Spaceship
Brooklyn, (New York) USA
creatives
Michael Lebowitz, David Chau,
Joshua Hirsch, Drew Horton,
Lisa Weatherbee, D. Garrett Nantz,
Daniel Federman, Andrew Payne,
George Murray
client
Universal Pictures
www.wimbledonmovie.com

creative firm
RainCastle Communications
Newton, (Massachusetts) USA
creatives
Erik Norwood
client
SoundBite Communications
www.soundbite.com

384

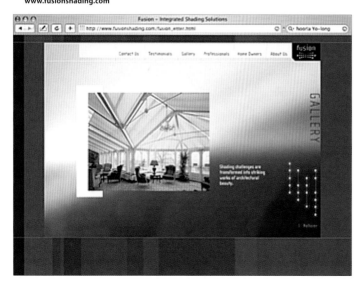

creative firm
E-lift Media
Millicent, Australia
creatives
Simone Burdon
client
Noorla Yo-long
www.noorlayo-long.com.au

creative firm
Fahrenheit Studio
Los Angeles, (California) USA
creatives
Dylan Tran, Robert Weitz
client
Virgin Records America
www.julietsounds.com

385

creative firm
WebDesigns-Studio.com
Beverly Hills, (California) USA
creatives
Madeline Y. Arenas, Bernard Aquino,
Ivy Baldoza, Den Marcelo
client
Sports Placement Service, Inc.
www.sportsplacement.com

creative firm
Big Spaceship
Brooklyn, (New York) USA
creatives
Michael Lebowitz, D. Garrett Nantz,
Edward Looram, Michael Dillingham,
Ron Thompson, Peter Reid,
Christian Stadler, Michael Trezza,
Karen Dahlstrom, Frank Campanella,
George Murray, Ian Bellomy
client
Warner Bros.
www.alexanderthemovie.com

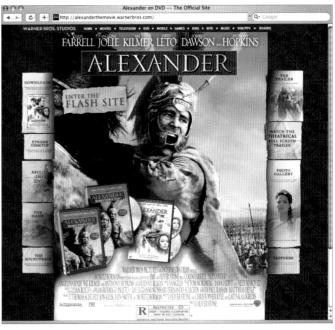

386

creative firm
JPL Productions
Harrisburg, (Pennsylvania) USA
creatives
Brandon Craig, Chelsie Markel,
Jamy Kunjappu
client
The Hershey Company
www.hersheys.com/payday/home.asp

creative firm
Campbell-Ewald
Warren, (Michigan) USA
creatives
Bill Ludwig, Susan Logar Brody,
Mark Simon, Joel Benay,
Marcia Levenson, Ilya Hardey,
Nancy Ritts, Sharon Condron, Mary Hildie,
Virginia Cusenza
client
The United States Postal Service
www.messagemaker.biz/

creative firm
McElveney & Palozzi Design Group
Rochester, (New York) USA
creatives
Matt Nowicki,
Ken Riemer
client
Ken Riemer
www.kenriemer.com

creative firm
MTV Networks
New York, (New York) USA
creatives
Audrey Chen, Jarrett Brilliant,
Lindsay Robertson, Rich Sullivan,
Jesse Willmon, Paul Beddoe-Stephens,
Karen La Chiana
client
Comedy Central
www.comedycentral.com/tv_shows/
drawntogether/

creative firm
Avenue
Chicago, (Illinois) USA
creatives
Bob Domenz, Ian Watts,
Justin Rhodes
client
Weber-Stephen Products Co.
www.weber.com/drtv/

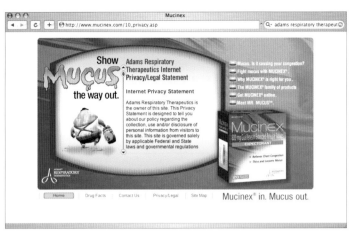

creative firm
Torre Lazur McCann
Parsippany, (New Jersey) USA
creatives
Jennifer Alampi, Steve Graff,
Vanessa Levin, Debra Feath
client
Adams Respiratory Therapeutics
www.mucinex.com

creative firm
Publicis Dialog
San Francisco, (California) USA
creatives
Jonathan Butts, Joe Lin,
Leanne Milway, Maria Tyomkina
client
HP

creative firm
Revolución
New York, (New York) USA
creatives
Alberto Rodriguez,
Roberto Pedroso,
Abby Lee
client
Palm Bay Imports
www.lancerswine.com

387

creative firm
Attic Design
New York, (New York) USA
creatives
Lori Reed,
Marshall Woksa
client
CMT/CMT.com
www.cmt/shows/events/
cmt_music_awards/2005

creative firm
Squarehand
New York, (New York) USA
creatives
Mónica Torrejón Kelly
client
Turn of the Century Pictures
www.turncenturypictures.com

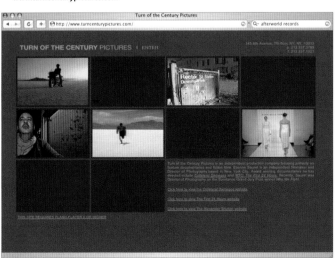

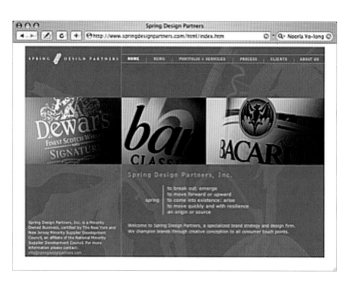

creative firm
Spring Design Partners
New York, (New York) USA
creatives
Ron Wong,
May Wong
client
Spring Design Partners
www.springdesignpartners.com

creative firm
WebDesigns-Studio.com
Beverly Hills, (California) USA
creatives
Madeline Y. Arenas, Bernard Aquino,
Rey Padilla
client
Landscape Development, Inc.
www.landscapedevelopment.com

creative firm
MTV Networks
New York, (New York) USA
creatives
Lindsay Robertson,
Jarrett Brilliant,
Nick Poppy,
Rich Sullivan,
Jesse Willmon,
Paul Beddoe-Stephens
client
Comedy Central
www.comedycentral.com/
tv_shows/lastlaugh2004/

388

creative firm
Keyword Design
Highland, (Indiana) USA
creatives
Judith Mayer
client
National Vietnam Veterans Art Museum
www.nvvam.org

creative firm
400lb.communications
Cheswick, (Pennsylvania) USA
creatives
Nathan Kress,
Clinton Godlesky
client
Vet Tech Institute
www.vettechinstitute.com

389

creative firm
Jowaisas Design
Winter Park, (Florida) USA
creatives
Elizabeth Jowaisas
client
Jowaisas Design
www.jowaisasdesign.com

creative firm
Liska + Associates, Inc.
Chicago, (Illinois) USA
creatives
Sabine Krauss, Kim Fry,
Todd Rosenberg
client
Hubbard Street Dance Chicago
www.hubbardstreetdance.com

390

creative firm
Open Eye Design, Inc.
Fullerton, (California) USA
creatives
Greg Herrington,
Dan Haard
client
Gener8xion Entertainment
www.8x.com/onenight

creative firm
LF Banks & Associates
Philadelphia, (Pennsylvania) USA
creatives
Lori Banks, Charlotte Markward,
Laura Hale, Craig Elkins
client
Chris DeCaro
www.chrisdecaro.com

creative firm
Very Memorable Design
New York, (New York) USA
creatives
Michael James Pinto,
Gwenevere Singley
client
Time for Kids Magazine
www.timeforkids.com

creative firm
Big Spaceship
Brooklyn, (New York) USA
creatives
Daniel Federman, James Widegren,
Matt Lipson, Drew Horton,
Edward Looram, Tai U, Lee Semel,
Andrew Payne, Christine Yu
client
Paramount Pictures
www.waroftheworlds.com

creative firm
BBK Studio
Grand Rapids, (Michigan) USA
creatives
Kevin Budelmann, Alison Popp,
Marie-Claire Camp, Scott Krieger
client
European Living
www.europeanliving.com

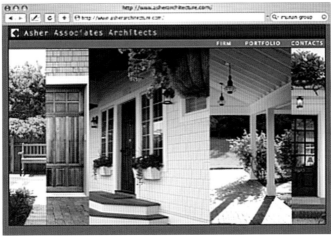

creative firm
Zygo Communications
Wyncote, (Pennsylvania) USA
creatives
Scott Laserow
client
Asher Architecture
www.asherarchitecture.com

391

creative firm
Roslyn Eskind Associates Ltd
Toronto, (Ontario) Canada
client
Kris Weston and Associates
www.kriswestonandassociates.com

creative firm
Didem & Alex Wong
Istanbul, Turkey
creatives
Didem Cariki Wong,
Alex Wong
client
Landographix
www.landographix.com

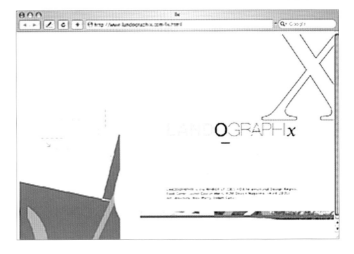

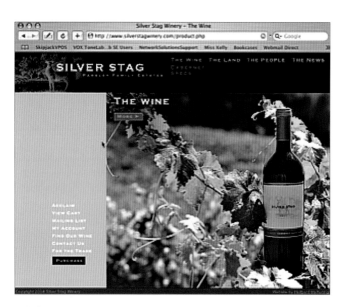

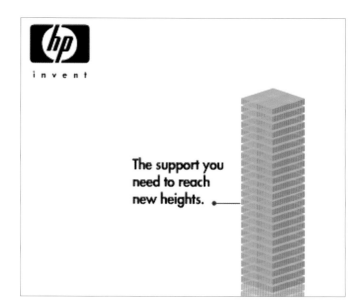

392

creative firm
Dezainwerkz
Singapore
creatives
Xavier Sanjiman, Kristal Melson
client
Dezainwerkz
**www.dezainwerkz.com/
master_wu_cny_tips**

creative firm
RainCastle Communications
Newton, (Massachusetts) USA
creatives
Erik Norwood, Stacey George
client
RainCastle
www.raincastle.com/holiday_card/

creative firm
3rd Edge Communications
Jersey City, (New Jersey) USA
creatives
Manny Dilone,
Frankie Gonzalez,
Melissa Medina Mackin
client
3rd Edge Communications
www.3rdedge.com

393

creative firm
LTD Creative
Frederick, (Maryland) USA
creatives
Timothy Finnen, Louanne Welgoss,
Kimberly Dow
client
LTD Creative
www.ltdcreative.com

creative firm
aijalon
Lincoln, (Nebraska) USA
creatives
Lance Ford, Quiller Caudill,
Melissa Kirchner, Jason Petersen
client
aijalon
www.40days.com

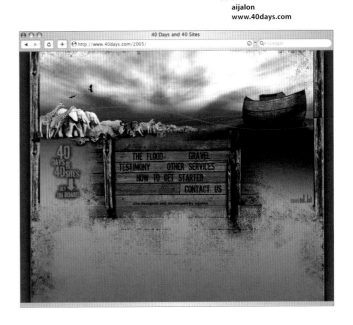

"Don't Blink"
Our Holiday Wish for you.

click to play

http://www.millerwhite.com/mw_holiday_card.html

creative firm
MillerWhite, LLC
Terre Haute, (Indiana) USA
creatives
Noelle Webster
client
MillerWhite
www.millerwhite.com/
mw_holiday_card.html.com

creative firm
Aquea Design
Las Vegas, (Nevada) USA
creatives
Raymond Perez, Chris Grav
client
Aquea Design
www.aqueadesign.com

394

creative firm
Open Eye Design, Inc.
Fullerton, (California) USA
creatives
Greg Herrington, Scott Krakoff
client
The King in Yellow
www.thekinginyellow.com

creative firm
KPR
New York, (New York) USA
creatives
Bernard Steinman, Scott Frank,
Jim Walsh, Jonathan Gough,
Brian Keys
client
KPR
www.kpr.com

creative firm
Rottman Creative Group, LLC
La Plata, (Maryland) USA
creatives
Gary Rottman, Robert Whetzel,
Tania Baumler, Mary Rottman
client
Rottman Creative Group, LLC
www.rottmancreative.com

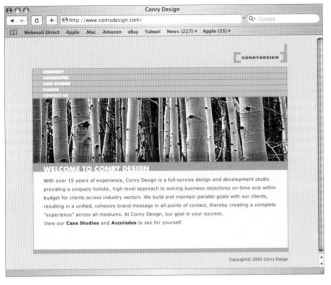

creative firm
Conry Design
Topanga, (California) USA
creatives
Rhonda Conry,
Paul Kane
client
Conry Design
www.conrydesign.com

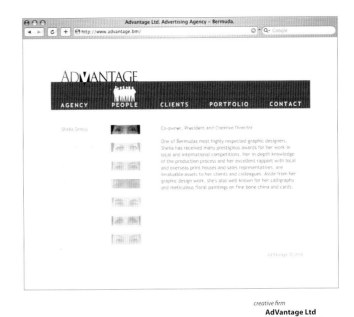

creative firm
AdVantage Ltd
Hamilton, Bermuda
creatives
Sami Lill,
The AdVantage Team
client
AdVantage Ltd
www.advantage.com

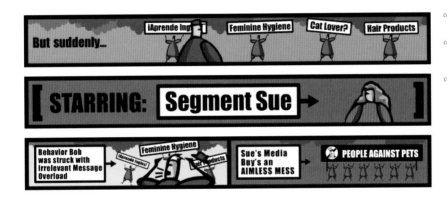

creative firm
Designkarma Inc.
New York, (New York) USA
creatives
Vitaliy Yasch,
Timofei Yuriev,
Sherri Valenti
client
24/7 Real Media Inc.
www.designkarma.com

395

creative firm
First Marketing
Pompano Beach, (Florida) USA
creatives
Dan Gershenson, Tom Olivieri,
Joe Paul, Jack Behar,
John Dragone, Larry Poccia
client
First Marketing
www.holifestigala.com

creative firm
Fahrenheit Studio
Los Angeles, (California) USA
creatives
Dylan Tran, Robert Weitz
client
Fahrenheit Studio
www.fahrenheit.com

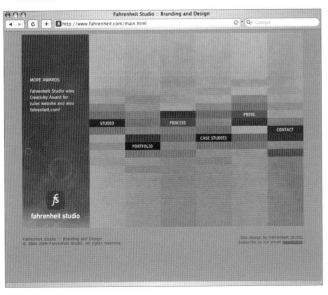

Index

Creative Firms

396

Clients

398

400